Nirvana — THE — *Foo Fighters*

DAVE GROHL

STORY

Nirvana THE *Foo Fighters*
DAVE GROHL
STORY

Jeff Apter

OMNIBUS PRESS

LONDON • NEW YORK • PARIS • SYDNEY • COPENHAGEN • BERLIN • MADRID • TOKYO

Exclusive Distributors
Music Sales Limited,
14-15 Berners Street,
London W1T 3LJ, UK.

Music Sales Corporation,
257 Park Avenue South,
New York, NY 10010, USA.

Macmillan Distribution Services,
53 Park West Drive,
Derrimut, Vic 3030,
Australia.

To the Music Trade only:
Music Sales Limited,
14-15 Berners Street,
London W1T 3LJ, UK.

Every effort has been made to trace the copyright holders of the photographs in this book but one or two were unreachable. We would be grateful if the photographers concerned would contact us.

Typeset by Galleon Typesetting, Ipswich.
Printed in Colombia by Quebecor World.

A catalogue record for this book is available from the British Library.

Visit Omnibus Press on the web at www.omnibuspress.com

For my parents Jack and Jean, the best in the business

Contents

Acknowledgements

One person's name may appear on the cover, but it takes a sizeable cast to help write a book such as this. Many thanks to those who contributed in their own way, be it big or small.

Chris Charlesworth, Andy Neill, Andrea Rotondo, Melissa Whitelaw, Alison Wofford and all at Omnibus Press for their support, above and beyond the call; my wife Diana Gonsalves and my daughter Elizabeth for understanding that a man needs a think hole; and to all the following people who either spoke on the record and/or steered me in the general direction of the truth: Greg Anderson at Southern Lord; Mark Andersen; Hannah Bentley; Steven Blush; Angie Carlson; Gerald Casale; Scott Crawford at Harp; Charles R. Cross; John Doe; Dante Ferrando at the Black Cat; William Flammia; Glen E. Friedman; Gillian Gaar; Gary Himelfarb at Ras; Larry Hinkle (he of the HG Hancock Band renown); Jake Hooker; Barrett Jones; Paul Jones at the peerless Foo Archive (www.fooarchive.com); Bobbie Lane at *Kerrang!*; Ian MacKaye; Scott McCloud; Joel McIver; Michael Meisel and Jill Berliner at Foo HQ; Vicky Miksis at the *Chicago Tribune*; Gordon Murray and Bob Allen at *Billboard* research; James Noll and all at www.slobfarm.com; Michael Palmieri (who told me the amazing truth about Dave Grohl's Oriental doppelgänger); Alan Paul at *Guitar World*; Michael Pilmer; Reuben Radding (ex-Dain Bramage); Keith Richmond; Henry Rollins; Steve Smith; Pete Stahl; Reegan Stark (thank you for the perfect seats); Paul Stenning; Bobby Sullivan and Johnny Temple of Lünchmeat, Soul Side and Girls Against Boys; Aaron Wilhelm, and Edgar 'Frankenstein' Winter.

A Tale Of Two Grohls

"To my dearest honcho, love Dave."
— Grohl autograph for author, 2002

ANYBODY with a passing involvement in modern music has at least one Dave Grohl story. This is not surprising, really, given that Grohl – the lucky man that he quite readily admits to being – has had two bites of the rock'n'roll cherry. His first was as the lank-haired, stripped-to-the-waist tub thumper behind accidental heroes Nirvana. Led by Kurt Cobain, who in his final months seemed hell-bent on fulfilling Neil Young's prophecy that it was "better to burn out than fade away", Nirvana blazed bright in the early 1990s, the dawn of what would become known as the alt-rock movement. That was, of course, before Cobain, weighed down by the double whammy of a raging heroin addiction and the pressures of being an idol to millions, blew off his head in his Seattle garage in April 1994.

As it turned out, that simply marked the end of Dave Grohl Mark One. Despite the weight of the grief he felt due to Cobain's suicide – Grohl later confessed that his "soul went dead" for some time after Cobain pulled the trigger – he bounced back only a year later. Grohl turned a series of home-made songs, some cut during his brief stint with Nirvana, into both an album called *Foo Fighters* and a band of the same name. Although originally intended purely for his personal listening pleasure, this would prove to be the beginning of an even more successful spell in the rock'n'roll spotlight for Grohl, this time as the good-natured, axe-wielding, power-riffing Foo Fighters' bandleader.

I guess I'm more fortunate than some, because I have two Dave Grohl stories. The first involves a hot room, an even hotter summer afternoon and a selection of mismatched trainers. It was early evening on the day of Sydney's first Big Day Out, a festival that was a bold attempt on the part of two local promoters, Ken West and Vivian Lees, to grab their slice of generation Lollapalooza. They'd checked out the first of Perry Farrell's counterculture roadshows the year before and were obsessed with bringing to Australia both its money-spinning success and its anything-goes line-up.

It was late January 1992 and, much to their bewilderment, Nirvana had somehow managed to become superstars in their own country, even though they were 12,000 miles away. After several months of increasing momentum, their second album, *Nevermind* – their first for major label DGC/Geffen – had finally reached the number one spot on the *Billboard* charts, elbowing aside Michael Jackson's *Dangerous* in the process. (*Nevermind* would go on to shift 14 million copies and be justifiably considered the defining LP of the grunge movement and one of the key albums of the Nineties.)

Nirvana's spot on the Big Day Out bill, however, didn't necessarily reflect their current world-beater status. They were wedged between the headliners, ageing college radio faves the Violent Femmes, and indigenous rockers Yothu Yindi. Not unlike Nirvana, Yothu Yindi had recently morphed from zeroes to heroes, in their case thanks to a chart-topping mix of tribal rhythms and deep groove called 'Treaty' – but that was all they had in common with the Seattle trio.

The Big Day Out was a multi-stage affair, liberally spread over a large area in the RAS Showgrounds, which was perched next door to the venerable Sydney Cricket Ground and about a mile from the city itself. Its epicentre was the Hordern Pavilion, a cavernous bunker that sucked in heat like a sauna and had all the acoustic qualities of a large canyon. Although ideally suited for around 5,000 punters, by late afternoon it seemed that the entire 10,000-plus crowd had somehow managed to wedge themselves inside the Hordern. Elsewhere, meanwhile, numerous local acts played to an empty field, unsure as to where the crowd had disappeared.

Nirvana's set wasn't quite the earth-moving experience many had expected – it was short, maybe 45 minutes maximum, and played at both blistering speed and volume – but the seriously expectant crowd ate it up. (It also helped, without doubt, that the 10,000 punters sucked down more than 55,000 cans of beer during the day.) While crowd surfing, moshing and stage diving were hardly new sensations in Australian music – Olympian standards were set at Nirvana's show the day before at Sydney's Phoenician Club – the sweat-stained punters on the Hordern Pavilion floor put in a Herculean effort that afternoon. Although most eyes were fixed on the charismatic Cobain, who was a blur of power riffing, matted hair and snarled vocals, it was the sight of Grohl, drumming at warp speed, that kept the whole mad punk rock noise together. They were no Steely Dan – muso chops weren't the issue here – but there was an intent of purpose about Nirvana's brawny mix of Sabbath power chords and youthful alienation, anchored by the wrist-snapping drumming of this Ohio-born drummer. And, unlike the troubled Cobain, Grohl appeared to be loving his time on stage. Every single sweat-soaked minute of it.

However it wasn't their roaring anthems that left the deepest impression on me. And neither, in all honesty, was it Grohl's express train drumming. No, it was more the aftermath of Nirvana's brief set. As the dust cleared and the assembled masses realised that encores didn't rate too highly in the puritanical world of grunge – Nirvana's set was over and they weren't coming back – the stinky, occasionally bloody punters dragged themselves away from the chaos, as the Violent Femmes' crew did their best to piece the stage back together. And then I noticed something totally new to me – the one-shoed army. The moshpit crew had become so totally immersed in the anarchy and sheer noise thrills of Nirvana that many of them had stomped on the feet (and, in some cases, the heads) of their neighbours, which meant that their shoes had been literally dragged off their feet and had got lost amid the carnage. Even if their owners had spotted the errant trainers, they'd be unlikely to reclaim them anyway, because, of course, shoes were just the thing to throw on stage, as a token of appreciation for their new rock'n'roll heroes.

So the one-shoed army limped their way out of the Hordern Pavilion, while Cobain, bassist Chris Novoselic and Grohl quickly and quietly faded into the Big Day Out crowd. And even though there was a lot more music to come, for much of the crowd they'd already had their Big Day Out, shoes or no shoes.

My second Dave Grohl story takes place 10 years later. A lot, of course, had happened since then, not the least being the changes in Grohl's physical appearance. His waist-length mane was long gone, updated with a thinking man's mullet, and sharply styled facial hair, that masked his still youthful 33-year-old face. While still a man of the people, at least on stage, Grohl was now a more urbane character away from music – he was a cheese connoisseur, amateur pilot and collector of erotic art, which was dotted about the bedroom of his massive LA spread (a home that, naturally, featured both a tennis court and skeet shooting range). Every inch the family man, Grohl's sister Lisa lived minutes away, in a house also purchased by her generous multi-millionaire brother. And his mother Virginia also spent most of her time on the West Coast.

Since the Big Day Out, of course, Kurt Cobain had taken his tragic short cut to rock'n'roll immortality, leaving Grohl to consider his musical future. But it somehow seemed wrong that Grohl, raised on a steely diet of raw punk and classic rock – Led Zeppelin's 'Stairway To Heaven' was among the first songs he recalled hearing – should walk away from music purely because his former bandmate took a poorly considered option.

The Foo Fighters' rise was swift. Although it wasn't something with which he was entirely comfortable, Grohl couldn't avoid the Nirvana factor and its influence on his musical fortunes. Their early records were by no means perfect, but there were strong indications that Grohl had developed sound melodic instincts of his own.

It was now 2002, and Grohl and his fellow Foo Fighters – garrulous, hyperactive drummer Taylor Hawkins, bassist Nate Mendel and guitarist Chris Shiflett, the two quiet achievers of the band – had returned for yet another Australian promo tour, talking up their new album *One By One*. By this time, four albums, hundreds of shows, thousands of quotable one-liners, and several million albums sales down the line, the Foos were rock'n'roll royalty, stadium-fillers all over the planet. While they would never capture the generational impact of Nirvana, the Foos were never known to let an audience down. Their shows were manic, their albums packed more anthems than Independence Day, and, just as importantly, with Grohl roaring away out front and Hawkins pounding a primal beat behind him, they weren't afraid to rock very hard.

It was a hell of a lot more than Grohl had ever expected of his life in music. There'd been more than one occasion, especially in his pre-Nirvana times while roughing it in punk contenders Scream, when Grohl was genuinely unsure if he'd ever make a living from music. (Famously, his first record sales royalty cheque, for $30, is framed on the wall of his home studio.) But Nirvana, of course, had added several zeroes to Grohl's bank balance, and the Foos were also doing their bit to make him one of the richest men in rock.

All this might explain the ear-to-ear grin Grohl wore when I connected with him during that afternoon in 2002. And the locale, Sydney's flash W Hotel, was a long way from the sweat-stained bunker of the Hordern Pavilion. The upscale, harbourside W was the first choice of any touring act with a record company's entertainment budget to spend. And its appeal wasn't restricted to musicians: Oscar-winner Russell Crowe dropped a lazy $12 million on a multi-level, waterfront apartment at the rear of the hotel. Grohl was keeping some A-list company.

My interview with Grohl and his Foos was conducted with the type of stealth usually reserved for hostage rescues – and visiting rock stars. Laid low with a sore throat, and with a "secret" gig to play that night, Grohl had been advised by the local rock doctor to cut the talking and save his voice for that evening's shouting, so he'd blown out numerous interviews (much to the dismay of the scribes assembled in the hotel's foyer). But, by sheer dumb luck, he'd agreed to one interview, which fell to me.

Grohl's humility is well documented – he's been tagged "the nicest guy in rock", surely both a blessing and a curse – but I still wasn't expecting him to stroll up, shake my hand and state, "Hi, I'm Dave." The sceptic inside me was very tempted to reply, "No shit, Sherlock" – his, of course, was the face that launched a thousand riffs – but I repressed the temptation. Instead, I realised that despite the millions in the bank and the pampered life of five-star hotels and flunkies whose only job was to say "yes", Grohl still had a reasonably firm grip on reality. And no subject was taboo, be it his ongoing sparring match with Cobain's widow Courtney Love over Nirvana's legacy (and money), his very public love life (he was now engaged to Jordyn Blum, having split with Hole bassist Melissa Auf der Maur), or even the recent OD and near-death experience of his Foo brother and best friend, Taylor Hawkins. It was a welcome relief from the soft-shoe-shuffle that typically passed for an interview, where your subject is either too jaded, too famous or, sometimes, too hungover to bother having a genuine conversation with you.

It was Grohl's parting gesture, just as much as his completely unnecessary introduction that said something about the man. He and Hawkins had been trading wisecracks about a tank top they'd bought that morning while checking out Oxford Street, Sydney's notorious gay strip. This sleeveless number, meant to be worn as tight as physically possible, featured the image of a tanned, buff torso; it was a total gay fantasy. There was no mysterious subtext, though; he and Hawkins hadn't been maintaining some mysterious love that dare not speak its name – they just found the thing funny.

When our interview ended, and the rest of the band had said their goodbyes, Grohl stopped me and asked for my pen. He then scrawled something on the tank top, before handing it over to me. It read: "To my dearest honcho, love Dave." It said something about the man: in spite of the sycophants and the upmarket setting, regardless of the esteem in which he was held because he was once the drummer in "that band", Grohl hadn't really changed since he was a teenage stoner in suburban Virginia lost in a Led Zep head trip. Although he'd left a few casualties on the roadside along the way, he was doing his best to remain an ordinary guy living an extraordinary life.

PART I

DC

CHAPTER ONE

The Family Way

"They were my first musical encounter. So maybe, subconsciously, I want to be Michael Jackson."

– Dave Grohl

AS years in music go, 1971 certainly had its moments. Though the lawyers were still sifting through the ashes of The Beatles, who'd finally disbanded officially a year earlier, it didn't seem as though the world – or former members of the band, for that matter – had spent too long mourning the loss. It was in 1971 that George Harrison, so long kept in the background by the songwriting firm of Lennon & McCartney, finally found an outlet for all the songs he'd been stockpiling over the previous four years and delivered his sprawling triple LP masterwork *All Things Must Pass*. Not to be outdone, John Lennon endured bagism, primal scream therapy, acorns for peace (and Yoko Ono) to record *John Lennon/ Plastic Ono Band* and *Imagine*, the latter being the most concise and radio-friendly set of his career. The album's title track was a utopian anthem that would go on to outlive its creator. Paul McCartney responded with *Ram* and the unlikely US chart-topper 'Uncle Albert/Admiral Halsey', which sounded like a *Sgt Pepper* leftover. Ringo Starr, meanwhile, was riding high in the charts with 'It Don't Come Easy', a Top Five hit on both sides of the Atlantic. The ex-Fab Four clearly had their solo mojos working.

There were rumblings in both the underground and the mainstream. With the help of Andy Warhol, who designed the racy zipper-fronted cover, The Rolling Stones' *Sticky Fingers* – and especially its sassy, struttin' lead single 'Brown Sugar' – was being played everywhere. (It was also a prelude to the Stones' eclectic double album, *Exile On Main Street*, recorded in France, which followed the next year.) A certain David Jones had grown his hair, discovered cross-dressing and re-emerged as David Bowie – who was about to morph into Ziggy Stardust. Former Velvet Underground poet punk, Lou Reed, was preparing to take his 'Walk On The Wild Side', in stride with a dazzling cast of New York freaks. Reed was also about to insinuate the term "giving head" onto mainstream radio, which was something of a ground-breaking achievement.

Another such American maverick in the making, Todd Rundgren, emerged from his former band, Nazz, with *The Ballad Of Todd Rundgren*. (Just like the Stones, his own masterpiece, *Something/Anything*, was also a year away.) Marvin Gaye brought a social conscience, not just his libido, to the charts with 'What's Going On', the Doors' final album with Jim Morrison, *LA Woman*, featuring the tracks 'Riders On The Storm' and 'Love Her Madly', helped to restore their dented credibility, and Three Dog Night were partying with 'Joy To The World'. Glam rock was teetering a few high-heeled steps into the future, while punk rock waited impatiently, ready to destroy everything that had gone before.

Musically speaking, it was a world of possibilities. Or at least it was elsewhere, but maybe not at the annual Ohio State Fair, held in the stifling heat of a Midwestern August afternoon. It was the site where two-year-old Dave Grohl would have his first musical experience, courtesy of Motown's favourite sons, The Jackson Five, and a press pass acquired by Grohl's journalist father. The Jacksons' latest single, 'Never Can Say Goodbye', was currently a runaway summer favourite.

Along with his father James, mother Virginia, and sister Lisa, who was three years older than her brother, Dave Grohl looked on as the Motown moppets – 14-year-old Michael and his siblings Jackie, Tito, Jermaine and Marlon – smiled and shimmied their way through a crowd-pleasing set. As life-defining musical experiences go, it didn't quite rank with bluesman Robert Johnson selling his soul at the crossroads, or an ambitious Paul McCartney checking out the Quarry Men at a local Liverpool fete.

Despite the less-than-cool connotations, Grohl would freely admit to being in the crowd at the Fair – which, incidentally, was a banner day for local girl Candy Franck, who won the double crown of Champion Twirler for her work with the baton, and Miss Majorette for her all-round charm. He would also readily confess, in his typically unedited fashion, that Michael, Tito and the rest of the Jackson crew didn't leave a life-changing impression on him.

"Although I don't really remember them because I was only two," he said many years later, "but they were my first musical encounter. So maybe, subconsciously, I want to be Michael Jackson."

Just like the Jacksons of Gary, Indiana, the Grohls were a music-loving family. They were also, in the words of their most famous son, the latest in the line of a well-established Pennsylvania Dutch family "where everyone is pretty frugal and hard-working". This latter quality in particular, a level-headed, workmanlike ability to make a living and get by when life isn't so comfortable, would prove especially useful to Grohl in the years before finding success as part of the rhythm section propelling Nirvana.

David Eric Grohl was born in Warren, Ohio on January 14, 1969. Located in northeastern Ohio, an hour's drive from the industrial hotspots of Pittsburgh, Cleveland and Akron, Warren was a town that took pride in somehow finding a balance between small-town, down-home rural life and the usual distractions of a reasonably sized city. Known to locals as "The Festival City", Warren could lay reasonable claim to being an active part of early European/American history, especially during the westward expansion. In 1799, 11 years after General Samuel Parsons of Middletown, Connecticut had made the first purchase of land in what was known as the Western Reserve, and European settlers in the eastern states had started to look west, the first log cabin was built in Warren by one Ephraim Quinby. Warren's original residence was situated at the southwest corner of what are now Main and South streets.

"Modern" developments came relatively quickly to this new town. Trumbull County – Warren's home county – was created in 1800, after a proclamation by Governor St Claire. A year later, in the first county election, General Edward Paine was chosen as Warren's delegate to the territorial legislature. In 1804, General Simon Perkins, the first Postmaster in the Western Reserve, settled there. Three years on, the Western Reserve Bank was established in Warren; the Western Reserve's first newspaper was also established in Warren, though not without teething problems. The paper's editor, one Thomas D. Webb, had hoped to name his rag *The Voice of the Wilderness*, a reasonable statement of the times, but finding that the letters V and W were missing in their proper size for the masthead, he had to settle on *The Trump of Fame*.

Warren's ensuing history was lively enough. Its library, complete with 1,000 volumes, granted its first lender's card in 1814, and in 1834 the State Legislature granted Warren a village charter. Wild fires in 1860 razed most of the business district; regrettably, it wasn't until 1882, some 22 years too late, that Warren would have its own fire department building. That same year, Warren's first telephone was installed. In 1913, severe floods paralysed the city's transportation, utilities and industry, while a more man-made crisis, a strike, brought the area's lively steel industry to a grinding halt in 1937.

By the time Dave Grohl opened his eyes to Warren in 1969, the city could also claim at least one space traveller. Apollo 11 astronaut Neil Armstrong – he of "one small step for man but one giant leap for mankind" legend – was an Ohio native who spent some of his early years in Warren. The city was also home to a sizeable manufacturing industry, as well as the National Packard Auto Museum. In census figures collated in the year 2000, Warren's mainly Caucasian population was a snip under 50,000; the median household income a few dollars over $30,000. It was a solid, safe and reasonable enough place in which to grow up, an unpretentious slice of Middle America, and a part of the country where a rock-solid, get-dirt-on-your-hands work ethic would clearly rub off on one of its most famous sons. Throughout his career, Grohl seemed to be a man in constant motion, not unlike much of the machinery that drove Ohio's industry.

The Grohls spent the first few years of their only son's life in Niles, which lay 10 miles outside of Warren, smack-dab in the heart of the Northeastern Ohio industrial area. This was the hometown of Grohl's paternal grandparents, who still live there along with other members of the Grohl clan. Though slightly smaller in scale – latest figures have Niles' population at just over 20,000 – the town's history, not surprisingly, paralleled that of Warren, its slightly larger neighbour.

Although originally given the not-so-poetic tag of Heaton's Furnace, it soon became Nilestown, which was simplified in 1843 to Niles, in honour of Hezekiah Niles, editor of the *Niles Register* newspaper. It didn't take Niles long to morph from just another pioneer outpost to a smoky industrial town, top-heavy with mills, as such captains of industry as James Ward, Sr. tapped into the high-grade black band ore that was found in the aptly named Mineral Ridge. Niles' profits even outstripped those of

Warren by 1870, although the town suffered during the Depression that hit three years later.*

Gradually, as ore supplies dwindled, steel took its place. By 1900, almost 7,500 people called Niles home, as such companies as Ohio Galvanizing, Sykes Metal and the General Electric Company established bases there. The First World War and the burgeoning automobile industry also gave new life to the area. The town had its share of flashpoints in local history, too. Among these was the Great Flood of 1913, which caused more than $300 million worth of damage, and the Anti-Klan Riot of 1924, where clashes between the local chapter of the Ku Klux Klan and their cultural opposites – the Knights Of The Flaming Circle – resulted in 18 hours of full-blown rioting and an ensuing 10 days of martial law, featuring a total of 104 indictments for members of both sides of the simmering racial debate. During the Steel Strike of 1937, employees of the Republic Steel Corporation, who'd dug in and actually refused to strike, could only receive food and other essentials by airdrop, while striking workers on the ground aimed their rifles and took potshots at the planes circling overhead.

By 1969, Niles was notable for one thing only: the establishment of the Eastwood Mall. It was the first major shopping mall on Route 422, and a worrying symbol of the rampant consumerism that today makes many American cities indistinguishable from each other. Sixteen years later, in 1985, a tornado picked up the town of Niles and gave it a horrific shaking, toppling a skating rink and shopping mall, levelling houses and claiming nine fatalities. However, by then the peripatetic Dave Grohl, and his family, had long gone.

Like most fathers and sons, David and James Grohl would have ideological differences, especially when it came to matters of politics, but they did share a passion for music. James Grohl was a classically trained flautist, something of a child prodigy, who later on became a true jazz aficionado. Dave Grohl described his father as "a really straight dude but he was a jazz freak". As a child, Grohl endured endless lectures on the Beats, of whom his father was a huge admirer – James often repeated a story that he was

---

* One of its many victims was James Ward & Company, which folded in 1874, taking the savings of many of the Niles locals down with it.

once hit on by Allen Ginsberg, the gay author of *Howl*, who, along with Jack Kerouac, was the high lord of the Beats. To reject the advances of a boho poet such as Ginsberg was an honour. Grohl's father was also tireless when it came to musical practice and this dedication rubbed off on his son. "He thought that unless you practised for six hours a day," Grohl said in 2002, "you couldn't call yourself a musician. That work ethic had a big effect on me."

Both of Grohl's parents were Ohio natives, although his father's blood-line had German roots, while his mother Virginia, a language teacher, was from an Irish/American background. Virginia's maiden name was O'Hanlon. Her great-grandfather, the first of her family to emigrate from Ireland, set up the public school system in Missouri. Virginia and James met while performing with community theatre and married soon after.

Like her husband, Virginia Grohl was a musician. She sang with local a cappella outfit the Three Belles, who undertook some touring and entered local competitions. Their repertoire was drawn from the Fifties, the golden age of doo-wop and sugary-sweet harmony vocals. Even as a child, surrounded by music and books, Grohl realised that his home life was quite different to most of his peers. As he put it, "I was definitely the exception in my neighbourhood. I didn't grow up to be a complete idiot."

There were, however, noticeable differences in his parents' outlook: his mother was left leaning and artistically inclined, while his father was more conservative, despite his bohemian connections. It wasn't a relationship that was built to last as Dave explained to Nirvana biographer Michael Azerrad, in the book *Come As You Are*, "My mother and father were pretty much at other ends of the spectrum – he's a real conservative, neat, Washington, DC, kind of man and my mother's more of a liberal, free-thinking, creative sort of person."

When not spinning jazz records, rejecting Ginsberg's advances or wailing on his flute, James Grohl was a reporter for the Scripps Howard news agency. Now known as the EW Scripps Company, this multimedia conglomerate was the brainchild of Edward E. Scripps, an Illinois native whose older brother James founded *The Detroit News*. When Edward sponged $10,000 from his well-heeled family in 1878, he set up a Cleve-land newspaper known as *The Penny Press*, targeting a new mass audience of urban workers. As well as launching the Scripps Company, Scripps also founded the United Press International news syndicate in 1907, as direct competition to the already established Associated Press. Scripps would be acknowledged as creating America's first "information revolution". Eventually the Scripps Company included numerous newspapers and TV stations; they even launched Charles Schulz's iconic cartoon strip, *Peanuts*, in 1950.

Like his son a few years down the line, when he arrived at Seattle just as generation grunge was starting to grow its hair and don flannel shirts, James Grohl had an uncanny knack for being in the right place at an absolutely ideal time. In 1972, while James was reporting for the Scripps news service, the family relocated to Alexandria, Virginia, where Virginia Grohl landed a job teaching English in the local Fairfax County education system. (Before that, they'd lived for a short time in Columbus, Ohio.) The move was brought about by James' reporting job, because this quiet slab of suburbia – which, just like Warren before it, was best known for the nearby Springfield shopping mall – lay on the banks of the Potomac River, just six miles south of Washington, DC.

James Grohl couldn't have dreamed of being a reporter at a more volatile (and newsworthy) time in post-war American history. In 1970, when his son David was barely a year old, James had looked on as the Kent State shootings, a.k.a. the Kent State Massacre, unfolded. The incident, intensified by the US invasion of Cambodia, exemplified the growing resistance among young, draft-able Americans to President Richard Nixon's ongoing war against communism in south-east Asia.

Student demonstrations at Kent State began on May 1; by the next day whispers started circulating in the nearby township and on campus that "revolutionaries" were planning to rip up the university and township and in the process kick-start a violent, anti-Nixon political revolution. Ohio Governor James A. Rhodes called in the National Guard. By May 3 the campus looked like a war zone, as 1,000 National Guardsmen tried to control the ongoing tension and violence. When 2,000 people gathered on the university commons, the National Guard ordered them to disperse and began firing tear gas. When 29 of the Guardsmen opened fire on the crowd, four students were killed and nine were wounded. Five days later, a crowd of 100,000, distressed by events at Kent State, marched on Washington protesting against the war. (Nixon would eventually invite some Kent State students to the White House in a transparent attempt at placation.)

The Kent State Shootings was a red-hot flashpoint in America's domestic response to their government's involvement in south-east Asia. *Time* magazine concluded that "triggers were not pulled accidentally at Kent State", while the President's Commission on Campus Conclusion tore shreds off both the protestors and the Guardsmen, stating that "the indiscriminate firing of rifles into a crowd of students and the deaths that followed were unnecessary, unwarranted, and inexcusable."*

This large-scale drama was fodder for a young reporter such as James Grohl, as was the Watergate scandal, which blew open on June 17, 1972, when a security guard working at the office complex of the Watergate Hotel in DC noticed tape on the door leading from the basement stairwell to the underground car park. This seemingly innocent discovery actually uncovered a break-in to the Democratic National Committee, and would result in Nixon's resignation on August 8, 1974. In the process it made household names out of such unlikely characters as E. Howard Hunt and G. Gordon Liddy. Grohl, of course, couldn't help but notice that the two reporters who broke the story, the *Washington Post*'s Bob Woodward and Carl Bernstein, became superstars. His career took an interesting twist when he became campaign manager-cum-speechwriter for Ohio Republican Robert Taft, Jr.

Taft, Jr.'s bloodline positively oozed politics: his grandfather, William Howard Taft, was the 27th US president, while his great-great grandfather Alphonso Taft served briefly as Secretary of War under Ulysses S. Grant not long after the US Civil War. Taft, Jr.'s father, Robert, Sr., was also a senator, widely known as "Mr. Republican". Grohl senior's posting with Taft was made even more interesting given that, many years later, his son Dave would campaign very loudly for Democrat hopeful John Kerry in 2004. While Dave would downplay any strong political convictions, and certainly didn't come on like Joe Strummer when it came to politicising his lyrics, he most definitely leaned to the left, just like his mother. Grohl, Sr.'s allegiances, however, were very much with the right; he even

---

* The shootings also led to some powerful artistic statements including Neil Young's 'Ohio'. Chrissie Hynde, of the Pretenders, then at Kent State, later said that Jeff Miller, one of the slain students, was a big Young fan. There was also Dave Brubeck's 1971 oratorio *Truth Has Fallen*, and a 2000 documentary, *The Day The War Came Home*. Strangely enough, the massacre was the catalyst for Kent State art students Mark Mothersbaugh and Gerald Casale to form art-pop oddballs Devo.

worked as a speechwriter for the Republican National Convention, about as right-leaning, politically speaking, as you could be without falling over.

With James Grohl on board, Taft, Jr. served as a US Senator for Ohio between 1971 and 1976, while the Grohls were based in Springfield. During his first attempt at office, Taft had a fairly smooth run to the Senator's job, even before he was voted into office, as the *Chicago Tribune* announced. "The rest of the Republican state ticket might do well to go into the hardware business," they reported. In much the same way that the name Bush has become an integral part of American politics over the past 15 years, the Tafts had a stranglehold on the seat of power. Taft knew that, too. When he instigated a series of TV spots in the run-up to his 1971 election, he used commercials that focused on his resemblance to his late father. He was usually referred to as "old Bob's son".

Taft, Jr. was also close to the Nixons, often playing host to the President and his wife Tricia, and their son-in-law David Eisenhower. Every inch the "Republican's Republican", Taft, Jr. was tough on poverty – in 1971 he voted to delete a $6 billion anti-poverty bill. During his spell as Senator, Taft was also voted chairman of the House Republican Research Committee.

Democrat Howard Metzenbaum would eventually defeat and replace Taft, Jr. in 1976, ending James Grohl's hot streak. Taft, Jr. died on December 12, 1993.* His *Chicago Tribune* obituary described the 76-year-old as "a scion of a wealthy Ohio family that helped define Republican politics in the US for more than a century". Curiously, he avoided the Taft family fondness for the White House and never ran for the presidency. Showing astute judgement, James Grohl would turn down an offer to work with arch Republican and Viagra spokesman Bob Dole, who in 1976 failed in his run for the vice-presidency under Gerald Ford, and then, much more famously, lost his 1996 campaign for the presidency to Bill Clinton.

Their conflicting political beliefs, however, didn't engender too much bad feeling between the male Grohls – although it undoubtedly caused some conflict between Grohl's liberal-arts-teaching mother and her husband. "My dad's a very smart man but very conservative," Grohl stated in 2005.

While his father was working on the conservative side of politics, Dave

---

* The same day as musical maverick Frank Zappa.

Grohl's youth was relatively uneventful, describing his early upbringing in Virginia as "grounded" and "normal". However, one trait that Grohl developed when he was quite young was a certain knack for showmanship. Asked about his childhood, Grohl admitted that he was "a show-off", "a little comedian", who'd stage impromptu productions for anyone willing to look his way. Interestingly, these performances – Grohl would describe them as "little shows" – sometimes involved innocent acts of cross-dressing, as he'd try on outfits stored away in the family attic, ideally "something as outlandish and ridiculous as possible". Cross-dressing, of course, would become almost a prerequisite in many of Foo Fighters' laugh-out-loud videos, so it wasn't as though dressing in drag was a new sensation for Grohl. He was a natural.

Before converting to the Washington, DC punk scene with evangelical glee, Grohl's musical upbringing was relatively conventional. Growing up in suburban America in the Seventies, what would become known as "classic rock" – a.k.a. "heritage rock" – was a staple part of his musical diet. Grohl boasted of owning a John Lennon toothbrush by the time he was six, but it was a less iconic musical figure who introduced Grohl to the world of rock'n'roll: Texan multi-instrumentalist Edgar Winter, the younger brother of albino guitar wizard Johnny Winter.

Born in Beaumont, Texas, Winter had briefly played in the backing band of his better-known brother, but soon split for a solo career. He started with more of a whimper than a bang: after his album debut, *Entrance*, sold poorly on its release in 1970, he formed the unfortunately named White Trash, who may have been a live drawcard – they were on the bill for the closing night of New York's legendary Fillmore East – but failed to sell records. Winter fared better with the forward-thinking Edgar Winter Group, whose first single, 'Hangin' Around', was backed by a weird instrumental entitled 'Frankenstein'. When the band's label, Epic, recognised that the flip-side was receiving all the radio attention, they edited the track and re-released it as a single. 'Frankenstein' reached number one on the US singles chart in May 1973, stomping all over such fluff as Elton John's 'Daniel' and Tony Orlando & Dawn's 'Tie A Yellow Ribbon Round The Old Oak Tree'.

Like much of America, a very young and impressionable Grohl was hooked, although he discovered the song a couple of years after its success

– and even then, purely by accident. Although the Grohls were a musically inclined family, with a guitar lying around the house from as far back as Grohl can remember, they didn't actually own a record player, so his mother would sometimes bring a school-issue sound system home for the weekend. "[It was] the biggest piece of shit you've ever seen," according to Grohl. On one occasion, Grohl, along with his mother and sister, went out record shopping and picked up a K-Tel Top 40 collection from the local drug store. Amid the usual chart fodder – Grohl swears blind that Chic were on the record, although he's got his timeline a little wrong, as 1978 was the year of 'Le Freak' – was Winter's 'Frankenstein'. Grohl was a true believer after one listen.

"To this day," he said in 1999, "[it's] still one of the most amazing songs you've ever heard in your life. My first favourite song was a prog rock instrumental. It changed my fucking life, I swear to God." In one of his bolder declarations, Grohl insisted that Edgar Winter opened his eyes to rock'n'roll.*

Saturday Night Live was a weekend staple in most American homes, and it was during the show that Grohl first set eyes on Athens, Georgia weirdos the B-52's. Named after the bouffant wigs sported by singers-cum-shriekers Cindy Wilson and Kate Pierson, and led by the dapper Fred Schneider, a man who preferred to talk rather than sing, the B-52's peddled a strange brew of New Wave, surf music, pop and retro kitsch. When Grohl saw them on the night of January 26, 1980, the band shrieked and shimmied their way through the tracks 'Rock Lobster' and 'Dance This Mess Around' from their self-titled debut album.

The effect was immediate – not just on Grohl, but on millions of others, as one starstruck viewer would reflect at www.amazon.com: "When they were doing the latter ['Dance This Mess Around'], my parents walked in from a night out and my mother said, 'What is THIS?' Of course, the very next day I got the album." Dave Grohl felt the same. "When the B-52's played 'Rock Lobster', they totally blew my mind. They definitely opened up a whole new world for me." Grohl snapped up a copy of the album and sat in front of his borrowed stereo, transfixed by the band's twisted tunes, songs that *Rolling Stone* magazine described as "a sound

---

* In late 2005, the author asked Winter about Grohl's championing of his signature song. The veteran rocker admitted that he found it "flattering".

unlike anything else on the scene". While the songs insinuated their way into Grohl's mind – so much so he'd still be talking up his young love of the B-52's 20 years later – he was equally fascinated by the band's look. From an early age, Dave Grohl was savvy to the image-conscious world of pop.

"The women looked like they were from outer space, and everything was linked in – the [record] sleeves, the sound, the clothes, the iconography, the logo, everything," he said. "I think when you're a kid, that's what you're after, a real unified feel to a band, and that's what the B-52's offered."

Also on Grohl's high-rotation list was cartoon rockers Kiss, plus U2 (their debut album *Boy* provided the soundtrack to Grohl's first couple of years in high school) and Canadian power prog trio Rush. He was also deeply enamoured of Devo, as much for the band's Ohio connections as their perverse takes on such tracks as the Rolling Stones' 'Satisfaction', which made their 1978 debut album, *Q: Are We Not Men? A: We Are Devo!* a strange sensation. "Everyone in my year wanted to be in Devo," admitted Grohl. "They were these aliens that you really wanted to know. It was really inspirational not only for a band [from Ohio] to take New York by storm, but also for them to be so far out." Not unlike the B-52's, the flowerpot men of Devo experienced success on a much larger scale with such subsequent releases as 1980's *Freedom Of Choice* and its snappy breakthrough single 'Whip It'.

However if there was one band that would have the deepest and most lasting impact on Grohl, it was Led Zeppelin. His teenage love of Devo and others eventually faded in favour of numerous angry bands from Washington, DC's underground, but Led Zep remained a Dave Grohl standard. In fact his love for them was so unconditional that his one as yet unfulfilled rock'n'roll dream was to fill the drum stool left empty by mad dog John "Bonzo" Bonham. (When Zep's John Paul Jones cameoed on Foo Fighters' 2005 double set, *In Your Honor*, Grohl's rock fantasy was partly fulfilled.)

Grohl credits his mother with accidentally introducing him to Led Zeppelin. He first heard the band's 1971 benchmark, 'Stairway To Heaven' on the AM radio she'd leave playing at home. A few years later, Zep's first two albums, the imaginatively titled *Led Zeppelin* and *Led Zeppelin II*, were handed down to Grohl by some local stoners, who were apparently heavy on the ground in Virginia. (Grohl once described his neighbourhood as comprising of "a lot of muscle cars and keggers and Zeppelin and acid and weed. Somehow they all went hand–in–hand.") Grohl's conversion was complete after hearing such Zep perennials as 'Rock And Roll', 'Black Dog' and 'Immigrant Song' each time he tuned his radio to local rock station DC101. Up until Bonham's premature death in 1980 and beyond, Led Zeppelin ruled the US airwaves.

To Grohl, Led Zeppelin was more than just a band. "They were the perfect combination of the most intense elements: passion and mystery and expertise." Grohl rated guitarist Jimmy Page as "freakier" than psychedelic bluesman Jimi Hendrix, while John Bonham, a massive influence on Grohl as a drummer, "played the drums like someone who didn't know what was going to happen next – like he was teetering on the edge of a cliff."*

This exposure to music unlike anything he'd heard before was ample motivation for Grohl to do more than absently pluck away at the acoustic guitar that lay around his Virginia home. Although Grohl would go on to make his name as a powerhouse drummer, a workmanlike guitarist and larynx-shredding vocalist, his first unlikely instrument of choice was the trombone, which he experimented with, briefly, in his pre-teen years but as he confessed, "That didn't last long." Grohl was in love with rock and, naturally enough, this steered him towards the guitar. He'd already strummed along to the records he was blasting from his mother's borrowed stereo, on a nylon-stringed Spanish acoustic also on loan from his mother's school. However, there was only so much 'Smoke On The Water' the family could take. They recommended guitar lessons (or preferably silence), which Grohl remembers taking, "When I was about 10 years old." He persevered with lessons for the best part of a year, but eventually grew frustrated with the more formal side "because it wasn't teaching me how to play music." To this day, Grohl still can't read or write music.

Curiously, over the years Grohl has clearly rethought the value of those early, fumbling beginnings. He has repeatedly given due credit to his first

---

* Grohl paid his respects by replicating Bonham's three-circle logo on one of his earliest drum kits; he later had the logo tattooed on his arm, while crashing at a Dutch squat with the band Scream.

and only guitar teacher (whose name has disappeared into the ether of time), citing him among his biggest musical influences, "Which is kind of weird, because I only took lessons for a year and quit because they were so boring."

Grohl had a totally different perspective on his first "real" guitar: a Sears Silvertone, a Christmas present from his parents in 1981. The Sears Silvertone was the archetypal American suburban dreamer's first guitar, the perfect weapon of choice for a kid like Grohl. Cheap and solidly con-structed, the Silvertone, which was sold through the Sears department store, hence the name, had rated well with many blues guitarists from the Thirties and Forties. Such bluesmen as Muddy Waters and Arthur "Big Boy" Crudup were early fans of this utilitarian six-string. Jimi Hendrix, Bob Dylan, and country legend Chet Atkins, all strummed their first few hesitant chords on a Silvertone.*

The model Grohl owned was the 1963 "amp-in-a-case" Silvertone, that featured a small amplifier built into the guitar's carrying case. It was everything the apprentice axegrinder needed. With his trusty Beatles songbook in hand, and Rush's *2112* on high rotation, Grohl was ready to rock – well, as much as a 12-year-old hopeful could rock, that is. The 300-plus pages of his much-thumbed Beatles songbook – a Christmas gift from his mother – kept Grohl engrossed, as he did his best to work out the songs and sing along. As musical beginnings went, Grohl was learning from the best.

The partnership of Grohl-Hinkle was unlikely to evoke the same kind of reverence as, say, Lennon/McCartney or Jagger/Richards. However, none of this mattered to Grohl when he chose schoolmate Larry Hinkle as his first musical collaborator. Grohl, who was 11 or 12 at the time, again leaned on his supportive mother for a cassette recorder to capture the tunes he was planning to record with his best friend.†

The dynamic duo was named the HG Hancock Band. Hinkle, who is now a cabinetmaker and part-time musician living in Fredericksburg, Virginia, still laughs at the memory. "It's silly," he told me in November

---

* Kiss' Paul Stanley, one of Grohl's teenage heroes, is now Silvertone's spokesman, as the company resurrected their guitars for the 21st century.
† Unsurprisingly, none of these early tapes have survived, although Grohl is clearly a cassette lover; his first solo recordings, issued in 1993 under the name Late, appeared on cassette only.

2005. "We were fans of Lynyrd Skynyrd at the time and the story we'd heard was that they'd named their band after their PE teacher. Our PE teacher's name was Ms Hancock. She was your typical PE teacher, a little butch as I recall, but really cool. [The] HG stands for Hinkle/Grohl. We thought we were cool." Hinkle and Grohl – along with another ever-present Virginian, Jimmy Swanson – became tight during fifth and sixth grade in school, first at North Springfield Elementary followed by Oliver Wendell Holmes Intermediate.

As a mandatory part of their schooling, Grohl and Hinkle had randomly chosen instruments to learn when they were in fifth grade: Grohl picked the aforementioned trombone while Hinkle opted for the less portable tuba. "Everyone would go to music class, and sit in a room with a music teacher who'd sing songs while the teacher played piano," Hinkle recalled. "But if you took an instrument, you could go and play with the band. I picked tuba and David played trombone. I think we both did it for one semester and we quit. I'm not sure why David stopped, but I stopped because I used to walk to school and in the wintertime this old tuba was hard to carry, and it was cold. It was a hassle."

The idea to record as the HG Hancock Band came to the pair when Grohl approached Hinkle with some handwritten song lyrics. Hinkle was blown away by what he read. "He came to me one day in class with some lyrics. He said, 'Hey, I've got this new song.' The lyrics were incredible, I couldn't believe it. Then later that day he played the song for me and it was genius . . . it turns out it was a Lynyrd Skynyrd song I hadn't heard, 'Gimme Three Steps'. Then David told me, 'Oh, yeah, it's a Lynyrd Skynyrd song.'"

When not breaching copyright laws, Grohl was also writing original songs that formed the basis of the now-long-lost HG Hancock Band cassette. Hinkle can't recall the names of the songs, but his memories of the bedroom recording sessions are still vivid. "It was David on acoustic guitar and I played drums, which consisted of his mother's laundry basket and knitting needles, maybe some pots and pans. [Hinkle's father had been a drummer.] David had this old beat-up classical acoustic guitar; he'd put steel strings on it, but it never seemed to have six strings on it at one time, there was always a busted string. But he could make it sound great, even back then. I started playing guitar after he showed me how."

Soon after these bedroom sessions with Hinkle, Grohl found out that his Silvertone guitar wasn't as indestructible as he'd first believed. After dropping it one day, the thing smashed into a thousand pieces. Grohl then graduated to a copy of a black Memphis Les Paul, as close as he could get to the guitar that Kiss' Paul Stanley sacrificed most nights during the band's blood-drooling, retina-burning live show.

As far as his musical tastes went, Grohl was still listening to conventional rock which even now holds a place close to his heart. "I'm not ashamed to say I live for that shit," Grohl stated in 2000, "Wings, Peter Frampton, Supertramp." Cheap Trick's 'Surrender' was another youthful favourite, while aforementioned southern rock rebels, Lynyrd Skynyrd, ranked highly. Grohl particularly admired guitarist Allen Collens, in equal parts for his killer riffs, poodle perm and Gibson Explorer guitar.

Grohl and Hinkle continued to get most of their musical education from Radio DC101. "Van Halen and AC/DC were the two big bands for us back then," Hinkle told me. This love of arena rock would be among the common denominators for Grohl when he met future Foo Fighter Taylor Hawkins, a man who knew the Queen catalogue inside out. Theirs was a bond forged on big hair, monster riffs and killer hooks – in short, classic rock.

There was nothing in Grohl's early years to hint at his subsequent conversion to the underground. His life was very much that of a fully functional American teen. Though prone to hyperactivity, a character trait that eventually drew him like a magnet to the fast, frenetic pulse of punk, he was a solid student, though hardly brilliant. As Grohl summed up in 1997, his school reports had a typically recurring theme of "David would be a great student if he could just stay in his fucking seat." As far as Grohl could recall, his school results were passable. "It was always enough to progress to the next year, anyway." One thing Grohl lacked, however, was drive. "I didn't have any ambition to be the best – I just didn't want to be the worst."

Larry Hinkle recalls that Grohl was constantly on the move; he was one of the greatest air drummers that Springfield ever produced. "David would beat on anything, he was constantly drumming, air drumming, pencils, knitting needles, anything, [he was] always beating out rhythms. I used to be really impressed that he could air drum to 'Working Man', the Rush song on *All The World's A Stage* – he could air drum perfectly to the drum solo in sixth or seventh grade – very impressive. He learned by listening to

Rush, the Police, Led Zeppelin, playing with whatever he could get his hands on."

Grohl was the everyman during his early school days, the kind of guy who "got along with the stoners, got along with the geeks". In fact, Grohl still maintains friendships from his earliest days at Annandale High School, in northern Virginia, which he attended for two years, and Bishop Ireton, a Catholic private school in Alexandria (a school "with a great reputation", according to one of the staff at Annandale High). While at Bishop Ireton, Grohl even mastered the gentlemanly sport of lacrosse. He also attended Alexandria's Thomas Jefferson High School, where his mother taught, and was voted vice president of his freshman class.

It was his move to Bishop Ireton that reflected a gradual change in Grohl, who insists that he shifted schools because "I was a naughty boy – just didn't care about anything, really." A heavy pot intake – he'd started smoking up to four or five times a day – and slipping grades was the main cause. He didn't care much for the school; he recalled his time there as "pretty scary". Founded in 1964, Bishop Ireton is owned by the Diocese of Arlington and run by priests and brothers of the Oblates of St Francis de Sales religious congregation, which might explain Grohl's uneasy memories.

Bishop Ireton also motivated Grohl to question his spiritual side, while confirming his other, stronger beliefs. "I was going to Catholic school and questioning God," he once said, "but I *believed* in Led Zeppelin." As an escape, Grohl would hang out at a nearby video arcade, pumping quarters into a Galaga machine. Like so many of his peers, Grohl's new-found lifestyle and school made an uncomfortable fit. His home life was also in the midst of a major upheaval.

Understandably, Grohl has never been especially forthcoming about his parents' divorce. He's revealed so little, in fact, that the date of their split and eventual divorce remains unclear, although it's most likely that the Grohls split in 1976, when their son was seven. James Grohl moved back to Ohio, leaving his family behind in Virginia. "By the time I got hold of the situation," Grohl said in 1997, "it was too late for me to have a freak-out. It just seemed abnormal for all my friends to have a father. I thought growing up with my mother and sister was the way it was supposed to be." Unlike many of his musical peers from the Nineties, who used a dysfunctional past as an excuse to unload their pain on the public,

Grohl has never complained of a difficult upbringing. Nor has it provided subject matter for his songs.

The upside of this domestic drama was that Grohl would become very close to his sister and his mother. Virginia Grohl would be a regular backstage visitor at her son's gigs – "I guess it's not what you'd call cool, but heck, who cares?" – and Dave has cited her as a constant source of inspiration. "My mother . . . she has put up with a bunch of shit and has to deal with teenagers and little fucking asshole punks her whole life being a teacher – and then she has one herself. She's a saint. [And] she has a beautiful voice."

Whenever the conversation turned to Grohl's father, he always spoke with a certain caution. "I've learned to accept the relationship we have," Grohl told a reporter bold enough to ask, "and he's a great guy, but growing up without a strong male influence had a strong influence on me." In another interview, Grohl admitted that whenever he stepped out of line while growing up, his father would deliver a sermon akin to "the State of the Union address. Imagine the lectures I'd get if I fucked up."*

With his father out of the picture, the Grohls were certainly not living in style, even though they were residing in one of the better-heeled parts of the country. Grohl has stated on more than one occasion that he was raised with very little, a fair comment given that his mother's salary as a state school teacher was hardly a king's ransom. There was enough money, however, to enable Grohl to visit a therapist soon after his parents' separation and eventual divorce. This was the first of several sessions that Grohl would pay to the analyst's couch; he went into therapy after the breakdown of his marriage and at other equally rough patches in his life.

"Everyone could do with a little therapy now and again," he said in 2002. "The best thing about therapy is reassurance, having someone talk back and give you a response that makes you feel like you're not alone and that what you're going through is understandable. Therapists may have a better understanding of human nature than your best friend who deals pot and works in a gas station." (Years later, Grohl's faith in therapy would be

---

* Grohl's situation wasn't unusual: a recent report has revealed that among Western nations, the US has the lowest percentage (63%) of children growing up with both biological parents. In 1980, the US divorce rate was 22.6 per 1,000 married women (currently at 17.7).

severely tested when an analyst told him that his life of hotels, stages and airports "was just not reality". Grohl responded by "getting the fuck off the couch, because this *is* my reality.")

Grohl appears to have had no great problems with adapting to his self-sufficient role as man of the house. "I could look after myself pretty easily," he recalled in 2002, "so I just focused on making sure that my family was happy. I've been doing it ever since."

Sandy Moran was the first girl to break Dave Grohl's heart. They met in the eighth grade and went out for all of two weeks. According to Grohl, "She was beautiful, the best-looking girl in the whole school. She dropped me like a hot potato, too." While this seems like standard teenage heartache, Ms. Moran's fickle ways did inspire the very impressionable Grohl. After copping the old "it's not you, it's me" line, he went home and had a dream. He was onstage in a massive arena, wailing away on guitar. "The audience were going nuts like they were loving me and I looked down and she was in the front row, crying. I think that was my initial motivation to become the biggest fucking rock star in the world."

While rock superstardom was a long way off in the teenage Grohl's future, its vices were having an insidious influence. Grohl has spoken freely about his teenage drug indulgences, which made for the perfect companion to his fast-developing appreciation of rock. A neighbourhood buddy – known only as Bobby – had been one of the first kids on Grohl's block to own a CD player and the first CD he bought was Led Zeppelin's *Houses Of The Holy*. "This coincided nicely with the start of my love affair with marijuana," Grohl recalled. Friday nights became almost a religious experience for the pair: they'd smoke up a storm and pick apart every single note played (or wailed) by the musical firm of Page, Plant, Bonham and Jones, while the rest of their schoolmates were hanging out at the local football game, ogling cheerleaders. "We'd turn into the saddest musos in the world," Grohl said in 1997, "because we'd never heard anything on CD before. [We'd say] 'Hey, you can hear John Bonham sniff in this speaker.' Jesus."

Smoking dope became almost as big a part of Grohl's life as his slowly advancing musical technique. "My best friend was my bong," said Grohl. Another smoking pal of Grohl's was Jimmy Swanson, who lived a block away and became a running buddy for life. "Me and Jimmy were bonded in pot; bonded by herb." But whereas Led Zeppelin was the soundtrack of choice for sessions with his other smoking pals, Grohl and Swanson dabbled with the harder stuff, namely Metallica.

A serious hard rock fan, Swanson had spotted a tiny ad for a mail order catalogue, called End of the Rainbow. He selected Mercyful Fate's album *Melissa* and Metallica's 1983 debut LP *Kill 'Em All*, a record cheerfully described by *Rolling Stone* as "an anarchic catharsis of gloom". Within 10 seconds of its lead-off track, 'Hit The Lights', he picked up the phone, called Grohl and screamed, "Get up here! Get up here now!" to Grohl down the phone. They'd never encountered anything like this primal roar – only Motörhead came close. "But this was, like, times 10," said Grohl. They were hooked.

In order to raise cash for pot, Grohl would sometimes help out at local concerts, manning merchandising stalls or whatever else was required of him. That's how this Led Zep-loving Metallica convert came to find himself at a prog rock show, hardly the right place for a teenager with monster riffs in mind. "Actually, what I was really doing was spending the whole day looking for pot." The only thing Grohl scored that night was a Genesis T-shirt, which his mother eventually used for a pillow case. Grohl still hangs onto this keepsake, a reminder of simpler times. "I was looking for pot and I ended up working at the Genesis concert. That phrase pretty much sums up my entire teenage experience."

Although impacting on his grades, and his eventual direction in life, Grohl insists that drugs were never a problem. As he saw it, "I've never got fucked up on drugs or got into such a bad place I felt trapped and couldn't get out." Grohl has insisted that he only dabbled with soft drugs and psychedelics – cocaine and heroin simply weren't his thing despite their use and abuse by those close to him. In fact, the only thing he'd admit to snorting was snuff. He eventually gave up most drugs by the time he was 20, when a token puff on a joint brought on a panic attack. "I'd wind up breaking out in hives and calling 911."

After Swanson turned him on to Slayer's *Chapel* EP, he spent a good chunk of 1984 "smoking as much weed as I could, taking acid on the weekends and listening to Slayer all the time". In many interviews, Grohl has spoken about his love of all things lysergic, admitting to "eating sheets of acid" as his musical tastes headed into darker, heavier territory.

Mushrooms were another favourite of Grohl's during his time in

Virginia. His first experience was in his early teens, on Christmas Day, no less; the mushrooms had actually been a Christmas gift from a well-meaning pal. Christmas at the Grohls was a big deal; typically there'd be 60 or 70 friends, family and teaching colleagues of his mother Virginia gathered in their house. "I tripped my fucking balls off right in front of my mother's friends, who were all teachers at my school. So it was kind of a nightmare." Grohl spent a good part of the day driving around in his mother's Ford Fiesta, his head protruding from the sunroof "imagining it to be a tank". Led Zeppelin's 'The Rain Song' was a particular favourite of Grohl's when he was on 'shrooms; he'd blare it so loudly that his entire street got to know the song note-by-blazing-note.

Hinkle was one of many regulars at the Grohl Christmas get-togethers. Although he can't vouch for Grohl's mushrooms experience – "I wouldn't doubt it, though" – he could speak for the quality of the festivities. "The parties were always really good."

As Grohl was fast turning into a typical teen stoner, in love with pot and rock in equal proportions, he managed to lose his virginity at the tender age of 14. The festivities were winding down at a keg party when a female basketballer from his school, two years his senior, pounced on Grohl in a bathroom, where he was busy writing messages on a mirror with lipstick. Grohl, who even then was conscious of his appearance – describing himself as "geeky", "dorky" and "kind of strange looking" – let his unnamed partner take over, as they moved to a pull-out couch downstairs. "She showed me the ropes. She ruled me like a caged animal." Although this was Grohl's only encounter with his cherry picker, he'd never have problems meeting and bedding women, even before he became "the guy from Nirvana". "I just started fucking," he aptly described in 2003.

While Zep-loving Grohl adored the lemon-squeezing wail of Robert Plant, Jimmy Page's sky-scraping riffs and John Paul Jones' consummate musicianship, it was John "Bonzo" Bonham's influence that convinced him to become a drummer. Bonham died on September 24, 1980, aged 32, at the end of a day of startling over-indulgence, beginning with a breakfast of ham rolls and four quadruple vodka-and-oranges, and ending with a drunken nap at Jimmy Page's house that turned into a deathly coma. When Page's assistant, Rick Hobbs, tried to rouse Bonzo the next morning, he'd been dead for hours.

The tales of Bonham's wild ways were almost as legendary as those of fellow maniac drummer Keith Moon of the Who. When he wasn't sleeping, Bonham was a man who could out-drink and out-drug most of his peers – until that fateful day at Page's house. As fellow drummer and friend Bev Bevan stated in a 2005 *Mojo* article on Bonham, "I think he felt he had a reputation to live up to, like Keith Moon. One of the last times I ever saw him was in the bar at the Hyatt in LA, and for my every one drink he'd order himself six Brandy Alexanders. [He was] knocking them back, one after the other."

As wayward and sometimes downright dangerous as Bonham could be, Grohl couldn't resist the appeal of this larger-than-life rock hero. Grohl not only felt that "drums, to me, always seemed like the greatest toy", but he had a ready-made role model. "John Bonham is the greatest rock drummer of all time," Grohl opined in 2005. "He had this manic sense of cacophony, but he also had the ultimate feel. He could swing, he could get on top, or he could pull back. Led Zeppelin, and John Bonham's drumming especially, really opened up my ears." Often without inducement, Grohl would happily reel off his favourite Bonham moments to journalists, including 'Achilles' Last Stand' ("A good example of Bonham's restless side"), 'When The Levee Breaks' ("It's pure chocolate fuckin' sex"), 'Immigrant Song' ("He's either drunk as hell or he's just having the time of his life") and, of course, Bonham's one-man performance, the epic 'Moby Dick'. "Drum solos are usually just wank, crap, but the one in 'Moby Dick' is the greatest drum solo of all time," said Grohl.

This irresistible mix of unrivalled musicality and drunken rebellion was enough for Grohl to put aside his guitar and turn to the drums, even though he didn't own a kit, and couldn't have squeezed one into his Virginia bedroom if he'd tried. Showing admirable ingenuity, he organised his bedroom furniture into something vaguely resembling a kit, and flailed away. Rush's prog-rock epic *2112* was another key soundtrack to his bedroom drumming. "I had a chair that was next to my bed," Grohl explained to a reporter from *Modern Drummer* magazine, "and I would kneel down on the floor and put a pillow between my legs to use as my snare. I would use the chair to my left as the hi-hat and use the bed as toms and cymbals. And I would play to these records [using a borrowed pair of oversized marching sticks] until there was condensation dripping from the windows." It was a brilliantly imaginative way to learn the basics of drumming, but it also meant that Grohl developed hands of steel. When he did eventually progress to a proper drum kit, he broke pretty much everything he touched.

Formal training on the drums was as useful for Grohl as his fumbling lessons on guitar. Along with his mother, Grohl attended a jazz workshop, held every Sunday at a Washington, DC club called One Step Down, where fledgling drummers were invited to sit in with the house band. While Grohl admits he "knew nothing of jazz", he once did get up and play, at his mother's insistence, as a birthday gift to her. The resident drummer was "very nice" after Grohl did his best to keep the beat for one song, so he asked if he would give him lessons. By this time, Grohl owned his first kit, a black Tama Swing Star five piece. ("It was fucking loud.") The teacher came over to the Grohl home and started by correcting Grohl's grip. "I held them like they were chicken wings or something," he recalled many years later. After a session of "paradiddles for $75 an hour", Grohl figured that he'd rather learn by ear than be formally trained. He hasn't had a lesson since.

CHAPTER TWO

Going Underground

"The DC hardcore scene was all about sharing, about being part of this big community."

– Dave Grohl

I T'S a recurring theme in rock'n'roll history: a hugely influential act, or sometimes an entire scene, emerges from the unlikeliest location. Liverpool's hole-in-the-wall Cavern, or Hamburg's Star Club, were hardly known until The Beatles put them on the musical map in the early Sixties. A downtown New York venue promising its customers "Country, Bluegrass and Blues" – a.k.a. CBGBs – seemed least likely to spawn such ground-breaking and influential acts as the Ramones, Blondie, Talking Heads and Television during the late Seventies. While a lot of things went down in Malcolm McLaren's 'Sex' boutique in London, even this shrewd operator could not have foreseen how big an impact punk rock would have when putting the Sex Pistols together in 1975. Even Seattle was better known for rain and coffee prior to the grunge revolution of the early Nineties.

Two high schools in the US capital, Washington, DC – Woodrow Wilson High School and Georgetown Day School – were up there in the "places least likely to start a revolution" stakes. With a school population that was roughly split between desperately poor African/American kids and the offspring of wealthy, ladder-climbing politicians – though rarely in the same classroom – it couldn't be said that Washington was big on the arts, even if Georgetown was one of Washington's few gathering places for the children of a small liberal elite.

Founded in 1945, Georgetown was the only private school (or state school, for that matter) in the US capital genuinely committed to diversity

33

and equal access for all students. Georgetown's founders included parents of black, white, Jewish and Christian students, and the school's mission statement was clear: "From the earliest grades, we encourage our students to wonder, to inquire, and to be self-reliant, laying the foundation for a lifelong love of learning."*

"The Georgetown Day School was in the upper north-west, a very elite school. You didn't have to wear shoes to class, you call your teachers by their first name, [and] your parents pay a lot of money to send you," said Steven Blush, a DC promoter and writer during the city's hardcore punk peak in the Eighties. The DC hardcore scene had its share of well-heeled players, including Marginal Man's Kenny Inouye, the son of a Hawaiian senator, and SOA's Ivor Hansen, whose father was an admiral in the US Navy. A native New Yorker, Blush enrolled at George Washington University in 1981, studying political science. He found himself drawn to the underground, which he chronicled in his book *American Hardcore: A Tribal History*, when he learned that "politics was even sleazier than the music business".

It's unlikely that Georgetown's founders could have envisaged the Eighties DC hardcore scene being nurtured in its classrooms, and neither could the staff at Wilson High, a state school just across the Potomac River in Arlington. Musical tuition and/or study definitely wasn't high on the curriculum, a fact confirmed by former student Bobby Sullivan, who, as part of the band Lünchmeat, would share a single with Mission Impossible, one of Dave Grohl's first bands. (The split single was Grohl's first "real" foray into a recording studio.)

Among Wilson's students were such future hardcore punks as Jeff Nelson, Brian Baker and Lyle Preslar (all of Minor Threat and other DC bands of renown), as well as Sullivan, Johnny Temple, Alexis Fleisig and Scott McCloud, who played in Lünchmeat and later Soul Side and Girls Against Boys. Some of these Wilson students had also attended Georgetown Day School. "A lot of people involved with punk were people I went to school with," Johnny Temple told me when we spoke in late 2005.

One of the most recognised graduates of these schools was Ian

---

* Enlightenment comes at a price, though – it currently costs roughly $20,000 per annum to pursue this "love of learning".

MacKaye.* Born on April 16, 1962, MacKaye cut a distinctive figure with his close-cropped skull and intense stare. He would become renowned for many things: he was founder of Dischord Records, the spiritual centre of the DC punk movement, and with one song he created the entire "straight edge" movement, which rejected the toxic excesses of the rock'n'roll life-style (a declaration that MacKaye would live to regret). With his passionate sermonising out front of such bands as Minor Threat and Fugazi, MacKaye proved to thousands of punks-in-the-making – Dave Grohl included – that you could find your way in the music business without having to sell out for the major label dollar. MacKaye was also a fifth-generation Washington native, a very rare thing in such a transient city. "If Iggy Pop is the godfather of punk," wrote www.allmusic.com's Greg Prato, with pinpoint precision, "then the godfather of hardcore would have to be Ian MacKaye."

What would become known as "hardcore" was a scene created by alienated suburbanites who'd been born too late for punk. As the move-ment developed, it veered away from what had come before. "The origi-nal punks were artistic; they were fans of Bowie and Warhol's Factory," explained Blush. "The music was this bleak, urban noise. A lot of these people were musicians to begin with and adapted punk to their style. They could play Bowie songs. It was great but it was dead by 1979, 1980: the Sex Pistols had broken up, the Clash were very different.

"Across America you had these kids getting into punk and then finding out it's over. So they create their own version of punk, what later becomes known as 'hardcore punk'. It was *hardcore*. The bands weren't musically good, they were just kids, so they put everything into energy and speed. All this fast music is starting to happen: the Dickies, bands like that. These weren't sophisticated; they were alienated kids from the suburbs."

Scenes quickly developed in such unlikely places as DC, Orange County in California, Boston and elsewhere, with audiences (and bands) comprised of educated, middle-class kids, slam-dancing right alongside the usual fuck-ups. "The initial impulse of most people was to pooh-pooh it," added Blush. "'Oh, the Sex Pistols did this, it's so five years ago.' The hardcore generation had been dismissed by 'serious' music fans as stupid.

---

* Even now, years after he graduated, a Wilson High website acknowledges MacKaye as one of its most successful alumni, along with a billionaire named Warren Buffett and Florida Congressman Cliff Stearns. MacKaye is simply credited as "punk rock icon".

'What are these kids doing? They're fucking up the place, dancing crazy.' No one wanted to deal with it.

"But the famous punk rock bands – the Sex Pistols, the Clash, the Ramones – they were all on major labels and on TV, it was a well-documented scene. That wasn't the deal with hardcore. If you find a live video of Black Flag it's probably at a VFW hall with one light and maybe a stage, if you're lucky. This was hardcore, a whole other level of punk. Most fans of punk had no time for it; they thought it was second genera-tion, a wannabe, when in fact much of the stuff in music today comes out of the hardcore scene, particularly the DC scene."

In his razor-sharp study, *Our Band Could Be Your Life*, writer Michael Azerrad* cites Ian MacKaye's band Minor Threat as the "definitive" hard-core punk band. Another of MacKaye's many admirers was Glen E. Friedman, later to find large-scale recognition with the skate-punk flick *DogTown – The Legend Of The Z-Boys*. Friedman is a photographer whose images of such hardcore punk immortals as Fugazi, Minor Threat, Bad Brains and Black Flag were invaluable documents of the Eighties punk scene.† Although based on both coasts – his divorced parents lived in LA and New York – Friedman was a familiar figure in DC as the scene there grew.

Friedman could see why Ian MacKaye became such an influential and revered figure; he was a man of the people. "Minor Threat were just awesome," he told me. "There was nothing like a Minor Threat show. Ian was truly at one with the audience; they looked at him like he was one of them." Friedman even rated MacKaye a better frontman than the wired coil of sweat, tattoos, alienation and anger calling himself Henry Rollins (a.k.a. Henry Garfield), who conducted public displays of catharsis with Californian punks Black Flag. "Ian was different from Rollins – he [Rollins] gave everything, but he detached himself, although Henry is fucking intense. [But] he was barely there with the band, whereas Ian was incredible. I never witnessed someone who saw Minor Threat that didn't love them. They were remarkable. I was the same age as these guys and was inspired by their music and their lyrics."

---

* Azerrad also chronicled Nirvana's rise in *Come As You Are*.
† These photos are best seen in his self-published 1982 "photo-zine" *My Rules* and two later books, poetically entitled *Fuck You Heroes* and *Fuck You Too*.

MacKaye's devotion to music began in the strangest fashion, particularly for a man who would steadfastly operate outside the mainstream. As a kid, he was mad for the rockumentary *Woodstock*, the defining document of the late Sixties hippie generation, three days of "peace and music" that made stars out of such acts as Joe Cocker & the Grease Band, Crosby, Stills, Nash & Young and Sly & the Family Stone. As great as they undoubtedly were, these acts didn't really make the type of music that would inspire a kid who'd eventually be known as "the godfather of hardcore" – even though the era's sense of community and possibility definitely influenced MacKaye. After endlessly watching the film, he came to a realisation. "I wanted to be in a band," he told Michael Azerrad for his book *Our Band Could Be Your Life*.

When MacKaye was 12, his father won a scholarship to Stanford University, so the family shifted to California for nine months. When he returned to DC, what MacKaye found would change the direction of his life as much as his beloved *Woodstock*. Most of his DC school friends had turned themselves into drugged-up juvenile delinquents. MacKaye was appalled. "Fuck that," MacKaye told Azerrad. "I was not interested."

If pot defined Sixties culture and the Woodstock generation, cocaine was definitely the drug of the Seventies. DC wasn't the only city hit by the crisis that so repulsed MacKaye; a late Seventies survey compiled by a group called Monitoring the Future put drug use by high school seniors throughout the US at around 39%. According to the High School Senior Survey (HSSS), cocaine use was on the rise at the time among high school seniors, from 2% in 1975 to 6% in 1979. Cocaine's dangerously addictive base form, crack cocaine (a.k.a. freebase), would reach almost epidemic levels in DC during the Eighties. Crime in the nation's capital, of course, increased hand-in-hand with the spread of crack use, as dealers fought over turf and customers fought with each other. It was no surprise that DC became known as the murder capital of America.

MacKaye's response to this drugged-up scene was to head in a totally different direction. Like his DC-born pal Henry Garfield/Rollins, MacKaye's act of rebellion was to go straight. At the same time, although he'd been a hard rock fan, a devotee of Zeppelin and Ted Nugent (himself an anti-drugs advocate), MacKaye – like Dave Grohl soon after – had a punk rock epiphany when he was turned on to the furious, politicised noise of such bands as Black Flag and Bad Brains. The songs that these bands spat out were rawer than a knife wound and played at a pace that even the speediest punter struggled to keep up with. MacKaye had seen the light.

For all his purist beliefs, MacKaye was no angel, as Blush recalled. "These DC kids, Ian and Henry included, would come up to New York shows and start trouble. They're painted as saints, but they were violent. They were troublemakers. They were hardcore punk rock kids with shaved heads and spurs on their boots; they were out to fuck you up. This was a scene of misfits; there was nothing cool about it."

The pick of MacKaye's hometown peers was Bad Brains, who formed in DC in 1979. Most of the band members were military brats, all-black pioneers in a predominantly white scene, and Rastafarians to boot. The band was brought together by guitarist Dr. Know (also known as Gary Miller), who'd outgrown his enthusiasm for jazz-rock fusion and started tuning into reggae and the Sex Pistols for fresh inspiration. Along with English-born vocalist HR (a.k.a. Paul D. Hudson), drummer Earl Hudson and bassist Darryl Aaron Jenifer, Bad Brains quickly got wise to the fact – as proved by such UK acts as the Clash – that reggae and punk weren't mutually exclusive. The proof is there on their legendary debut single, 'Pay To Cum', a song described by *Mojo* magazine as "one minute 33 seconds of dizzying, breathless positivity and blur-speed rhythms [that established] an essential blueprint for East Coast hardcore."

Bad Brains wanted to achieve two things: to become the fastest band on the planet and to spread the word of PMA (positive mental attitude), an ideology best heard in their signature song 'Attitude'. PMA was a very mainstream notion of self-help pioneered by Napoleon Hill in his best-selling book *Think And Grow Rich*, which was published in 1937 and was pitched at wannabe millionaires. It was clear that Bad Brains' philosophy was a world apart from the nihilistic anarchy of the Sex Pistols.

Soul Side's Johnny Temple was a big fan of the anything-goes style of many DC bands, especially Bad Brains. "Fortunately, DC was a very musically inclusive scene. I was never interested in listening purely to punk and hardcore, although I really admired the great bands, such as Bad Brains and Minor Threat and Scream," he told me in 2005. "One of the great things about the DC scene was that the punks and their music, although it's not always recognisable, had a deep appreciation of soul music. There's this local DC funk style called Go-Go, which can be heard in bands like Bare Essence and Trouble Funk [who would share the bill at Minor Threat's final show, which Steven Blush promoted]. I was into reggae, as were a lot of other people on the scene."

"There were thousands of aspiring Go-Go bands in DC," Soul Side's Bobby Sullivan recalled, "and rap came second to Go-Go. The DC scene was not ever about one kind of sound."

Regardless of musical style, most of the DC bands shared a mutual dislike of what was happening in the mainstream at the time. This was the not-so-golden age of big hair, puffy shirts and even bigger production, when it was deemed essential to make drums sound as though they were recorded in a wind tunnel, in the process sucking the soul right out of each and every note. Even the ass of blue-collar hero Bruce Springsteen was up for grabs, as he wiggled it feverishly during the clip for his hit song 'Dancing In The Dark' and placed it very prominently in the artwork of his *Born In The USA* album. Such previous innovators as David Bowie felt the need to use what passed as "cutting edge" technology, especially the ubiquitous synthesiser. Neil Young, who'd given the entire singer/songwriter genre a much-needed shake-up during the previous decade, had fallen into a creative black hole, with such albums as *Trans* and *Everybody's Rockin'* barely rating with either critics or the public.

It was OK to call your band A Flock Of Seagulls, Kajagoogoo or Air Supply, and have Epic Records blow $70,000 on the video for Michael Jackson's 'Beat It', which featured a cast of 150 extras – and Eddie Van Halen.* What passed as "rock" was an airbrushed travesty with Bon Jovi, Def Leppard, bland AOR acts like Foreigner and REO Speedwagon, along with a seemingly endless procession of imitators ruling the airwaves with their overblown power ballads.

Acts like Australia's Men At Work watered down the rock/reggae fusion pioneered by the Police, scoring big with 'Who Can It Be Now?' and their grating signature novelty tune 'Down Under'. With 'The Boys Of Summer' and 'You Belong To The City', ex-Eagles Don Henley and Glenn Frey respectively squeezed out dull, lifeless odes to life on rock's exclusive A-list. Warhorse bands like the Rolling Stones and the Who were playing stadiums, in the process enhancing the distance, both

* MTV was still a work-in-progress at the time, having been in operation for only two years, so no label had previously risked that much on a video clip.

physical and emotional, between band and audience. It was clear that the DC bands and their audiences had plenty to rebel against, not least being former B-movie star Ronald Reagan, whose repressive era of Reaganomics began with a nationwide recession almost as soon as he moved into the Oval Office in 1981.

As Bobby Sullivan told me, "If you think of the popular era of Eighties music and you remember how soft everything was, then you look at what was happening in the punk scene, you can see where the heart really was in American music."

Bad Brains was clearly a band with a heart. They were one of many DC acts that would play a huge role in the punk rock conversion of Dave Grohl. "I have never ever, ever, ever seen a band do anything even close to what Bad Brains used to do live," Grohl confessed in 1997. "Seeing Bad Brains live was, without a doubt, one of the most intense, powerful experiences you could ever have." Bad Brains also made a convert out of Steven Blush. "Bad Brains were the big guys. You talk to Ian MacKaye and these guys and they'll tell you they learned from the Bad Brains, who really kicked it up a notch. The first time you saw them you wouldn't move at all, you'd be so stunned by the speed and the ferocity of what you were experiencing. Also the musical dexterity was off the map; they were fusion musicians – they were into Return To Forever and John McLaughlin. It was very empowering to people."

Also looking on with both shock and awe was MacKaye and his equally intense pal, Henry Rollins. "I have fond memories of those days," Rollins, as ever on the road, wrote to me via email. "I saw some of the first-ever Bad Brains shows."* By the time of his Bad Brains experience, Rollins was already making a racket of his own in Black Flag. Rollins was actually their fourth singer; their first, Keith Morris, who'd been described as "Johnny-Rotten-as-psychotic-beach-rat" when the band's 1978 debut, 'Nervous Breakdown', set the US hardcore scene in motion, split to form Circle Jerks in 1980. A DC native – and also a skinhead – Rollins, who was born on February 13, 1961, had found that the easiest way to apply for the

---

* Sadly, a much hoped-for Bad Brains comeback went sour in May 1995. Minutes before a show in Montreal, opening for the Beastie Boys, singer HR went berserk, breaking the nose of manager Anthony Countey before attacking drummer Earl Hudson. HR was then busted for possession of pot at the Canadian border, although he was eventually allowed to return to LA.

singer's role in his favourite band was to jump onstage at a New York show and join in. When then-Flag singer Dez Cadena shifted to guitar, Rollins was officially given the gig.

As with Minor Threat punk photographer Glen E. Friedman was an instant Black Flag convert. "My favourite band of that era was Black Flag, who I'd pick over the Bad Brains, who were also incredible."

When Blush caught them live, he surrendered to hardcore. "My fate was sealed."

Just like Bad Brains, Black Flag liked to mash up musical genres, throwing metal and jazz into the mix. They were also proudly and defiantly independent. Their relentless, albeit microscopically low-budget touring schedules would develop new routes for other bands in much the same way as the early American pioneers had opened up the great divide more than a century earlier. Black Flag's angry, driving songs, best heard on 1980's *Jealous Again*, established a sonic blueprint for hundreds of post-punk bands. Guitarist Greg Ginn founded SST Records, which became the label of choice for such revered acts as Sonic Youth, Minutemen, Hüsker Dü, Meat Puppets – and Seattle hopefuls Nirvana. "Kurt Cobain's absolute dream," according to Blush, "was to make a record for SST."

Dave Grohl was so taken by the sheer intensity of Black Flag that he used the band's logo – a stylised flag comprising four vertical black rectangles, a creation of Raymond Pettibon, who'd later design a Foo Fighters' album cover – as one of his first home-made tattoos. Years later, Grohl finally had the chance to pay a more public tribute to the band, "borrowing" a drum riff from Black Flag's Bill Stevenson for the title track to Queens Of The Stone Age's breakthrough album *Songs For The Deaf*.*

Ian MacKaye's staunchly independent Dischord Records rose from the ashes of his first band, the Teen Idles (formerly the Slinkees). By the late summer of 1980, when the Idles decided to split, MacKaye had $600 savings – proceeds from the band's 35 gigs – locked away in a cigar box in his room. MacKaye (on bass) and the other band members – singer Nathan Strejcek, guitarist Geordie Gringle and drummer Jeff Nelson – decided to

---

* When I asked him about Grohl's work, Henry Rollins responded: "I don't know the guy and have heard about three of their songs, none of them I remember. I don't think I would be much of a help."

mark their demise with the recording of an eight-track EP entitled *Minor Disturbance*. With the advice of Skip Groff, a friend of the band who as well as operating a Maryland record store Yesterday and Today, ran his own small label, Limp Records, MacKaye learned the basics of putting out a record. Fully aware that no "real" record label would touch them, 'Minor Disturbance' became Dischord Records No. 1, released in December 1980. MacKaye shifted from bass to vocals and formed the now legendary Minor Threat with Jeff Nelson.

The Dischord/DC scene grew swiftly. Strejcek formed Youth Brigade; MacKaye's brother Alec was playing in a band called the Untouchables. Rollins, who prior to his Black Flag tenure had been a Teen Idles' roadie – the "fifth Idle", according to MacKaye – formed SOA (State Of Alert). Meanwhile, on the campus radio station at George Washington University, sometime DJ Steven Blush invited MacKaye and Rollins into the studio to spin some discs. Blush insists that it was "absolutely the first time any hardcore of that type had been played on the radio anywhere". Chicago's Touch and Go Records also started to make a noise in the underground, releasing records from local acts the Necros, Fix, Meatmen and others.

"DC's biggest successes [were] bands like Fugazi and Minor Threat," said Soul Side's Johnny Temple, "who succeeded on a completely independent level." Hugely inspired by LA punk label Dangerhouse Records, who'd released discs from X, the Weirdos and the Dils, MacKaye realised that there was more to Dischord than the Teen Idles' one-off.

Dischord's second release was SOA's *No Policy* EP, jointly financed by Rollins through his job at an ice-cream store and the sales of *Minor Disturbance*. By the end of 1981, Dischord had rolled out releases from Minor Threat, Government Issue and Youth Brigade. The famous "Dischord House", the label's HQ, threw open its doors in October 1981. This bungalow-styled home in Arlington, Virginia, just across the Potomac from Washington, was rented by the members of Minor Threat for a princely $545 a month. It was a lively place – the label operated out of a small room off the kitchen, bands rehearsed in the basement and willing volunteers pieced together record sleeves and lyrics sheets wherever they could find some space.

Dischord House also became the drop-in centre for such out-of-towners as Glen E. Friedman, who usually stayed there during his frequent trips to DC, as he began to document the hardcore scene on film. Soul Side's Bobby Sullivan brought a youthful Dave Grohl to Dischord House a few times. (It was a short stroll for Grohl, who lived nearby.) Sullivan's older brother Mark, who played in the Slinkees with MacKaye, actually lived in Dischord House, while he was with the band King Face. (The brothers Sullivan later recorded together for another Dischord band, Sevens.)

Friedman, who'd witnessed both the LA punk and New York hip-hop scenes first-hand, could sense that DC definitely operated on another level altogether. "It was a much different scene from LA or New York, there was way less in-fighting. It was a real family thing; these people were like brothers and sisters. They were hardcore; they were totally into this thing. It was just young people starting a scene and being totally into it.

"The scene seemed to be devoid of ego," Friedman continued. "If one guy left a group they'd break up and start a new band. It was an incredible creative process for those guys in the early years. If someone had to go to college, the band would break up – Minor Threat broke up for six months. I wouldn't say it was incestuous, that word has too many negative connotations, but it was a very friendly, communal, familial scene down there, with some of the friendliest people I've ever met."

"That community was the single most influential thing in my life," Bobby Sullivan said to me. "In it, I saw the power of people in action, the ability to promote and organise in an underground way that wouldn't be exploited by the music industry and all the larger business interests that go along with it, because so much gets lost when things get too big."

"The DC hardcore scene was all about sharing," Dave Grohl stated years later, "about being part of this big community."

In January 1982, Dischord released *Flex Your Head*, a compilation of 32 songs from 11 DC area bands, a clear indication, as Johnny Temple told me, that "the DC scene was really fertile at that time". The title, *Flex Your Head*, was Dischord's retort to New York critic Lester Bangs, who'd called the DC crew "muscleheads". The album remains an essential document of the time.

Not long after the release of *Flex Your Head*, the label experienced its first major cash-flow problem, even though the always-driven MacKaye was working at three jobs, on top of running the label and leading Minor

Threat. Distributors weren't paying their bills on time, and the label couldn't get any credit with record pressing plants. With the help of John Loder, from London's Southern Studios, who'd released records from influential UK punk band Crass, Dischord were able to keep going. (Their partnership continues today.)

According to Sullivan, "Dischord did a great job of being very discerning about what they put out – every release was significant. But the records were really just cheap imitations of the live experience. This was the true essence of the [hardcore] genre – the audience and band were locked into a shared experience. [And] there was little, if any, barrier between the dance floor and the stage."

By 1984, MacKaye and Dischord – alienated by a DC scene that punk purist MacKaye felt was fast becoming violent and disjointed – turned inwards. It didn't help that MacKaye's early ventures outside DC, for two Teen Idles shows in LA in 1980, and for some Minor Threat gigs there the year after, were poorly attended. As MacKaye stated in a brief history of the label, "The Dischord community became more of a scene within a scene," releasing new records by such bands as Rites Of Spring, Beefeater, Dag Nasty, Embrace (MacKaye's latest band), and Lünchmeat (soon to become Soul Side).

When I asked others about the levels of violence in the DC scene, no one felt it was as extreme as LA, for instance, where clubs such as the Starwood had been shut down due to wild scenes of blood-spilling at punk shows. "DC was a pretty lawless place in those days," said Johnny Temple, "so kids beating themselves up at a punk show wasn't a big issue for the cops. They would show up, but mainly if a kid stabbed someone, things like that. LA had much, much worse violence."

As a highly politicised label, Dischord became involved with an organisation called Positive Force DC, an altruistic collective that arranged benefits, free concerts, demonstrations and "teach-ins" with the purpose of "fundamental social change and youth empowerment". One of its founders was Mark Andersen, who documented the DC scene in his book *Dance Of Days: Two Decades Of Punk In The Nation's Capital.*

"They are a great, great social justice agency," said Temple. "They organised a lot of the punk benefits and helped steer the ship, as it were, when it came to political issues. South Africa was a big issue then, as was homelessness, a big issue in DC and throughout much of urban America at the time." Positive Force later assembled a compilation album, *The State Of The Union*, released, of course, by Dischord.

If there was a "golden age" for the DC punk scene, it was probably in the mid Eighties. As part of Soul Side, Johnny Temple was right in the thick of the action. "People point towards the summer of 1985, which got dubbed the 'Revolution Summer'," he told me. "There was a real conscious effort then to jump-start the DC music scene and make it vital and make it matter and represent good values. That was through bands like Soul Side, Rites Of Spring, Embrace – Scream [whom Grohl would later join] was there throughout. All those bands made great records. The arc of the DC music scene is very up and down, but if you draw a line from Minor Threat to Fugazi, then '85 through to '87 was a peak. There was a lot of great stuff happening."

What also set the DC scene apart from future flashpoints such as Seattle was that, with the exception of a brief bid for Dischord, there was absolutely no interest expressed by major labels. Nor was there any misguided notion among most of the bands, both with Dischord and elsewhere, that punk rock could lead to the mansion on the hill. Temple, again: "Part of the DC ethos, if you will, is the idea that you shouldn't look to music to pay your bills. I don't subscribe to it myself, but I think it's a great principle and idea. It's true that a lot of the music that was made, and this whole social movement on a small scale, benefited by the absence of commercial concerns."

"Many of us were looking for ways to stay underground," said Sullivan, "while others [Dave Grohl included] chose to compete for success. There were a lot of ideals wrapped up in that scene and I'm glad now that I was guided by them."

"DC had a very insulated scene," Temple added. "DC never got besieged like any other city. LA, San Francisco, Austin, they were all plundered – this never really happened in DC."*

When Ian MacKaye formed Fugazi, the majors eventually started circling but as MacKaye explained in the brief history of Dischord, selling his

---

* Temple strayed from DC's purist ideology when his post Soul Side band, Girls Against Boys, were signed to Geffen for 1998's *Freakonica* album. With the proceeds, Temple set up Akashic Books, who published *Dance Of Days*. "I'm a very pragmatic person," he said, laughing, when I asked him about this apparent act of heresy.

soul for big bucks was never part of the master plan. Dischord didn't even use contracts – or lawyers – when signing new bands. MacKaye did everything he could to live up to the label's righteous slogan: "Putting DC On The Map". "We understood the value of self-determination, and because the label [by that time] was so well established we weren't faced with the same circumstances as many other bands and labels at that time."

If Dischord was the home of the DC scene – or, as MacKaye saw it, the "scene within a scene" – there were several venues that hosted most of the bands, namely the 9.30 Club and the DC Space. "9.30 was always the biggest underground rock club," said Temple. "It moved about 10 years ago from being a hole in the wall to being a premier rock'n'roll club. But the old 9.30 was definitely a seminal rock'n'roll club. DC Space got gentrified out of existence a long time ago."

The original 9.30 Club was located downtown at 930F 10th Street, about 10 blocks from the White House, in a "tiny little room", according to Steven Blush. Before becoming hardcore ground zero, the 9.30 had hosted such international acts as Goth rockers Bauhaus and expat Aussies the Birthday Party (featuring Nick Cave). Blush, who was at both of these shows, recalls that the response from DC punters was underwhelming. "Bauhaus played to about eight people, Nick Cave and the Birthday Party to about five. No one was into this stuff in DC." Things changed when Bad Brains became the surrogate house band; they also blazed away in other local venues, including Madame's Organ, a venue run by idealistic yippies, located in nearby Adam's Morgan.

Just as many shows happened under the radar; all-ages gigs, held at whatever venue was willing to play host, were punk rock essentials, and the starting point for Dave Grohl's musical apprenticeship. Blush would organise many of these shows, although he became a promoter purely by accident. Blush was at a TSOL show in New Jersey when he was cornered by Mike Varney, the manager of both TSOL and the Dead Kennedys, who complained that punk provocateurs the Kennedys couldn't get a gig at the 9.30 Club. On his return to college, Blush rented out the campus cafeteria as an alternative venue. The Kennedys' first DC show, which included such local acts as Void on the bill, was a huge success. According to Blush, "It just exploded from there."

"It was kind of always the same crowd," said Temple. "It was a small scene. You might have 300, 400 people at a good show [or] only 50 at others. It'd be a pretty diverse crowd from in and around the city – people with funny haircuts, eccentric, artistic tastes. A lot of young people – it was good."

"It was kids putting on shows for the public in very neutral settings like the YMCA, VFW or church halls," Sullivan recalled. "The shows were very inclusive and almost always All Ages. It was this way intentionally."

"I think people came from different backgrounds, but they were mostly middle-class white guys," added Temple. "DC, however, is a city that's 70 per cent black, so it definitely had more racial diversity than other punk scenes. But I wouldn't say it was totally integrated. I think that there was some economic diversity; some kids came from pretty privileged backgrounds, but some were from working-class backgrounds, other kids were homeless."

Surprisingly, for a city with such a chronic drug problem as Washington, DC, the punk rock scene that Dischord spawned was relatively clean. Clearly, Minor Threat's anthem of sobriety, 'Straight Edge', had hit home with some punters. "I'm sure plenty of people in bands did drugs, but drugs weren't really a part of the DC scene," Temple told me. "Minor Threat spawned this movement called 'straight edge' – [but] although most people weren't straight edge, there wasn't a lot of gleeful drug-taking going on."

Of course, Washington, DC wasn't the only centre of underground action while Dave Grohl was growing up. There were numerous other scenes developing in the late Seventies and early Eighties, each as lively in their own way as what was going down at DC all-ages gigs, the 9.30 Club and in the Dischord House basement.

Once New York club owner Hilly Kristal got beyond the fact that the Bowery venue he opened in 1974 wasn't going to play host to "country bluegrass blues" acts, this grungy hole-in-the-wall, situated directly beneath a flophouse, became the birthplace of New York punk rock. Bands such as Television, the Heartbreakers, the Ramones, the Dictators, Richard Hell & the Voidoids, and Blondie would soon be calling CBGBs home. By 1976, Kristal had organised a "network" of sorts with "sister" venues The Hot Club (Philadelphia) and Boston's The Rathskeller, although there wouldn't be a genuine punk circuit until Black Flag hit the road a few years later and proved that there was some kind of nationwide interest in hardcore – even if they were only playing for free beer and enough money to buy gas to reach the next city.

As Kristal wrote in his history of CBGBs, "We called this music 'street music' and later 'punk'." *Creem* magazine writers Lester Bangs and Dave Marsh had used the word "punk" in the late Seventies, but it was then a broad term for anything vaguely resembling rock'n'roll that was operating under the mainstream radar (usually in someone's garage). It's been suggested that the term "hardcore punk" was coined by New York producer and manager Bob Sallese when he was promoting a 1981 show in Bayside, Queens by a little-known band named The Mob. Another possibility is the album *Hardcore 81* by Vancouver band D.O.A. Whatever its origin, the term gradually insinuated itself into the punk lexicon.

Key among those who spread the word was LA scenester Rodney Bingenheimer, a nervy, Warhol-like character keen to affiliate himself with whatever was new and hip. His KROQ radio programme *Rodney on the ROQ* preached the gospel according to English punks, the Sex Pistols and the Clash and New Yorkers the Ramones, as well as various Orange County runts who were starting to make some noise. San Francisco-area public station KPFA featured the *Maximumrocknroll* radio show, hosted by DJs Jeff Bale and Tim Yohannon, who provided rare airplay for many upcoming northern California bands. The pair later formed a fanzine of the same name. *Slash* was another key mouthpiece of the burgeoning scene, along with fellow 'zines *Ripper, Flipside* and *Guillotine*.

It wasn't long before many West Coast bands tuned in, including San Francisco hardliners The Dead Kennedys, led by Jello Biafra, a man whose strident political and social preoccupations drove such signature rants as 'California Über Alles', Nazi Punks Fuck Off' and 'Too Drunk To Fuck'. (Biafra's career was marked by a righteous defence of obscenity charges against the band, and, later on, his political aspirations.) Other OC hardcore pioneers included JDs Adolescents, best heard on their 1980 debut single 'Amoeba', and the Descendents, LA chroniclers of alienation, whose 1982 single 'I'm Not A Loser' has been described as racing by "in a super-quick caffeinated blur – equal parts Ramones, Beach Boys and Black Flag."

LA music writer and Blondie fan club president, Jeffrey Lee Pierce, formed the Gun Club; their single 'She's Like Heroin To Me' was another key song of the early Eighties punk movement. A human firebrand (and

Vietnam vet, allegedly) named Lee Ving led LA punks Fear, who briefly included future Red Hot Chili Peppers bassist Flea, and whose 1982 single, 'Let's Have A War', succinctly summed up their raison d'être. In 1979, the Germs, including future Nirvana/Foo Fighters guitarist Pat Smear, released their *GI* album, presenting a sound that characterised much of what defined the punk formula at the time: warp-speed tempos and fast, choppy chord changes. Grohl thought the Germs were "the baddest motherfuckers in the world".

Punk, and later hardcore punk, wasn't strictly a New York/LA/DC phenomenon. Hüsker Dü formed in St Paul, Minnesota in 1978, as a New Wave outfit that got wise to punk's sheer noise thrills, hitting a sonic peak with 1984's *Zen Arcade*. Not only was it a rare punk double-disc, but *Zen Arcade* was strictly all killer and no filler. Punk bands emerged from such locales as Victoria, British Columbia (The Neos), Detroit (The Fix), Austin, Texas (The Dicks, Big Boys) and Chicago (The Effigies, Strike Under and especially Naked Raygun, the first punk band Dave Grohl ever witnessed live).

As Michael Azerrad pinpointed in *Our Band Could Be Your Life*, if there was a holy trinity of hardcore bands, it consisted of LA's Black Flag, DC's Bad Brains and Minor Threat. It was this trio that would have a huge impact on the young Dave Grohl, whose first close encounter with punk rock happened, in typical Grohl style, purely by accident.

CHAPTER THREE

The Conversion

"I stood there and I thought, 'I could do this, I can play drums – and you don't even have to sing, you can just scream your balls off.'"

– Dave Grohl

EACH summer, the close-knit Grohl family would spend a few weeks with relatives in Evanston, Illinois. Their annual pilgrimages were relatively uneventful experiences until Dave's cousin, Tracey Bedford, met him at the front door in the summer of 1982. On previous visits, she'd struck him as little more than a typical tennis playing, jock-dating suburban girl. But things had changed. "This was punk Tracey," Grohl said, "complete with bondage pants, spiked hair, chains, the whole nine yards. It was the most fucking awesome thing I had ever seen." Grohl and Jimmy Swanson might have been dallying with the darker sounds of such metal bands as Metallica and Mercyful Fate, but this was something else altogether: Tracey hadn't just taken in the music, she'd embraced the lifestyle as well.

Larry Hinkle was accompanying Grohl on the trip. "It affected me the same way it affected David," he told me. "She was a year older than us and had all these cool records: Bad Brains, Dead Kennedys, Black Flag. She had this record, *Decline Of The Western Civilization*, a live record, that we listened to a lot that week."

Grohl was fascinated. Over the next seven days, his cousin opened up a punk Pandora's Box, talking Hinkle, Grohl and his sister Lisa through the extensive network of fanzines, labels and bands that all played their part in the hardcore underground. It had the same effect on the 13-year-old Grohl as Led Zeppelin, Metallica, pot or Edgar Winter's 'Frankenstein' had had in the past – he became a total convert. Up until then, "punks" were only something Grohl had seen in passing on TV shows like *Chips* and *Quincy*.Tracey was the real deal. "She was part of this unbelievable underground network that I totally fell in love with." Also during this visit she popped her cousin's punk rock cherry, as it were, by sneaking him into his first show – hardcore or otherwise – at a Chicago hole-in-the-wall called Cubby Bear, located directly across the street from Wrigley Field, the home of the Chicago Cubs.

The bands Grohl and Hinkle saw play that night were Rights Of The Accused (R.O.T.A.) – who were friends with Bedford – and Naked Raygun. Both were Big Black-affiliated acts. The splatter-movie-graphic Big Black was an influential punk outfit led by misfit Steve Albini, Chicago's answer to Ian MacKaye, who actually lived at Evanston while studying art and journalism at nearby Northwestern University. Originally called Negro Command, Naked Raygun were clearly a confrontational outfit on the Chicago punk scene – any band that could pull off a song with the name 'Potential Rapist' was either incredibly ballsy or just plain stupid. Led by singer Jeff Pezzati, the band peaked when they blitzed the 9:30 Club along with the equally legendary Mission Of Burma in 1983.

Grohl took plenty away from the Cubby Bear experience. He was especially enthralled by the closeness of the band and the punters – it was hard to tell one from the other. "Since then," he recalled, when asked in 2000 about his first punk gig, "I knew that a live gig should always be in a small club. The band and the audience should be so close together that you don't need a mic to communicate." Grohl did his best to stay true to that ideal, even when his punk rock aesthetics were severely challenged by the commercial success of Nirvana and Foo Fighters, bands that would spend as much time rocking arenas as they would dingy clubs.

The Naked Raygun gig provided a catalyst for Grohl's nascent musical plans. While surveying the on-stage carnage, Grohl realised that musical chops – cribbed from his beloved Rush and Led Zeppelin – weren't essential to being in a band. Attitude was just as important. "I stood there and I thought, 'I could do this, I can play drums – and you don't even have to sing, you can just scream your balls off.' " During the same visit, Hinkle, Grohl and his sister also got to check out other bands, including Channel Three and Violent Apathy.

When Grohl returned to DC, he was a changed man, and *Maximumrocknroll* was his new Bible. He was thrilled to learn that a hard-core revolution was happening in his own neighbourhood. "We were just blown away," Hinkle admitted to me. "After that [Chicago visit] we came back to Virginia and we were punkers. Very shortly after we got turned onto punk we realised that DC had a lot of cool bands." Grohl discovered Ian MacKaye's Dischord label and, among their many bands, he was especially hot for Minor Threat.

Hugely motivated by the hardcore revolution, Grohl knew that he had to form a band. His limited repertoire wasn't going to hold him back, nor was the fact that his buddy Larry Hinkle had since relocated to the other side of DC. Still playing the guitar at the time, Grohl coaxed a few neighbourhood buddies into forming a nameless covers act, who tried to master the songbooks of such classic rock acts as the Rolling Stones and the Who. If the band could score a legitimate gig, Grohl would receive extra credits at school. They did just that, rocking a nursing home with a cover of the Stones' version of 'Time Is On My Side'. Grohl's recollection of his public debut is vague, although he did recall that "people danced". It was hardly Madison Square Garden, but it was a start.

Thanks to his immersion in hardcore, Grohl's list of favourite drummers expanded considerably, as he studied their every move. Whereas in the past it had contained simply one name – John "Bonzo" Bonham – he was now big on such iron-fisted tub-thumpers as Bad Brains' Earl Hudson, Circle Jerks' Chuck Biscuits, as well as Bill Stevenson from the Descendants and Black Flag. When he combined their aggression with melodic wallop of Bonham's playing, Grohl began to understand what constituted a great drummer: "Heavy on the bottom, graceful, powerful, capable of countless styles."

There was a downside to this volatile blend of left-leaning punk and the mind-numbing pot Grohl was still wilfully consuming: his grades started to slip. "I was a little pothead punk," Grohl has said of this time in his life. Nothing mattered for him at the time apart from discovering more music and pulling cones. "I couldn't give a shit about anything [else]." Grohl's disenchantment with formal education had begun. There's no doubt that this "pothead punk" was ambitious, but straight A's didn't feature on his list of immediate goals.

Scream, formed in 1981, were based in Alexandria, Virginia. Their roots lay even further out in the suburban wilderness, in a dust-speck called Bailey's Crossroads, Virginia, where brothers Franz and Peter Stahl were raised. (Bailey's Crossroads was formerly the winter home of the Barnum & Bailey circus.) Franz, born on October 30, 1962, was the elder Stahl. As uncool as their hometown clearly was to DC scenesters, the Stahls remained proud of their roots; each Scream record would be inscribed with the letters BXR, shorthand for Bailey's Crossroads.

There was music in the Stahls' bloodline; their father had managed a DC outfit called The Hangmen, who had a regional hit with 'What A Girl Can't Do' in the midst of Beatlemania in 1965. Steven Blush recalls some discussion of their father's musical cronies. "They were hanging out at hippy parties when they were growing up. They had some exposure to the music business."

Franz Stahl, who played guitar, had been in a few local Virginian bands with a badass black bassist called Skeeter Thompson, who was then recruited into Scream, along with Pete Stahl on vocals and drummer Kent Stax. Thompson, meanwhile, found a blood brother and role model in Bad Brains singer HR and formed a handy alliance with DC's premier hardcore outfit. "Scream showed up through the Bad Brains, because they both had a black guy, so they had this thing in common," recalled Blush. (Blush remembered there being "probably a dozen black kids" on the DC scene at the time, including a skinhead woman going by the name of Lefty, who even today remains a fixture at DC shows.)

Even with such solid connections, the crew from Bailey's Crossroads were looked upon as outsiders. "They were considered sort of rednecks," Blush recalled. "They were from the suburbs; they were getting out there. [Bailey's Crossroads] is a shitty little suburban town."

Scream spent some time finding a sound to call their own. The band admitted in early interviews that they had no idea whether their style of music was a comfortable fit with the aggressive DC sound of such home-grown heroes as Minor Threat and Bad Brains. Drummer Stax actually thought that Ian MacKaye's Teen Idles "sucked", but Thompson had liked what he heard of the band, and stood at the back of a few of their shows, taking it all in. Curiously, until then he had been a jazz-fusion fan, hot for the slick sounds of guitarist John McLaughlin's Mahavishnu Orchestra, as well as Jimi Hendrix. While at school he was a pot-smoking jock, hardly the perfect CV for a future punk rocker. (Thompson would later develop a dangerous fondness for crack cocaine, which effectively ended the band.)

Thompson saw the light when he caught Bad Brains, knowing, "That's definitely where I want to be." He didn't necessarily want to replicate their cut-and-paste style, but was won over by their all-inclusive attitude. "They let me relax [because I] was very intense when I used to go to shows. I would dress punk, but not like everybody else." Knowing that in HR there was another African American playing hardcore was just the affirmation Thompson needed.

One of Scream's early shows was an all-ages gig at the Wilson Center, a hall in DC's Hispanic neighbourhood that housed an employment office, a free clinic and social services facilities. The basement, hired out to bands by the organisation to raise much-needed cash, could hold a crowd of about 300, maybe 350, although MacKaye insists that Fugazi once squeezed 600 punks into the space. Steven Blush booked some gigs there. His attitude for finding venues such as the Wilson Center was simple: "OK, who can we rent a hall from that won't freak out? It was a church basement in upper northwest DC. That's where I first saw Scream."

The multi-band bill included Bad Brains, Minor Threat, SOA, Void and numerous other local acts, including Scream. However the crowd was not amused with what they witnessed. "The first time people heard us they weren't sure what we were trying to do," Thompson told *Touch And Go* fanzine, "and the crowd naturally rejected us because we were outsiders."

A subsequent gig at Arlington's Woodlawn High School was received with similar indifference, much to the dismay of Scream supporter Jello Biafra, who'd also played on the bill. Afterwards, Thompson admitted that the crowd's reaction was so bad that he didn't want to play in DC ever again. Much of this apathy was related to the way Scream looked – unlike most of the DC area punks, Scream weren't big on spiked hair and combat boots. Some purists felt that Scream were heretics because they dared to wear tennis shoes on stage. Pete Stahl admitted that the indifferent reaction to their music was reasonable, "because we were still developing our sound" at the time.

Thompson wasn't so understanding. "The hippies didn't like us because we were too fast," he figured, "and the punks didn't like us because we wouldn't fit their image." Scream did like to mix things up when playing live. According to Thompson, "We always had a 'throw-it-in-your-face' style. We weren't total trash, we were like melodic thrash."

Another DC ideal that Scream rejected was the notion of "straight edge", which supported avoiding the usual type of rock'n'roll vices. Advocates were impossible to miss: they had the letter X scrawled in marker pen on their shaved heads and/or hands. Scream dismissed the movement when they spoke with *Flipside* mag in December 1982. "Some kids are into drinking and drugs, some aren't. People make too much of a big deal about straight edge."

As raw as their early sound clearly was, Scream understood the value of sonic dynamics. The band's songs, which were mainly written by Pete Stahl, usually contained three "changes". "They don't even have to be chord changes or key changes, but, like, climactic changes," described Thompson.

Prior to their Wilson Center spot, Scream's early gigs had taken place at beer blasts. The response from the partygoers boiled down to the precise equation "the bigger the keg the better the reaction". Thompson, again: "People would get so drunk that they would almost start to get into it, even though in the back of their minds they were hating it."

It also helped that there usually weren't any seats at these drunken free-for-alls. Pete Stahl would "just run and jump into people", while drummer Kent Stax also played the antagonist, staring down sloshed punters from behind his kit. "We created something they'd never seen before," said Franz Stahl. "[And] they started to understand it."

Often the Fairfax County police would bring these gigs-cum-riots to an early end, as Pete Stahl told *Touch And Go*. "We used to have lots of trouble . . . I guess they had nothing to do except bust up parties."

Scream, however, were winning some converts of their own, including the Soul Side crew, who would go on to share some bills with the band in 1983 and 1984, well before Dave Grohl joined. "I loved them, always loved them," Johnny Temple told me. "Scream was a little more rock'n' roll than other bands on the DC punk scene. I think they were a little more grounded in hard rock than other bands, too. It was all about their musical values – they were soulful, really soulful. Pete was an incredible singer; Franz was an amazing guitar player; Skeeter was a larger-than-life person and Kent was an incredible drummer."

Soul Side's Bobby Sullivan cites Scream as one of his biggest early influences. "I really liked their lyrics and I liked that Pete could really sing. I was into reggae as well and Scream also had that influence. They reminded

Grohl has never gotten by on movie star looks, variously referring to himself as 'geeky', 'dorky' and 'kind of strange looking'. However, it didn't prevent him losing his virginity at 14. 'She showed me the ropes. She ruled me like a caged animal.' *(Mick Hutson/Idols)*

Grohl was the everyman during his early school days, the kind of guy who 'got along with the stoners, got along with the geeks'. He still maintains friendships from his earliest days at Annandale High School and Bishop Ireton, a tony Catholic private school in Alexandria.

When Grohl attended Alexandria's Thomas Jefferson High School, he was voted vice president of his freshman class. His mother Virginia taught there. Things changed, however, when he discovered pot and punk. 'I just didn't care about anything [else], really.'

It was at such venues as Washington 9.30 Club that Grohl underwent his hardcore metamorphosis. 'The DC hardcore scene was all about sharing, about being part of this big community,' he said. '[And] you don't even have to sing, you can just scream your balls off.' *(Jim Saah/www.jimsaah.com)*

Grohl keeps the beat for Mission Impossible, at the Lake Braddock Community Center, July 25, 1985. '[They] were a pretty cool band; musically, they were doing stuff that is pretty clichéd now, but then wasn't,' says Johnny Temple, whose band Lünchmeat shared the double bill. *(Amanda MacKaye)*

'You've got to hear Grohl play drums. He's better than [Minor Threat's] Jeff Nelson!' Mission Impossible, doing it for the kids in Richmond, Virginia, 1985. (From Left): Bryant Mason, Grohl and Dave Smith. *(Mark Smith)*

Ian MacKaye, frontman for Minor Threat and Fugazi and the man who kept the Dischord House in order. MacKaye proved to thousands of punks-in-the-making – Dave Grohl included – that you could find your way in the music business without having to bend over for the major label dollar. *(Jim Saah/www.jimsaah.com)*

The wired coil of sweat, tattoos, alienation and anger calling himself Henry Rollins (aka Henry Garfield), out front of Black Flag. Dave Grohl was such a huge fan that one of his first homemade tattoos was a likeness of the Black Flag band logo. *(Jim Saah/www.jimsaah.com)*

Dain Bramage's Reuben Radding and Dave Grohl (from left), caught at a Washington DC show in 1986. 'We just didn't fit in,' says Radding. 'We weren't hardcore, but we were way too loud and experimental for the janglier pop scene in DC.' *(Mark Smith)*

Grohl at the same Mission Impossible DC show. When the band split in 1987, Radding simply couldn't find a replacement for Grohl. 'After you've spent a couple years with Dave Grohl as your drummer, it's easy to feel like no other drummer exists.' *(Mark Smith)*

Scream, the hardcore outcasts from Bailey's Crossing, circa 1987. (From left): Franz Stahl, Dave Grohl, Skeeter Thompson and Pete Stahl. When Grohl was asked to join, Dain Bramage fell apart. 'Scream were our heroes so I don't blame him [for joining],' said Grohl's close friend, Larry Hinkle. *(Tomas Squip)*

Nirvana, August 1988. (From left): Drummer Chad Channing, Kurt Cobain and Chris Novoselic. Grohl met Nirvana while touring with Scream, and was not impressed. He described the Seattle crowd as 'total Olympia hot chocolate drinking Hello Kitty people'. *(Alice Wheeler/Retna)*

Nirvana as a short-lived quartet in June 1989, featuring Jason Everman (second from left) and drummer Chad Channing (third from left). From day one, Channing was a fringe-dweller. 'It was like any important decisions . . . regarding the band had nothing to do with me at all,' he said. *(Ian Tilton)*

Cobain and Novoselic with Dan Peters who was 'on loan' from Mudhoney, 1990. Cobain was a frustrated drummer, which also made him one tough bandleader. *(Ian Tilton)*

An early shot of Grohl (far right) with Cobain and Novoselic. Grohl had immediate reservations when he first met the men from Nirvana. 'I did not see myself fitting into that picture at all when they first picked me up from the airport,' he said. *(Martyn Goodacre/Retna)*

'Everyone wanted [success], but Dave really wanted it,' said former Scream manager Glen E Friedman.
'[He] was always the nicest, hardest-working guy. And he was a bad-ass drummer.'
(Tony Mottram/Retna)

me of the Clash. They were also tight with the Bad Brains, who were just about gods to me at the time." Scream had enough potential for MacKaye to grant them a handshake deal with Dischord for their first album, *Still Screaming*. Nineteen tracks were recorded at the Arlington-based Inner Ear Studios, between October 1982 and January 1983, with the band, MacKaye, Eddie Janney and Don Zientara co-producing.

At a time when mainstream America was mad for the slick sounds of Toto, Daryl Hall & John Oates and Phil Collins, *Still Screaming* was a particularly hard sell. However, the album had a huge impact, especially inside the DC hardcore world. At 19 tracks, with a catalogue number of Dischord #9, it was also the first full-length album that Dischord had released to date. The reaction of Blush was immediate: he was overwhelmed. "It's the best album to come out of DC," he says, casting his mind back to 1982. "To me, they're the best band in town. They had an amazing singer – it's an amazing band. And they actually wrote songs."

"Scream were our heroes," Larry Hinkle confirmed to me.

The one hardcore ideology that Scream readily embraced was the idea of breaking down the barriers between band and audience (an anything-goes notion that helped Henry Rollins snag his dream gig with Black Flag). Sullivan recalls being at a Scream show where a DC local willingly jumped on stage to shout the lyrics to 'American Justice', a standout from *Still Screaming*, so Pete Stahl offered the mic to the crowd, as he would do at most gigs. "Even though this local couldn't sing very well," Sullivan recalls, "Pete always offered it up. Inclusiveness was way more important than precision. Many [Scream] shows were all-out singalongs."

One punter in the Scream pit, and many other DC moshpits, was a young Dave Grohl, who gradually became visible on the local hardcore scene. "I knew Dave," Blush says, "but as a face in the crowd."

Grohl recalled seeing Scream play "countless times", and felt a strong sense of connection with his fellow Virginians. Although Grohl was diving headfirst into the DC scene, he was still something of a fringe-dweller, mainly because he didn't attend Wilson High or live downtown. He simply dug the way Scream played. "They were the coolest hardcore band in Washington, DC." Grohl was especially taken by the band's willingness to mess with the formula, throwing in classic-rock twists, including Steppenwolf's 'Magic Carpet Ride' and 'Green Eyed Lady', from one-hit-wonders Sugarloaf, into their sets.

Fanzine reaction to Scream wasn't so dazzling. *Capital Punishment* figured they were "a bunch of jocks trying to be punks", while many others thought they were a Stooges covers band, mainly because their set included a song by the name of 'Search And Destroy'. Therefore, it was no surprise that the band from Bailey's Crossroads felt like outsiders – a point made very explicitly in the *Still Screaming* cut 'We're Fed Up', where Stahl wailed: "We're from the basement / From underground / We'll break all barriers with our sound / We're sick and tired of fucking rejection / But we're not down, we got a direction." Enough said.

Scream were also smart. Taking a lead from Bad Brains and Black Flag, they packed up a van and searched for punk horizons outside of the DC area. As vibrant as that scene was, a few gigs at the Wilson Center or the 9.30 Club wasn't going to be enough to pay the rent. They also couldn't shake the bad vibes from their early DC show at Woodlawn where the crowd either turned their backs or walked out of the hall.

One of their first out-of-town ventures in 1982 was to Seattle, for a show that Steven Blush helped organise. In the crowd were such future grunge heroes as the members of Soundgarden and 15-year-old Kurt Cobain. "Scream was a huge band in their world," Blush says. "They grew up on Scream." Scream also toured California, playing as many parties as clubs. One standout was a house-wrecking party in Santa Cruz, where the joint was gradually torn down around Scream as the band destroyed the Beatles' 'Helter Skelter'. They even won over a go-go crowd at a beach house, even though the house owners "were negative" about the gig until the band talked them round. They also swung through Texas and Arizona, sharing a bill at the Backstage with Civil Defense. The Arizona show inspired a song that never made it to disc, which Thompson described at the time as "hardcore a cappella. It's gonna be a first."

By 1983, Scream realised that they needed to flesh out their sound – there were only so many bases that could be covered with a four-piece line-up. Just like Minor Threat and Black Flag before them, the band added a second guitarist but in typical Scream style they chose the man least likely: a full-blown rock axegrinder who, in both looks and playing style, couldn't have been more out of place. His name was Robert Lee Davidson, but was known to most as Harley. Just like the Stahls, "Harley" was from the suburbs, where he'd played in a local metal covers act called Tyrant, and he met the Stahl brothers when he started dating their sister.

Harley stunned the DC purists – he represented almost everything that they'd been trying to destroy in music. Others, such as Steven Blush, got the joke. "It was 1983, it's not the age of Metallica, and here's this metal guy from the suburbs with a feather earring. He was a trip; he'd come out in eye make-up and a leather glove. It was great, but it was so uncool. Everyone else was a skinhead and here's this motorcycle rock guy."

Also looking on was noted DC historian and activist Mark Andersen, who'd become heavily involved with Scream through his work with Positive Force DC, at a time when the band were doing as many benefits as regular gigs. "They gave so much," says Andersen, "maybe even to the point where they hurt themselves as a band financially."

One of his first Scream shows was at Georgetown club The Bayou, in late 1984. Andersen admits to being slightly annoyed by Pete Stahl's on-stage hijinks during 'Spanking The Monkey', the band's ode to jerking off – "[I was] thinking, 'this is almost heavy metal'" – and found Harley's flashy string work "a bit superfluous at times". However, Andersen was won over when Scream dedicated 'I Look When You Walk By' to DC activist Mitch Snyder, who'd almost died during a hunger strike. Scream clearly had a social conscience. "They weren't afraid to be explicitly, radically political from day one," says Andersen. (Ironically, despite the blight of Reaganism, many DC hardcore bands shied away from making blunt political statements.)

Twenty years later, Andersen is more than willing to list Scream's qualities: "They clearly knew how to play; they never made a show of being 'punk', fashion-wise; they were racially integrated – not unique in DC, but significant; [and because] they were from the mid-to-outer VA suburbs, [which was] seen as the 'wilderness' by many DC/Maryland-centric punks, they weren't part of what some saw as the 'ruling clique' of DC hardcore.

"Scream was great on an off-day and a full-on world-crushing juggernaut when hitting on all cylinders. There was a certain swagger to Scream that could border on machismo at times – note songs like 'Hygiene' or 'Monkey' – but this, fortunately, was undercut by their obvious vulnerability and the sincere passion shown in their songs.

"[And] they were a sexy band; these were good-looking guys with some serious animal magnetism, much more than most of the DC scene. Above all, though, I would say that their passionate soul set them apart from [many] other early DC bands. They didn't express just anger but hope, idealism, love and lust. That 'soul' has a name: Pete Stahl."

While Scream were busy recording the songs for their *This Side Up* LP – which, in one of their many unfortunate screw ups, wouldn't be released for a full 10 months after it was recorded – Dave Grohl was planning to become more than a face in the crowd. If there was one DC band that he hoped to play with, it was Scream. He loved them with a passion that he'd formerly reserved for Bad Brains. But first he had to work his way into the drummer's seat.

Grohl was at a Void show in the summer of 1984 when he made a handy connection in Brian Samuels, another familiar face in the DC crowd, who told Grohl about his band, Freak Baby. Their line-up at the time was Samuels on bass, Dave Smith (drums), Bryant Mason (guitar) and singer Chris Page. Taking a cue from Scream, Samuels told Grohl that they needed a second guitarist – did he want to audition? Within days, Grohl was officially in the band. "I was accepted," he recalled years later, "and my career as a punk rocker [officially] began."

Freak Baby barely rates a mention in the DC hardcore scene's legacy; none of the insiders I spoke with could actually recall seeing the band play. Their gigs were restricted to a few suburban high school shows but they did make a key connection with engineer/producer Barrett Jones. Grohl and Jones established a loyal professional and personal bond that continues to this day.*

Jones ran the Laundry Room studio, so called because its original base had been in the washing room of his parents' house: the "control room" was in the laundry, while the band played in Jones' bedroom, a mere seven feet away. In 1984, when Jones and Grohl connected, Laundry Room was based in Arlington, Virginia.† At the time, Jones was playing in a DC band called 11th Hour and Grohl was especially drawn to Jones' do-it-yourself spirit, which he'd inherited from the hardcore scene. Although Grohl was a 15-year-old who could only play a few chords and was still mastering drums, this sense of independence had a lasting impact on him.

---

* When we spoke for this book, Jones only agreed on the proviso that the questions I posed could be answered with either a "yes" or a "no".
† Laundry Room's base has shifted many times over the years; it's currently in Seattle.

In the Laundry Room, Grohl observed while Jones recorded songs on his four-track deck for 11th Hour, bouncing between instruments and the desk. "He was recording some of his own songs, playing drums, bass, guitar, everything, [by] himself," said Grohl. "And I thought, 'Man, I want to try that.'"

Not much came of the Freak Baby Laundry Room sessions, although, more than 20 years afterwards, Jones remembered them as "fun". If there was a standout track it was 'Different', a song tagged by previous Grohl biographer Martin James as "stuffed to the gills with adolescent anger, but somewhat lacking in the precise power of punk at its best". Regardless, the zealous Grohl had a few cassettes prepared and wandered into Smash, a local record store, where he convinced the owner to display the tapes at the counter. Sadly, the Smash deal didn't achieve much for Freak Baby, apart from getting "four or five local skinheads" on board, according to Grohl. Given the proliferation of skins in and around DC, that was hardly a huge achievement.

In between ever-diminishing appearances at school, and infrequent Freak Baby gigs, Grohl endured the usual dead-end teenage jobs. He endured a summer "smelling of pepperoni" at a pizza parlour called Shaky's. Grohl's assessment? "That job fucking sucked." He eventually got his revenge, purloining a keg of beer from the cellar without being caught. He also stacked racks at DC's Tower Records, where, years later, during a signing session, he was propositioned by a pair of "typical American housewives", who slipped Grohl a snap showing the two of them proudly posing topless. Grohl smiled and passed on the offer. ("It was kind of obvious they'd both breast-fed . . . their nipples looked like old chewing gum.")

Grohl spent six relatively uneventful months in Freak Baby but it was obvious that his hours in the Laundry Room with whiz-kid Jones had been time well spent. By now, Lünchmeat's Bobby Sullivan had become buddies with Grohl, either meeting at each others' parents' homes or at the Dischord House. Sullivan found Grohl "easy to hang out [with]; he was always fun." He also got to know Virginia Grohl, who'd become her son's closest adviser over the years. "She was so nice and so involved in his life," Sullivan recalled. "I remember thinking that when faced with Dave's talent and positive disposition, I couldn't help thinking he must have had a great mum. Guess what? He did." Grohl's father, however, was nowhere to be seen, nor did Sullivan recall Grohl mentioning him. Larry Hinkle, however, does remember James Grohl. "David would always have to straighten up when he went to visit his dad."

Grohl and Sullivan often jammed in the basement of Virginia's house, where Sullivan discovered Grohl's fast-developing skills as a multi-instrumentalist. "I was amazed at his talent on guitar and bass," Sullivan told me, "because I knew him as a drummer. I remember how into the first DRI [Dirty Rotten Imbeciles] 7″ [single] he was. [And] he liked to play the fastest beats he could. He could do with one bass pedal what other drummers would do with a double-kick drum." Grohl had bought the single from the band's singer, Kurt Brecht, after a DRI show. Twenty years later they'd reconnect for the Probot project, when Grohl called him and said, "Hey, man, it's me. I bought a single out of the back of your van 20 years ago. You'd be amazed at how little I've grown up."

After a Freak Baby rehearsal one afternoon, Grohl sat down at Smith's kit, while Smith picked up Samuels' bass. Smith was a rudimentary time-keeper at best, and, as it turned out, he was also a closet bassist. When Grohl – the best air drummer in Springfield – began playing, the band knew they had the potential to unleash a far more powerful sonic beast, even if it meant discarding Samuels in the process. Perhaps the Freak Baby line-up change wasn't that surprising because Grohl considered that "the drummer was awful".

Grohl had plans for the band. His new musical love was *Zen Arcade* by revered Midwest trio Hüsker Dü. In guitarist Bob Mould and drummer Grant Hart, the 'Dü had a pair of exemplary songwriters, the Lennon & McCartney of hardcore pop. *Zen Arcade* was arguably the band's peak, a 23-track, double-album masterwork that mixed such haunting cuts as 'The Tooth Fairy And The Princess' with typically breathless blasts of raw power ('Whatever'). It was one of the major underground releases of 1984 and a record that Grohl believed was worthy of emulating. When Grohl eventually got to see Hüsker Dü play, he stood at the front of the stage, transfixed: "The music was just a distorted melodic mess with these sweet harmonies over the top . . . for me it's still the kind of music I enjoy the most."

With Grohl now in the drumming and driving seat, Freak Baby renamed itself Mission Impossible, fleshing out their short, sharp sets with a cover of the TV theme that gave the band its name. Through Grohl's friendship with Bobby Sullivan, Mission Impossible and Sullivan's band Lünchmeat formed a teen alliance, of sorts, often sharing the bill at all-age gigs.

A precursor to the much better known Soul Side (and later Girls Against Boys), Lünchmeat was another band to stumble out of Wilson High. Sullivan and Chris Thompson, bassist and main driving force, were next-door neighbours and had formed the band when they were 17 and still attending Wilson High. When hooking up with Mission Impossible, Sullivan realised both bands had plenty in common: they were mad for the same bands, especially the big names of DC hardcore, and they'd also had some experience in the studio. They were also painfully young.

The first gig that Lünchmeat and Mission Impossible shared was at the Lake Braddock Community Center in Burke, Virginia, on July 25, 1985, the first of a number of joint shows there. "It was quite a turning point for us," Sullivan admitted to me. As well as agreeing to split door takings – which ranged from zilch to $200 – the bands would also divide both sides of a seven-inch single, in true egalitarian fashion.

Sullivan has vivid memories of the Lake Braddock show. "It may have been their first time headlining [and] the audience was so enthusiastic for both bands. They had a great scene there, and many of the people [at the show] had demos of the bands, so they were singing along with a lot of the songs."

Johnny Temple, soon to join Soul Side, was also at many of the Mission Impossible/Lünchmeat double bills, which is where he first met Grohl. To Temple, Mission Impossible were "a pretty cool band; musically, they were doing stuff that is pretty clichéd now, but then wasn't – the slow-mosh parts, followed by the super-fast stuff. It's one of the modern rock dynamics that you hear a lot now."

On the advice of his pal Sullivan, Temple spent a good part of Mission Impossible's set checking out the human dynamo playing drums. "My friend Bobby said, 'Man, you've got to watch the drummer, he's incredible.' I'd definitely never seen anyone play the drums so fast and so proficiently. He was passionate but solid as hell – really fucking solid. A lot of people who play solidly can be sterile, but he wasn't."

Just as impressed was Dischord main-man, Ian MacKaye, who recognised some familiar traits in both bands. "Mission Impossible were a great live band," he told me, "and the first time I saw them I was impressed. It is fair to say that Mission Impossible and Lünchmeat were both energetic, young bands that stirred things up in DC when they started playing."

Also looking on was Dante Ferrando, a fellow drummer in punk acts Iron Cross and Grey Matter and Grohl's future business partner in DC venue the Black Cat. "The stuff he was playing was simple, but he played it with incredible precision and power," Ferrando wrote via email. "I was a little envious when I found out that he had only been playing drums for six months. I had been playing for about five years and I don't think I was as skilled as him." Grohl's switch from guitar to drums had clearly paid off.

Grohl and Mission Impossible began their recording career at a pivotal moment in the DC hardcore scene, the so-called "Revolution Summer" of 1985. Minor Threat, DC's premier hardcorists, were no longer in existence, having played their swansong on September 23, 1983 at Washington's Lansburgh Center. Despite MacKaye's of-the-people-for-the-people attitude – or partly because of it – the situation between himself, Jeff Nelson and the rest of Minor Threat had fractured to the extent that inner-band communications simply didn't exist. Nelson advised MacKaye of Minor Threat's demise by pinning a note to his door that announced: "The band has decided to break up, so just split the money up."

MacKaye threw himself into his work at Dischord, but was disenchanted by the increase of mindless violence at DC shows, so he began to develop plans for his "scene within a scene". As far as he and the Dischord crew were concerned, the out-of-control skins could have what remained of the DC scene, as they slam danced each other into bloodied pulps. Dischord House inmate Tomas Squip summed up their new goals precisely: the skinheads and slam dancers could keep the "aggressive thing"; they were now in search of "the heartfelt thing". Speaking in the book *Dance Of Days*, Squip added: "The original punk philosophy was 'fight bullshit' and 'do something real'. The punk scene was doing neither of these things [in 1985]. Revolution Summer was about getting back into fighting bullshit again." The label had to find new ways of keeping it real.

Dischord started donating what cash it could afford to such forward-thinking organisations as the American Civil Liberties Union, Planned Parenthood, Handgun Control, even the Union of Concerned Scientists. Dischord then made an even louder noise when they set in motion the first "punk percussion protest", outside the South African Embassy (apartheid was still in force at the time). The scene was documented in *Dance Of Days*: "Several dozen punks [were] pounding on drums, trash cans, buckets, or anything else that made a noise when struck. The din even puzzled the regular demonstrators at the embassy, whose invitation to the punk group to join them across the street was politely declined."

MacKaye, who'd been impressed by Mission Impossible and Lünchmeat's teen spirit, clearly had his hardcore passion back. "We want to show that we give a fuck about something that we think is totally wrong," he said after the South African Embassy demo. "And just like the civil rights movement in the Sixties, this is a chance for us to all band together." Rites Of Spring, another revered Dischord band that MacKaye was currently championing, played the first show of Revolution Summer that same day, June 21, at the 9.30 Club.

MacKaye then co-founded the band Embrace. Whereas Minor Threat had railed against everything they saw around them, MacKaye now turned inwards, changing the whole focus of the band's message (and unintentionally establishing the "emo" template). His more personal direction was made readily apparent when he bellowed such lyrics as "I am the fuck up that I can't forgive". Embrace's music was more melodic than typical hardcore, influenced by everything from metal to mid Seventies hard rock to a long-forgotten English prog-rock act called Empire, whose few releases were a huge hit with the Dischord crowd.

The DC scene that Mission Impossible and Lünchmeat entered in 1985 had been shaken up: while the players were predominantly the same, the goalposts had shifted considerably. New bands formed (Embrace eventually lead MacKaye to the biggest group of his career, Fugazi), while the Dischord crew rediscovered their sense of political and social conviction with that 90 minute pots-and-pans jam outside the South African Embassy. It was a new dawn in the DC hardcore underground and both Mission Impossible and Lünchmeat were keen to get involved, if only operating from the suburban fringes of the scene.

The split single with Lünchmeat actually wasn't Mission Impossible's recording debut. They'd contributed a pair of tunes, the youthfully assertive 'Helpless' and 'I Can Only Try', to a WGNS/*Metrozine* compilation called *Alive And Kicking*. There was ample proof in these two tracks that Mission Impossible was quickly turning into what Grohl described as "a super fast hardcore delight".

When Lünchmeat and Mission Impossible decided to work together, Dischord, naturally, wanted to get behind them, as did Skip Groff from the Yesterday and Today record store. However they would have to share the record with the newly formed Sammich Records. A lousy pun on Lünchmeat, Sammich was run by Ian MacKaye's teenage sister, Amanda, and the equally youthful Eli Janney, soon to be Soul Side's producer and, later, a member of Girls Against Boys. Sammich was a collaborative effort and was justifiably dubbed Dischord Jr.

As Sullivan recalled, "Sammich was started by a group of around 20 people in our immediate circle at the time." Everyone chipped in, pasting together covers, packing records for shipping, circulating flyers, the works. "Looking back at the larger scene at the time," Sullivan added, "it's amazing how many people came together to make that happen.

"Bands from Dave's generation and mine were of the younger set around the DC scene, so there was a lot of guidance and influence from the older bands, promoters, activists, etc." There were, of course, some problems that came out of receiving possibly too much guidance. "I would say all the music and ideas were being critiqued in a way that made it hard at times," Sullivan admitted, "but also very strengthening. It encouraged an evolution in everybody's music – and especially their ability to play it."

The split single featured Mission Impossible's 'Thanx' on the A-side and Lünchmeat's 'Getting Shit For Growing Up' on the flip. *Flex* fanzine granted the record a 7/10 review, declaring: "Both bands play decent HC [hardcore]; Lünchmeat are a little calmer, M.I. are a little faster. Nothing spectacularly new but good solid HC." For Grohl, it was a reasonable enough start.

Despite this apparent solidarity, the recordings were actually made separately – Lünchmeat cut their song in the autumn of 1984 at Black Pond Studio in Rockville, while Mission Impossible made it into the studio in spring 1985. The photos appearing on the Xeroxed sleeve were taken from their shared bill at the Lake Braddock Community Center and to document this historical moment, the sleeve was plastered with optimistic slogans reading, "Revolution summer is for always". However the forward progress of both bands was interrupted by schooling. By the time of the record's release, Sullivan, for one, had enrolled at college and two Lünchmeat members actually had to fly back from school in Colorado, without telling their parents, to play the band's final gig.

By the summer of 1985, Mission Impossible was also closing up shop due to school commitments, playing their final show in Washington's Fort Reno Park. Although Grohl wasn't going to let school get in the way of *his* new life, he had no regrets over bandmates Bryant Mason and Chris Page calling it quits in order to study. Though together for barely six months, Mission Impossible had experienced some high times, as Grohl would document. These included Ian MacKaye's very public approval of the band, as well as an opening slot for the legendary Troublefunk at a high school prom. The way Grohl saw it, "It was 1985 and I was living my hardcore dream. Mission Impossible . . . was a chance to try out all the tricks that I had learned from my growing record collection – on a real drum set even! I hadn't the slightest idea how to set the fucking thing up, but I sure loved beating the shit out of it." Grohl admitted that many of the breaks in their original songs were written for no other reason than it gave them the chance to "jump just like the pictures we'd seen in *Maximumrockandroll* and *Flipside*".

During this period, Grohl had an important discussion with his sister Lisa. Despite the pure thrills of "beating the shit" out of his drums, he was considering moving back to guitar. Lisa, however, put him straight. "My sister told me, 'No, you're turning out to be an okay drummer, and drummers are hard to find. Guitar players are a dime a dozen.'" It wasn't the last time he'd receive good counsel from his family.

CHAPTER FOUR

Grave To The Rhythm

"You've got to hear Grohl play drums. He's better than [Minor Threat's] Jeff Nelson!"

— Dain Bramage's Dave Smith

IF nothing else, 1986 would remain a banner year for Dave Grohl as a gig-goer. It was the year he witnessed what he'd describe as "one of the greatest shows I ever saw", a free-for-all that left an indelible impression on this wide-eyed muso-in-the-making. Slayer, an act of sheer sonic aggression, crawled out of LA's Huntington Beach head-banging scene in the early Eighties. An easy target for the moral majority who jumped all over their songs which touched on such prickly subject matter as Nazi death camps, serial killers, sadism and Satanism, Slayer proved that rock actually was the devil's music when five teens on a "Kids Who Kill" episode of *Geraldo* cited them as their number one band. Talk about the kiss of death.

By the time they played at DC's stately, elegant Warner Theater in 1986, Slayer had just released their *Reign In Blood* album.* The show was enough to make Grohl recognise the potential power of rock'n'roll as theatre. "I remember these two huge glow-in-the-dark, upside-down crosses illuminating as the crowd rushed the stage and trampled the first 10 rows of 150-year-old velvet chairs. It was definitely a moment." (It was also a moment for future Foo William Goldsmith, who witnessed similar Slayer carnage at the Paramount in LA. "It was insane. People were coming out all bloody.")

A few months prior to that night, the restless Grohl had connected

---

* An album that Grohl would regularly cite among his all-time favourites.

with another local DC band, then going by the name Age of Consent (conveniently shortened to AOC). Originally known as Consenting Adults, they had formed in 1981, but really started to move in the right direction when bassist/vocalist Reuben Radding joined drummer Peter Levine and guitarist Dan Kozak in 1982. Like Freak Baby, they took whatever gigs they could, playing school dances and parties in the northern Virginia region, and adding a percussionist and backing vocalist, Sam Imhof.

"The group began heavily influenced by Gang of Four, the Jam, the Who, PIL, and other mostly English New Wave bands," Radding explained when we talked in 2005. "We probably thought of ourselves as punk, but the hardcore scene didn't." Radding's knowledge of hardcore, according to Grohl, was "negligible", something Radding didn't deny, although he did have a sound working knowledge of the New York No Wave bands. "I had seen Minor Threat and the Bad Brains, but not a lot else from that scene," Radding said. "I was younger than those guys and didn't have a way to get from the suburbs into DC to see shows much until later on, and when I did I was more into local pop and psychedelic bands like the Velvet Monkeys and the Insect Surfers. Hardcore wasn't my favourite music."

The DC-born son of classical musicians – his mother was an opera singer, his father a violinist in the National Symphony – Radding had sung in the school choir, but preferred rock's rawness over what his father considered "proper" music. Part of his attraction to playing rock'n'roll was that old teen standard: rebellion. "My father thought it [rock'n'roll] was nonsense."

Like Grohl and Kurt Cobain, Radding was a Beatles freak. He bought his first guitar at the age of 11, and became completely obsessed with his axe. "I saved my milk money for a year and bought a guitar and became a rock'n'roller," he explained. "I did take guitar lessons, and some theory, and played in the jazz band in school. I was over-educated for a rock guy, but I *was* a rock guy. In those days, I was all about Beatles, Buddy Holly, surf music, Cheap Trick, and AC/DC. In high school I became more into the Police, the Jam, REM, and Mission Of Burma." From there he graduated to "old blues and hard rock", before being exposed to the Sex Pistols' *Never Mind The Bollocks* when he was barely a teenager.

Radding's musical education really flourished when he attended high school, first at Yorktown High and then at HB Woodlawn, the site of numerous hardcore shows (or "dances" as they were called, even if a mirror ball and dance floor were conspicuously absent). Radding caught his first Minor Threat show at HB Woodlawn, as well as other early hardcore acts and various Go-Go bands.

Radding also got the chance to check out Mission Impossible there, when the teen punks opened for Troublefunk. Above anything else, he was impressed by their open-mindedness. "To me," Radding figured, "they were a hardcore band that was willing to play some slow riffs – they had different influences. And they could be complex; they'd even play songs in a minor key," he laughingly added.

Radding had seen Grohl play as far back as the days of Freak Baby, mainly because Radding was a friend of Mission Impossible bassist Dave Smith, who lived in nearby Arlington. "I met Dave soon after he joined Freak Baby, the precursor to Mission Impossible, as a guitarist, in about 1984, I think," Radding said. "I remember thinking he was a little kid. He was only a couple of years younger than I, but at the time that seemed like a big deal.

"He would come with other MI guys to hear AOC a lot, but we didn't talk much. Later, when he switched to drums, Dave Smith called me up and said, 'You've got to hear Grohl play drums. He's better than [Minor Threat's] Jeff Nelson!'" Straightaway, Radding was dazzled by Grohl's form. "He was a remarkably talented guy," he told me. "I'd never seen a better drummer at such a young age. I was completely blown away."

In 1985, Radding's band, AOC, split. "[We] began to get a small but fierce following at this point, but gigs in DC were hard to come by," he said. "We just didn't fit in. We weren't hardcore, but we were way too loud and experimental for the janglier pop scene in DC. So we played a lot down south: Richmond, VA, Norfolk, VA, the industrial triangle in North Carolina, Athens and Atlanta, GA." Finally, though, the cost of trying to maintain what Radding described as "the most under-appreciated band on the East Coast" led to its demise.*

"At the time," Radding recalled, "Barrett [Jones] was still living with his parents in Arlington. He had been recording his own music in his bedroom, but wanted to try recording a live band, and we were his guinea pigs." When he started playing with Dave Grohl, Radding had moved

---

* They did, however, release one record, 'As Time Ticks Away', a cassette-only single recorded with Barrett Jones. It was Jones' first gig as producer.

into a house with Jones in South Arlington, and this became the new Laundry Room studio.

Around the same time, Dave Smith had written a chord progression that was proving too complicated for anyone he knew to play. He mentioned this to Radding, who admits he was "a pretty cocky guy", so he took up the challenge. ("It was this Hüsker Dü-like riff," he recalled.) This was also the ideal chance to jam with Grohl. "Since AOC had just broken up I was hungry to play," Radding admitted. "Plus, I really wanted to try playing with Grave [as Grohl was then known; to avoid confusion, Dave Smith was Smave]. So I asked to audition. I had been a bassist for a few years, but I figured switching back to guitar would be well worth it to play with those guys."

Their first session took place in Virginia Grohl's living room. Radding started playing the challenging riff, and when the two Daves joined in, he could sense something was right about their combination. "It was memorable," he told me. "And Dave had that spark. I was struck by his energy and his sense of drama when playing. We always compared him to Keith Moon." Grohl's first bandmate, Larry Hinkle, had also jammed with Radding and Smith, another close friend of Hinkle's, with a view to forming a band. Nothing came of it apart from a 40-plus-minutes desecration of Iron Butterfly's interminable prog-rock monster 'In A Gadda Da Vida'.

Not only were there sparks straightaway between Radding, Grohl and Smith, but at least four songs were written during their first living room jam, as Radding scatted vocals, jazz style, over the top of the racket. Such an outpouring wasn't unusual for Radding, who told me that AOC had written something like three or four tunes a week for the three years they were together. "It was pretty fast," he said of his new trio's output, "but business as usual for me."

But unlike any band he'd played in previously, Radding found that he, Grohl and Smith shared common tastes – and were actually willing to check out each other's recommendations. "It was really a jolt for me," he said. He turned his bandmates onto such acts as Lou Reed, Television, and Mission Of Burma, as well as jazz, and "they were really receptive [to my tastes]." At the time, Radding recalled, Grohl was a "champion of metal".

The trio quickly decided to move out of the living room, but first needed a name. Short of ideas, the three came up with the tag Dain Bramage while out driving in the van belonging to "Smave". The name was a blatant steal from a skit that they had seen on *Saturday Night Live*, in which a punch-drunk footballer tried to convince those around him that he wasn't suffering "dain bramage", despite a few too many blows to the head. "It felt right for us," Radding told me, although those close to the band weren't so sure. It would prove a nightmare for anyone putting together handbills for gigs; more often than not the band's name would be written on flyers as "Drain Bamage" – or variations thereof – much to their dismay.

The band's first show in December 1985 was way out in the middle of nowhere at the Burke Community Center in Virginia – "Real suburbia," Radding recalled. It was Radding's first gig as a hardcore player, so he had no idea what to expect. What he found was vastly different to the anarchy he'd witnessed at DC Space and the 9.30 Club. "I walked in, and one of the kids who had organised the show had set up a stand selling hotdogs. It was really cute. The room was full of kids in leather jackets, there were Mohawks everywhere – and there were their parents, too, standing against the wall, looking on."

There was no actual stage at the Community Center, just some tape that marked off the area where the band would play. "These kids' faces were inches from mine, yet none of them touched me," Radding said laughing. "There was no shoving, like the [hardcore] shows I'd seen before. These kids were extremely polite; they were really well behaved."

According to Radding, it took all of one song for Dain Bramage to gauge crowd reaction. "We weren't sure what response we'd get, but by the end of the song they were all flipping out."* Grohl was just as turned on by Dain Bramage's potential as Radding. "This band was where I really started to utilise my growing interest in songwriting: arrangements, dynamics, different tunings, etc. We were . . . usually experimenting with classic rock clichés, in a noisy, punk rock kind of way."

It also helped that friends of the band – or possibly the band themselves – appreciated the marketing potential of graffiti which helped boost Dain Bramage's profile considerably. When I asked Steven Blush about the

* A one-camera video shoot of this show circulates widely amongst bootleggers.

band, he said that they were hard to miss. "I recall his band Dain Bramage, because you'd see that [name] spray-painted all around DC."

Dain Bramage entered Barrett Jones' Laundry Room to record two sets of demos. The first, cut in late 1985, not long after their live debut, featured five tracks – 'In The Dark', 'Cheyenne', 'Watching It Bake', 'Space Cat' and 'Bend'. Things loosened up considerably at the second session, judging by the songs laid down, including such classics as 'Home Sweet Nowhere' and 'Flannery' (both made the cut for the band's one and only album), along with the rarely heard 'Baltimore Sucks (But Booje Needs The Bucks)', a jam that was designed purely to use up spare tape, as Radding recalled. "We'd finished the songs we'd intended to do, and Barrett told us we still had tape left and to do something. I mean tape was expensive, why waste it?"

During that second session the band also put their own spin on Grand Funk Railroad's 'We're An American Band', a white trash suburban anthem. Although Grohl loved classic rock, the Grand Funk cover was Radding's idea. "I heard it on the radio and thought it would be perfect for us. I played the opening drum break for Dave exactly once off a cassette and he walked right over to the drums and played it right the first time." It was another sign of Grohl's drumming skills.

With a little help from former AOC drummer Reed Mullin, then playing with Corrosion Of Conformity, the demos found their way into the hands of promoter Bob Durkee, who had organised shows at such Hollywood spots as the Cathay De Grande, and later worked as an engineer with the highly credible Mountain Goats. Durkee had just established his own label, the poetically named Fartblossom Records – "Fartblossom? What the hell is that?" Radding wondered out loud when he first heard the name – based in Pomona, California. The label commenced operations early in 1985 with the Justice League's 'Think Or Stink' single. North Carolina punks Subculture, featuring future Squirrel Nut Zipper drummer Chris Phillips, were another early Fartblossom signing.

After signing Dain Bramage, Durkee's next move was to get the band into the studio. From July 20 to 24, 1986, the trio squeezed into the 24-track RK-1 Recording Studio in Crofton, located not far from Annapolis. "It was some god-forsaken suburb in suburban Maryland," said Radding. "It was a really small space, like the rec room of a house, with an incredibly small control room that couldn't even fit three people at the one time." Co-producing the sessions were house engineer Eric Larson (who preferred to be known as "EL"), and Dan Kozak, erstwhile guitarist of AOC. The latter – who'd written the album's title track, which AOC had included in their live set – had some empathy for Dain Bramage, but the band quickly realised that they should have stayed in Jones' Laundry Room. There was no magic happening in Crofton.

Radding now accepts that he was partly to blame for this mistake. "[But] I didn't want to admit it, because I'd played a big role in choosing the studio. We wanted to feel like we were getting somewhere, but the quality was no better than what we were used to [with Jones]."

The result of these sessions was the *I Scream Not Coming Down* album. Radding feels that the newer tracks, such as 'Flannery' and 'Drag Queen', worked out best, but overall the demos cut with Jones were still far superior to the finished LP. *I Scream* did have its supporters, however, such as *Flex!* "I sort of expected generic Eighties hardcore from this label," admitted their reviewer, "but this LP is quite the opposite, surprisingly fresh and original music. Melodic and complex stuff which reminds me of some Minnesota bands, but especially of the first Moving Targets LP (like them, Dain Bramage have a great drummer). Great."

To Grohl, *I Scream Not Coming Down* was an accurate document of Dain Bramage's short life. "It was a fine demonstration of our blend of rock, art punk, and hardcore," he summed up.* If the album had a centre-piece, it was the opening number, 'The Log', which the band usually transformed into a 10-minute-plus epic live. Understandably, Fartblossom talked the record up with extreme prejudice when it finally made record stores on February 28, 1987. "This new power trio from Arlington, VA, features two former members of Mission Impossible," declared their advertorial blurb. "With a lot of conviction and guts, they deliver 10 songs of incredible depth and power. A real rock'n'roll record." However, Fartblossom's hype came too late.

Not much came of *I Scream Not Coming Down*, apart from a smattering of gigs and a guest spot on local alternative station WHFS. It was the first time that a band of Grohl's had received any genuine publicity, and he was

---

* The album has become something of a collector's item, too, nowadays fetching upwards of $25.

justifiably enthused.* Yet throughout his short stint as drummer for Dain Bramage, Grohl had his eyes on a larger prize: the drummer's stool in Scream. In March 1987, while shopping for drumsticks, he spotted a flyer in Fall's Church, Virginia's only music store, reading: "Scream looking for drummer, call Franz". Grohl knew it was his big chance to join the band of his dreams. Unfortunately, what Grohl didn't realise was that Scream circa 1986 wasn't the same outfit that had made such an impression during Revolution Summer.

Scream's long-delayed second album, *This Side Up*, was finally released in May 1985 and in separate sessions from October 1985 and January and May, 1986, they recorded tracks for the album that would become *Banging The Drum*. Not released until September 1987, almost two years after the album's original sessions, *Banging The Drum* contained several songs that stretched to a very un-punk-like five minutes.

Scream became the first hardcore band since Bad Brains to try a different tack. This band of Bailey's Crossroads misfits, who'd never truly belonged to the DC hardcore scene despite their many high-profile fans, and were rarely seen or heard in Washington, took tentative steps outside the USA, playing a mixture of squats and small-scale gigs through Europe and the UK in summer 1986. They returned the following year with the band Fire Party in support.

As exciting as these adventures seemed in theory, the reality was altogether different. Punks and hippies ran the squats along the lines of communes and their residents were actively involved in left-leaning politics. They raised most of their survival money by hosting gigs; bands were usually paid in accommodation and/or dope.

Speaking in *Our Band Could Be Your Life*, Fugazi's Brendan Canty summed up life on this less-than-salubrious circuit, describing squats as "a series of stinky rooms, and/or a series of rooms where people are staying up all night, smoking hash next to you while you're trying to sleep. Or waking up to Black Flag being played at eight o'clock in the morning."

---

* For years Grohl kept a cassette copy of the interview – as late as 2002 he was still bragging about Dain Bramage's very brief moment in the sun. "I remember thinking that it was so fucking cool that there was a DJ introducing our band's songs, going out to maybe a thousand people."

Often the visiting American bands would learn after the show that they'd have to sleep on the side of the stage, which at that point of the evening was usually a mess of half-empty beer cans and puke, not to mention the toilet facilities, which rarely came with running water and were usually overrun with rats. Vermin, in fact, was a major problem, as Canty recalled. "There's rats running around, so we all get in our sleeping bags and we just pull the drawstrings up as close as possible so the rats won't get in."

Admittedly, there was another, more positive take on the European hardcore community. Writing in *Dance Of Days*, Mark Andersen noted that one observer viewed the scene there as "a hotbed of counter-culture, larger and more permanent than the Haight-Ashbury hippie experiment ever was." Sleeping and toilet facilities, however, weren't mentioned.

Scream had their own internal problems. Bassist Skeeter Thompson had graduated from "pot smoking jock" – a few shared joints were part of Scream's pre-show ritual – to a full-blown crack addict. His problem was no secret to DC insiders. "Everyone who was down knew what was going on with Skeeter," said Blush. It was more than enough for drummer Kent Stax, whose decision to leave Scream was twofold: he couldn't deal with Thompson's erratic behaviour and he'd also become a first-time father. Hence the ad spotted by Grohl.*

"It was probably a good time for Kent to leave," Blush added, "because that was around the time that Skeeter was going off. Scream were totally falling apart at this point – the energy of the band was fading. A lot of this had to do with Skeeter's drug problem, which was just out of control. He was pawning their gear – he did this two or three times – for drug money. It was pathetic."

Dave Grohl had no real idea of the situation he was buying into when he spotted Franz Stahl's "drummer wanted" ad: he was 17, ambitious, and about to jam with one of his favourite bands. That's all he truly cared about.

The story of Grohl's audition for Scream has been told often enough for me to suspect it's the literal truth. Many of the people I spoke to for this book confirmed Grohl's version of events that played out as follows: after several attempts, Grohl got through on the phone to Franz Stahl and asked

* Stax kept in touch with the band; Larry Hinkle recalled spotting him helping Grohl out during the latter's first rehearsals with Scream.

if he could audition, not really expecting anything more than a one-off jam to boast about to his buddies. Grohl spilled out his résumé to Stahl, telling him what bands he'd played in and what music he lived for. When Stahl asked Grohl how old he was, the 17-year-old bumped his age up by five years. That was their first conversation, and Grohl thought it went well enough to score an audition.

However, a few months passed without Stahl phoning back to confirm a time or place. Grohl called again, and this time convinced Stahl to check him out. By now, the savvy Grohl had learned all the parts to almost every recorded Scream song. "Seeing as how Scream records were among those I used to play drums to on my bed when I was first learning," Grohl has said, "I knew all their songs by heart." The tenacious Grohl had gone a step further by somehow managing to get his hands on a demo tape of the songs that became *Banging The Drum*. To say he was well prepared was a major understatement.

When Grohl set up his kit in Scream's rehearsal room, Stahl asked what he'd like to play – some Zeppelin or Black Sabbath, perhaps? Grohl had a better idea; he rattled off several Stahl originals – 'Solidarity', 'Fight/American Justice', 'Amerarockers'. "Can we play those?" he innocently asked. Stahl was even more impressed when, over the next two hours, Grohl pulled off perfect takes on all these songs and more. Yet Stahl didn't offer him the gig straightaway; that wouldn't happen until they'd jammed a few more times.

Ironically, when Grohl was formally offered his dream job, he didn't accept immediately. While his heart was fully with Scream – even though he didn't know what bad shape they were actually in – he also had a heavy conscience: what about his buddies in Dain Bramage? They were the first band with whom he'd cut an album, and their intelligent take on hardcore was starting to win converts. Was it the right time to bail out?

Grohl's reading of the situation boiled down to: "Leave my greatest friends in the dust and travel the world with one of my favourite bands ever. Or stick with Dain Bramage and hope it all works out." Surprisingly, especially for a true Scream fan and one with burning ambition, Grohl said no to Stahl's offer – at least at first. He explained the position he was in but Stahl shrewdly persuaded Grohl to attend Scream's next show, which just happened to be one of their best shows Grohl witnessed. Not surprisingly, he changed his mind soon after and officially joined Scream in March 1987.

Of course, there are at least two versions to every story, especially in the often poorly documented world of rock'n'roll. Dain Bramage's website* maintained by band historian Keith Mitchell, suggests that the nature of Grohl's departure wasn't quite so heartfelt or compassionate. "Dain Bramage ended in March 1987 when Dave G. quit without any warning to join Scream," it reads. "Reuben and David S. tried to form a new band, but in the words of Reuben, 'After you've spent a couple years with Dave Grohl as your drummer, it's easy to feel like no other drummer exists.' Dain Bramage was no more."

Radding confirmed this when I asked, adding that it took Grohl some time before he spoke with him and Smith about his future with Dain Bramage. Even then, Grohl was vague about his intentions. He told Radding that Scream had asked him to fill in, but not necessarily join full-time, and that he'd refused, insisting that he had more creative input with Dain Bramage. Radding was unconvinced. "Part of me was not reassured by this – why didn't he say anything until now?" Radding was underwhelmed by Scream, even though he knew Grohl idolised both the band and their former drummer Kent Stax. "I thought they were a pretty good band, but too rock-star-ish."

Admittedly, Dain Bramage's future was limited. There were only so many gigs they could play in and around DC, while Fartblossom's delay in releasing *I Scream Not Coming Down* had stalled any forward momentum. To Radding, they'd peaked with a house-full DC Space show in January 1987 "and then things started to go downhill".

One of the people Grohl approached for advice was Larry Hinkle. "I remember Dave asking me, 'I got an offer to join Scream, there's a European tour coming up, what should I do?' I told him to stay with Dain Bramage, I thought they had it going on. But Scream were our heroes so I don't blame him [for joining]."

Radding was genuinely annoyed with Grohl, who, after their first hesitant conversation on the subject, took a long time before advising him that he was leaving Dain Bramage. "We were the last to know," Radding told me. "I recall talking to him on the phone [and being] really pissed off at him."

It took several years for Radding to forgive Grohl completely for his

---

* www.pooldrop.com/dainbramage/history

badly handled departure although he did admit that this was partly compensated by Grohl's luck with the ladies, which helped liven up the quieter times in Dain Bramage. Radding wasn't actively involved, having a steady girlfriend at the time, but he watched Grohl's many conquests "with amazement".

Radding and Smith auditioned other drummers in an effort to keep Dain Bramage going, but eventually accepted that a player of Grohl's precision and power probably didn't exist. Some years later, when Grohl was playing in New York with Nirvana, he called Radding totally out of the blue and invited him to a show. (Radding relocated to Manhattan not long after Dain Bramage split. Smith, meanwhile, ended up in Portland, Oregon, and would work for a time on Foo Fighters crew.)

"I held a grudge," Radding confessed, "I really did, and I didn't know how I'd feel." After spending some time backstage with Grohl, Radding realised that they were still friends and that Grohl didn't appear to have been touched by celebrity, despite the sycophants that now hovered around him. Grohl was still the same hyper, charismatic character he'd been while in Dain Bramage. "I let it go," Radding said. "He did the right thing." Eventually, Radding, Grohl and Freak Baby's Steve Page would stage a DC reunion, of sorts, in the mid Nineties, at a friend's studio.*

In early 1987, Grohl had another key decision to make. Unlike Mission Impossible, Freak Baby or Dain Bramage, Scream was a legitimate working band – albeit for little more than beer and gas money. Because of his time on the road, Grohl decided to quit high school before graduating.

The former straight A student had let his grades slip ever since discovering punk rock and drugs, so college had never really been a serious consideration. Nonetheless, his mother, who was then teaching at Grohl's high school, had some serious doubts about her son's career choice. "It didn't go over too well," was Grohl's understated take on the dinner table discussions he had with his mother. Eventually, however, she came round, but with a proviso of regular home rent being paid. She also insisted that he attend night school in order to finish high school. Grohl agreed, even if

---

* There have been ongoing talks between the three about reissuing *I Scream Not Coming Down*, together with a remixed version of the finished album, plus the Jones demos and live tracks.

he never quite got around to fulfilling his side of the deal; he blew his night-school tuition money on pot.

Grohl has made only one comment about his dad's reaction to the news that he was dropping out of tuition: "My father wasn't too into that idea." Grohl accepted this, but informed his father that he was no fool; he knew how to survive. "That's why I left high school – I knew in 10 years I wouldn't be using much trigonometry." The only people Grohl neglected to tell about his decision were his new bandmates, who were blissfully unaware that he was still at high school in the first place. Grohl also scored a roadie gig for his pal Jimmy Swanson, making them the two youngest guys in the Scream van by seven or eight years.

Even today, Grohl has few regrets about dropping out, genuinely believing that life in the Scream van made him more worldly wise than a dozen years at college. "I honestly believe that by dropping out of high school and touring the world I learned more than I would have sitting in a fluorescent-lit room with someone pointing at a chalkboard and treating me like a robot. Of course," he added, "I've been very lucky."

Grohl admits that he's not as well read as he'd like to be, "and my vocabulary isn't as big as I wish it was." None of this occurred to him, though, as he drove around Virginia in the VW Bug he owned at the time, *Led Zeppelin III* set on the car stereo's repeat mode, as he "contemplated my direction in life".

Grohl might not have made good on his promise to attend night school, but he did manage to bring some money into the household. This came mainly from odd jobs he picked up outside of Scream, who went into a heavy six-month rehearsal period soon after Grohl joined. When not in the rehearsal room, he worked in a furniture warehouse and a newspaper plant – "just blue-collar shit", as he described it, although he actually developed a fondness for the furniture gig. "That was cool," he told *Metal Hammer* in 2003. "I liked it while I was there."

Mark Andersen was at one of Grohl's early DC shows with Scream. While he could immediately see that Grohl had "broader gifts" as a drummer than the rock-solid Stax, it wasn't as though Scream had undergone a radical makeover. "[There was] no perceptible change to begin with," he told me, "other than, if possible, the band was even tighter and more awe-inspiring in concert."

Steven Blush had a slightly different take. "I don't think he [Grohl] was a major contributor to the band, he was just brought in to drum. He didn't really have a voice."

By spring 1987, Grohl and Scream were buried away in the studio, working on tracks for the band's fourth album, *No More Censorship*, the record that marked their (unsuccessful) shift from hardcore HQ Dischord to reggae label RAS (a.k.a. Real Authentic Sounds of Reggae). RAS was the brainchild of a certain Doctor Dread, who set up the label in 1979 with the goal of spreading the Rastafarian word, and its music, across the United States. This grand notion must have appealed to Bad Brains-lovers Scream – especially Skeeter Thompson, who wouldn't be playing music if it wasn't for rockin' Rastafarians Bad Brains. Unfortunately, RAS' efforts to get involved with a rock band, and Scream's attempt to escape the Dischord straitjacket, were a brave failure. When the album belatedly appeared in 1988, *Flex!*, for one, was underwhelmed. "Their worst record," they wrote. "A lot of boring and generic rock music with some hardcore influence, few good tracks. Good lyrics, though."

During the autumn of '87, Scream hit the road for Grohl's first US tour. Even though the band was collapsing around him, Grohl found the punk life a natural fit. "The feeling of driving across the country in a van with five other guys, stopping in every city to play, sleeping on people's floors, watching the sun come up over the desert as I drove, it was all too much. This was definitely where I belonged."

Life on the road was tough; the band survived on a $7 per diem, which, admittedly, was a punk rock luxury (Black Flag had gotten by on $5). Once Grohl loaded up on cigarettes – a vice he has found impossible to shake – he'd sometimes go two or three days without eating. At some shows there'd be more people on stage than in the crowd. Life was no easier for Jimmy Swanson. At one point in the tour, for some unexplained reason, Swanson kept his shoes on for a week; when he eventually removed them, a stubborn wart came right off along with his battered sneakers.

Sometimes the guys would go a week between showers, and even when they found a bathroom, as Grohl told a reporter in 2000, facilities were third-world standard, at best. "There is absolutely no toilet paper in the dressing room and you desperately need a crap. What do you do? You can usually fashion something into toilet paper. You just have to look around."

Grohl's secret – his age – didn't last long in the back of the van. Pete Stahl realised there was a hefty age gap between the rest of the band and their new recruit, and he became a sort of "father figure" to Grohl. Like a punk sage, Stahl would hand down all his hard-won wisdom to Scream's new recruit. Most importantly, Stahl taught him how to cope with the increasingly erratic Skeeter Thompson, who'd taken it upon himself to initiate Scream's newcomer. When it was least expected, Thompson would hold Grohl down "and put his stinking feet in my face".

Scream almost came to an abrupt halt during that US tour. One night, with Grohl and Swanson taking turns at the wheel, they very nearly totalled the van, and the band. While driving, Grohl and Swanson were working their way through an "enormous" bag of pot, smoking it with a device called the Easy Rider Aqua Pipe. "It's portable and doesn't spill. Very nice," recalled Grohl. As the rest of Scream slept, the van gradually filled up with smoke, while the dynamic duo up front, now unable to see each other, burst into a fit of giggles. "All of a sudden the van starts rumbling because we were way off the road, going about 70 miles an hour." When his startled bandmates came to, Grohl and Swanson were banished to the back of the van, and Thompson's feet.

Grohl also took advantage of the usual distractions on the road. When the band played Denver, he barely made it through the show, having taken one too many mushrooms. Hallucinogenics, he quickly learned, weren't conducive to breakneck-speed drumming. He was so out of it that he even missed the skinhead riot which erupted that night in the venue's lobby. A more coherent Grohl got the chance to open for another of his punk heroes, Circle Jerks, in the unlikely locale of Mormon HQ Salt Lake City; roaring away at the Speedway Café, a venue Grohl recalled as "awesome". The conditions at these gigs were primitive. Monitors, sometimes even PAs, were a hardcore luxury. Most nights the band had to get by with what they could hear on stage coming directly from their amps. It was a useful education for Grohl in working with the bare essentials.

Grohl's baptism of fire in Scream continued when they returned to Europe in February 1988. The itinerary of Grohl's first European tour read like a backpacker's wet dream, taking in Holland, Germany, France, Italy, the UK, Spain and much of Scandinavia but even a backpacker's hostel would have seemed like luxury for Scream. Once again, they were playing and staying in squats, as well as youth centres and the occasional bar. While living rough was chipping away at the already fragile nature of the band, new boy Grohl was ecstatic. He was visiting foreign countries, playing in a band he truly admired. Scream, being one of the first US hardcore acts to tour Europe, also managed to draw reasonable crowds. "My first trip to Europe was amazing," was Grohl's summation.

The trip also helped to expand Grohl's musical vocabulary and introduce him to a band that would prove pivotal. Stuck between gigs in Amsterdam – a time Grohl described as "killing time, staying at a friend's house, smoking weed and doing nothing" – he got his hands on a copy of the Melvins' album *Gluey Porch Treatments*. The Melvins were underground legends in the US northwest, hailing from the backwoods logging town of Aberdeen, also the home of Kurt Cobain. Buzz Osborne, a Richard Simmons* lookalike and also a diehard Trekkie – led this bunch of iconoclasts. The Melvins either influenced or worked directly with most of the key bands to emerge from the Seattle area, including Mudhoney and, crucially, Nirvana. *Rolling Stone* magazine succinctly wrote: "Every last grunge star cited the Melvins as a major influence in their sound, but none of them produced anything as heavy."

The Nirvana connection was strong with the Melvins. Dale Crover was one of the many pre-Grohl drummers in Nirvana and his house-cum-rehearsal-space was the ultimate Aberdeen hang-out; Crover dubbed the motley crew who gravitated there the "Cling-Ons", due to their *Star Trek*-ish geekiness. (A young Kurt Cobain often hung out to jam and get high.) The Melvins' heavyweight, sludgy, Sabbath-on-Valium sound was the sonic blueprint for what would be dubbed "grunge", typified by *Gluey Porch Treatments*, their 1987 album released on the poetically named Boner Records. Grohl found the album by chance, as he was flicking through the record collection of his Dutch host. Although at first dismissive – "Here's another hardcore record," he thought – Grohl was quickly hooked. "I had never heard anything so heavy before," he said, "and the fact these were teenagers from Aberdeen, Washington, playing music heavier than Black Sabbath – or any metal record I had heard – was unbelievable. It really fucking blew my mind. They were bordering on prog rock genius."

Grohl was especially turned on by Crover's drumming and his bizarre,

---

* A popular American fitness guru on daytime television.

unexpected time signatures. (Years later, he'd admit just that to Crover, who laughed and revealed that he'd recorded the album with the "biggest piece of shit drum kit" he'd ever used.) Grohl played *Gluey Porch Treatments* virtually every day for the next two years, with no idea how instrumental Buzz Osborne would be in his musical future.

Grohl made one more useful connection during this tour. While in Birmingham, England, he crashed on the floor of Lee Dorrian, the screamer of doom metallers Cathedral and Napalm Death, and label boss of Rise Above Records. When they met, Dorrian was a promoter, helping Scream find UK gigs. "Oh God," Dorrian recalled in 2003. "Dave stayed at my flat where there was no furniture, no carpet, all the windows were broken and we just slept on the floor. I remember Dave from then; he was a cool guy."*

---

* As spartan as Dorrian's digs were, Grohl repaid the favour by granting him a track on *Probot*, Grohl's death-metal all-stars album from 2003.

CHAPTER FIVE

Scream And Scream Again

"Everyone wanted it, but Dave really wanted it. [He] was always the nicest, hardest-working guy. And he was a bad-ass drummer."

– Scream manager, Glen E. Friedman

FOR the next couple of years, Scream was Dave Grohl's life. The way Steven Blush saw it, Grohl had joined a great band that was fading fast. "It was like *INXS: Rock Star*," Blush said. "He'd joined a band past its prime. Your fucking bass player is pawning your gear – it's a ridiculous situation. But Dave kept the Stahl brothers going; the Stahl brothers are an important part of this whole Grohl thing."

Evictions and disconnected phone lines, as well as "missing" equipment, were the norm in Scream's world. Whenever Skeeter Thompson bottomed out he'd be temporarily replaced. One of Scream's short-term bassists was Ben Pate, from the band the Four Horseman, a supergroup of sorts pieced together by Def American label's Rick Rubin. However, this couldn't put the brake on the band's unstoppable slide.

Thompson, who has since recovered and now lives in Little Rock, Arkansas, with his three children, had plenty of supporters in DC, including Andersen. "I liked – and like – Skeeter a lot," he told me. "He is a genuine, good-hearted guy, or at least as much as anyone could be who had some of his addiction issues . . . Skeeter wasn't the only one who indulged, but he was the only one whose life got fucked up as a result.

"I suspect the coke started coming in when they were exhausted on the road, as they often were, as a pick-me-up for their energy-drenched gigs. Alas, in Skeeter's case, it apparently went from snorting powder to free-basing and then into crack. As they tend to, drugs came as a dinner-party guest who then moved into the spare room, then took over the whole house – with terrible implications for the whole band."

87

Scream were also the victims of bad timing. The days of Revolution Summer were well and truly over and key DC bands, such as Minor Threat, had split.* Government Issue, Void, Faith and others had also broken up. As Blush saw it, "Scream were hanging on to the ghosts of the scene. And the other guys [in the band] were getting old, it was really falling apart."

Scream made an impact on people, for better or worse. In the midst of the *Banging The Drum* sessions in London, the band stayed at the flat of Peter "Pinko" Fowler, a Southern Studios employee and part of the label's strong connection to Dischord and the DC underground. Thompson, every inch the ladies' man, would proposition local girls from the apartment window, advising interested parties that they should "come around and ask for Pinko." The next day, a posse of neighbourhood men did just that, advising a startled Fowler that he'd best stop propositioning the local ladies "if he wanted to keep the use of his legs." By then, of course, Scream and Thompson had moved on.

Grohl got the chance to document an eventful day in the life of Thompson with 'Just Another Story About Skeeter Thompson', a track which appeared on the rare and much bootlegged *Pocketwatch* tape of 1993. To the backdrop of what sounds like a speeded-up Velvet Underground guitar drone, Grohl documents a misadventure of Thompson's that occurred while Scream were squatting in Amsterdam during Grohl's second European trip with Scream. It transpired that Thompson hooked up with a good-looking, well-heeled local, who began buying him clothes and supplying him with "the best herb, the best hash", as Grohl spells out in his droll, spoken-word style. She also had a little secret that she didn't let Thompson in on. One day, while Grohl was absently flicking through a copy of *Maximumrocknroll*, "reading my little [Xeroxed] punk magazine, not really paying attention", Thompson walked in, dropped his stash on the coffee table and proceeded to unzip. When Grohl looked up, "He's standing there, with his dick in his hand," which he then pointed in Grohl's direction, before asking the teenage drummer: "Does that look like pus to you?"

During Grohl's time in the band, Scream racked up five tours of

---

* Thompson once joined Minor Threat on stage to belt out 'Guilty Of Being White', quite a statement for a six-foot-plus African/American punk!

America and visited Europe three times, recorded a live document –
1989's *Live At Van Hall In Amsterdam* – and continued to play as many
Positive Force DC benefits as humanly possible. They also contributed a
track, 'Ameri-dub', which opened *State Of The Union*, a 16-track benefit
sampler compiled by Mark Andersen for the ACLU & Community for
Creative Non-Violence.*

In spite of all this, the Stahls knew that something had to work in the
band's favour soon, or else they'd have to start considering other, more
fiscally rewarding forms of employment. It was at this stage in Scream's
slide that Glen E. Friedman had a key conversation with Ian MacKaye.

Since his early involvement capturing the anarchy and energy of the
DC underground on film, Friedman had become involved with the music
business, managing seminal Venice Beach punks Suicidal Tendencies, and
producing their self-titled 1983 debut album. Still considered a hardcore
classic, the album was a huge breakthrough for the punk underground: not
only did it sell mad amounts – according to Friedman, "We thought we'd
sell 5,000 copies, if we were lucky; it turned out to be the biggest punk
rock record of the decade" – but its standout track 'Institutionalized'
gained widespread MTV airplay and made the soundtrack of the cult
classic flick *Repo Man*. The song also turned up in the more mainstream
Miami Vice with the Cali punks even scoring a cameo in the slick dick
drama.

It was during this time that Friedman met John Silva, who, as part of the
Gold Mountain team, would go on to manage both Nirvana and Foo
Fighters. Silva was then a managing hopeful, who'd looked after The
Three O'Clock and Redd Kross and had once been a housemate of Jello
Biafra's. Silva was in a relationship with Lisa Fancher, one of the first
women in LA to run her own record label, Frontier, that put out both
Suicidal Tendencies and the first Circle Jerks record. As Friedman recalled,
"[Silva] never made a penny; he'd leeched off her for years." Friedman did
admit to liking Silva, though, "before he became a manager", but he
found the guy odd. "He used to get around in Beatles boots and paisley
shirts, like he was straight out of the Sixties, looking like a real pansy.
And," he added, "the Suicidal Tendencies record was making a lot of

---

* Released in April 1989, Fugazi, Shudder To Think, Soul Side and Marginal Man also
contributed to the album.

money for Frontier Records, so the way I saw it, John, through Lisa, was living off the record."

Things went sour for Friedman and Suicidal Tendencies, even though Friedman had been a close pal of frontman Mike Muir (he'd known his brother from the time he was first involved with the Dogtown skate crew). "I'd gotten them on MTV and everything," Friedman recalled, "but halfway through their run on MTV they became, well, I don't know how to put it politely. I'd turned the worst band of the year, a real bunch of assholes, into the biggest selling punk band of the decade. I'd help create the monster, but I had to leave it." After the experience, Friedman swore blind that he'd never get that close to a band again.

Back in DC, Friedman had a fateful conversation with MacKaye. "Ian had mentioned to me that it was really time for these guys [Scream]; they want to be big, DC isn't big enough for them. They want to move on. Ian asked me if I wanted to help out, because I was associated with Def Jam, and bigger stuff, at the time." MacKaye, renowned for his reluctance to document the DC scene, has no clear recollection of the conversation. "I don't remember steering Glen in the direction of Scream," he admitted to me, "and it's not like me to push for management or label-seeking. After all, I co-own a label and I've never worked with management – whether for my bands or any other bands on Dischord. I think Glen probably approached them on his own as he was a fan of the band and wanted to help them out."

Friedman had become friendly with New York hip-hop impresario Russell Simmons, and super-savvy producer Rick Rubin, and, with their help, was planning his own label, to be called World Records. As far as Friedman was concerned, Scream were the ideal first signing for the label. "I really thought Scream were great," he told me. "I loved their earlier records and thought that the new demos they had, which would become the *Fumble* record, were [also] great."

Friedman was especially smitten by Grohl, the youngest and by far the most zealous member of the band. Grohl livened up even more when Friedman signed the band to a production deal, with a view to making them World Records' first release. Friedman readily used $10,000 of his own money to sign the band. "He [Grohl] was totally exuberant and really excited about having me on board and trying to get them a label deal. Dave called me more than the other guys, and we became good friends. Everyone wanted it, but Dave *really* wanted it."

Grohl became Friedman's go-between, as he tried to set up showcases for Scream. "Dave was always the nicest, hardest-working guy. And he was a bad-ass drummer." Friedman actually arranged two such showcases in Canada, where he travelled to meet the band, but bad weather screwed up his plans. As Friedman remembered, "One A&R guy, who years later signed up Britney Spears, couldn't come, and all these different problems happened." It seemed as though Scream couldn't shake off the bad luck that had delayed the release of various albums and burdened them with a crowd-pleasing bass player who had issues offstage. "From what I heard," Friedman admitted when I asked about Skeeter Thompson, "he had serious problems with addictions, but seemed to be a really nice guy. On stage he was like so many DC bands of that era: energetic, all over the place."

Yet Friedman persevered, handing out demo tapes wherever he could, but when he did get A&R people interested, he'd have to deal with typically short-sighted responses. "They'd say, 'Well, I don't know about Pete, he's losing his hair' – which hurt me because I thought Pete was amazing, but record company people at major labels say that kind of stupid shit. [Then they'd say] 'But that drummer is incredible. What's *he* doing?' People were asking about Dave separate from Scream, which I thought was an abomination."

While Friedman dealt with the sharks, Scream kept touring, hoping things would work out with both their troublesome bass player and a new manager. In the rare periods of band downtime, Grohl hung out at Barrett Jones' Laundry Room. Jones was now working with another band, Churn, and Grohl would drop by the studio and try out ideas on Jones' four-track set-up. Grohl quickly learned the best methods of recording. "I realised that if I were to write a song, [I should] record the drums first, then come back over it with a few guitars, bass and guitars. [Then] I could make it sound like a band." Once he mastered this DIY technique, Grohl boasted that he'd laid down a trio of songs in less than 15 minutes. "Mind you, these were no epic masterpieces, just a test to see if I could do this sort of thing on my own. It was the beginning of a beautiful relationship [with Jones]."

Grohl was being overly modest, because at least one of these tracks was much more than a dry run. 'Gods Looked Down', which ended up on the final Scream record *Fumble* in altered form, was the first clear sign that

Grohl was far more than a heavy-handed, lank-haired, tub thumper. Jones described 'Gods' as "incredible". When I asked him about the song, many years after it was first recorded, he hadn't changed his mind. "It is still one of my favourites [from his sessions with Grohl]," he told me. "I don't remember exactly what the Scream one sounds like, and of course I am a little biased, but I still like that one better. I listened to it recently and it's very raw – it's the first thing he ever recorded [with me], but it's still great."

Clearly excited, Grohl kept working on these sonic sketches, some of which appeared on *Fumble*, while others were "hidden away for later use". He also kept attending gigs, taking in the Monsters Of Rock, his first genuine stadium show. The line-up, featuring Metallica, Van Halen, Dokken, Scorpions and others, was extremely hairy – and Grohl was extremely high, having dropped some choice acid. The experience was more than enough to reinforce his punk rock, keeping-it-real outlook, where the only thing separating band from audience was a few feet of sticky, beer-stained carpet. "I found the whole thing extremely comical, and couldn't for the life of me understand the appeal of something so contrived and phoney," Grohl said, ironically adding, "Good thing I would never have to do that."

By spring 1990, Scream left the States for what proved to be their final European tour. Skeeter Thompson's situation hadn't improved. As the band shuffled through another customs check in yet another European airport, Thompson would brazenly carry his stash in a large brown plastic bag, on full display. "He was the craziest person I've ever known in my life," Grohl described.

Grohl described Scream's last European tour as "a real ballbuster". The band played 23 shows in 24 days, while crashing at the usual assortment of squats and hovels. One member, presumably Thompson, disappeared after a couple of weeks, but the band soldiered on, even cutting another live album, this time in Germany. However, the craziness was taking its toll on Grohl. After a show in Germany, he got involved in one of the few fist fights of his life. "This guy stole T-shirts from our stand," he explained, "and we kicked him out [of the gig]. As we were leaving he was banging on the windows of the van and I just had a total loss of control. I just beat the shit out of his face." Since then, whenever possible, Grohl has sworn off violence. He's a lover not a fighter.

The entire band must have wanted to punch the shit out of someone when they got back to DC. Pete Stahl was bravely sharing a place with Thompson, and among their unread mail was an eviction notice, dated one day hence. The only solution was to get back on the road, so the band fuelled up the van and headed off on what would be their final American tour. In hindsight, Grohl admits that the tour was booked "rather hastily", which helped to explain the low crowd numbers and numerous cancellations. "It was apparent," he said, "that something had to give. That something would be our bassist Skeeter."

The underground scene was also changing, as a groundswell of new bands started to emerge from another unlikely spot, the Pacific Northwest. Bobby Sullivan, whose post Lünchmeat band, Soul Side, had also bounced between squats and gigs in Europe, thanks to various Scream contacts, felt that Scream's latter-day hard rock sound alienated an audience getting more into punk rock.

"If Scream had not evolved and had kept their punk sound," Sullivan figured, "they may have become a lot more famous. This pre–Sub Pop disposition to incorporate more rock'n'roll elements into the hard edge sound that punk had was not welcomed by the punk community. It wasn't until there was more of a mainstream interest in punk/indie music that the Sub Pop phenomenon happened. It's too bad that Scream and King Face, two immensely important bands in the DC scene, didn't get to ride that wave."

Sullivan and Soul Side got to catch an unforgettable Scream set, when they shared a bill in St Louis. Sullivan's bands had spent so much time playing shows and hanging out with Scream that "they were like our big brothers, so it was a big moment to see Dave playing with them. I remember seeing a picture from that night of Dave, and his hair was flying off his head in a perfect S-shape, due to the way he was shaking his head while he was playing. I don't think you could have gotten a picture of his footwork without it blurring. He was really fast."

Friedman hadn't given up on Scream, despite their diminishing returns. As their new manager and with $10,000 of his own money invested in them, he started fielding calls from the band who, at the time, were heading towards the West Coast. They needed money, badly. It wasn't really the sort of news Friedman needed to hear. "I wasn't the kind of guy who handed out money. I was just trying to get them a deal."

The next despatch from Scream to Friedman bore even worse news: Skeeter Thompson had once again gone AWOL. The band was falling to pieces. "I heard that Skeeter had to get back home, or got lost, or something like that," Friedman told me in late 2005. (Officially, Thompson's defection has euphemistically been put down to "girlfriend trouble".) "I also heard that he'd fallen back into some drug problems. It was all fucked up. They were stuck in LA with nothing to do, no place to live [and] they had no money to get home. They were in pretty bad shape."

Thompson's defection left the band no choice but to blow out the rest of the tour. The remaining members limped to LA, where they crashed for a month at the house of the Stahls' sister, Sabrina. It was September 1990 and the band was stranded. Admittedly, there were some diversions: Sabrina lived in a fine Laurel Canyon house that she shared with two female mud wrestlers working at the nearby Hotel Tropicana, who supplied Grohl with free drinks when he came to watch them perform. The only money coming in was courtesy of one of the crew, a Canadian roadie called Barry, who'd receive the occasional welfare cheque from over the border. This didn't last long, so the ever-pragmatic Grohl found some labouring work, helping his friend "Lumpy" build a coffee shop in Costa Mesa, tiling floors.

In one of his few interviews, Pete Stahl – who, like Barrett Jones, agreed to speak with me only on specific subjects – admitted that this was the low point for a band who'd had their share of despair. "Man, that was a really depressing time," he said in 2004. "We were all so broke, just sitting on my sister's couch, all of us wondering if that was it."

Gluttons for punishment, the band briefly started searching for a new bassist. Grohl put in a call to Buzz Osborne from the Melvins, whom he had finally met a few years earlier. Their friendship started with a joke: while on tour with Scream in Memphis, Grohl bought an Elvis Presley postcard and tracked down the King's uncle, Vester Presley, for an autograph. He sent it signed to the Melvins, then based in San Francisco, inviting them to an upcoming Scream show. Grohl's warped sense of mirth appealed to the indie iconoclasts. Just prior to the show, Grohl discovered that Scream would actually be sharing the bill with the Melvins. They bonded over backstage beers and have been friends ever since.

When calling Osborne, Grohl asked whether he could be put on the doorlist for their upcoming LA show, and if he knew of any bassists-for-hire. Osborne didn't, but he did mention that a couple of guys he knew from Aberdeen were looking for a drummer. "Maybe you should give them a call," Osborne said.

What Grohl didn't realise is that he'd already met Kurt Cobain and Chris Novoselic, albeit briefly, on a few occasions. Both were huge Scream fans and had seen the band play in Olympia, Seattle. Scream was invited along to a post-gig after-party, hosted by "Slim" Moon in a nearby apartment. There were roughly 20 people squeezed inside, with the women standing on one side of the lounge, the men on the other. Grohl wasn't impressed by the gathering. Speaking in the Nirvana bio *Come As You Are*, he described the crowd as "total Olympia hot chocolate drinking Hello Kitty people" – in short, indie posers who'd fallen under the spell of K Records label boss and Beat Happening leader Calvin Johnson.* Grohl tried to turn them onto a Primus tape, which he fetched from the band's van, but it made no impact.

The men from Scream were standing around, sipping beer, feeling out of place, when a woman shut off the stereo and plugged in her guitar. She began playing what Grohl described as "total bad teen suicide awful music". Unimpressed, Scream quickly headed for the door. As it turned out, the woman with the guitar and the morbid hang-ups was Cobain's then-girlfriend, Tobi Vail. (Grohl subsequently found out about the relationship when halfway through a tirade about the "sad little girl with the bad fucking songs". Cobain – who remembered the Scream crew as "real rocker dudes; I thought they were assholes" – replied: "Oh, yeah, that's my girlfriend.")

On another occasion, during a San Francisco stop on Scream's 1990 swansong, Grohl went backstage after a Melvins show, where Cobain and Novoselic, in town rehearsing with then-drummer Dale Crover, were also hanging out. Although he didn't speak with either, they did leave an impression on Grohl. Novoselic, who was partial to a drink or 10, was exceptionally rowdy. "Who *is* that guy?" Grohl asked Osborne, pointing to the tallest, drunkest man in the room. Cobain, meanwhile, sat in a corner, scowling.

Scream played a show at Frisco's I-Beam on that same trip. Osborne, who was one of Scream's loyal supporters, recommended the band to

* They were known as "Calvinists".

Cobain and Novoselic. Already fans of the band, they were blown away by Grohl's warp-speed, no-surrender style of playing. According to Nirvana biographer Michael Azerrad, Novoselic left the gig full of praise for Grohl. "Wish he'd be in our band," he told Cobain.

As fate would have it, Novoselic also mentioned this to Buzz Osborne, which led to his tip-off to Grohl. A few days later Grohl called Novoselic. After polite preliminaries, the lanky bassman said that he did remember Grohl from his playing in Scream, but there was a problem: they'd recently hired Mudhoney drummer Dan Peters and were already in rehearsals for an upcoming UK tour. Grohl wished Novoselic luck and told him that he should get in touch when he was next in LA. After all, it didn't look like Grohl would be leaving the City of Angels anytime soon; he was still marooned on Sabrina Stahl's couch, in between lugging building supplies for "Lumpy". Later that same night, Novoselic called Grohl back, and asked him if he could possibly fly up to Seattle and meet with him and Cobain. They'd changed their minds about Dan Peters.

Once again, Grohl had to make a key decision: just as he was forced to choose between Dain Bramage and Scream, he now had to figure out whether bailing for Nirvana, a band with a serious buzz but who were virtually unknown to Grohl, would be worth the risk. Grohl realised that he owed a lot to the Stahl brothers; they'd hired him to play with his favourite DC band, and they'd also given Grohl some crucial lifestyle lessons about getting by on very little. They were the closest he'd ever come to real brothers. "It was the toughest decision I ever had to make," he admitted afterwards. Once he'd made up his mind, Grohl couldn't get to the airport quickly enough. "I got the hell out of LA and there was no looking back."

Of course, there were plenty of reasons to move on from life in Scream, Skeeter Thompson being several of them. As great a band as Scream undoubtedly were, they were past their prime, and the frequent album release delays had also stalled any genuine forward momentum, a problem Grohl had already lived through with Dain Bramage. *Fumble*, the album that featured Grohl's 'Gods Looked Down', wouldn't be released until July 1993.

It was a tough decision to leave Scream, but also inevitable. As Steven Blush told me, "By 1988, no one wanted to know about this [hardcore] stuff until a few years later when Bad Religion made a comeback and people got interested in punk again." Blush, for one, knows Grohl made the correct decision. "It was the right thing to do. Nobody could blame him for leaving that kind of situation. This great band had gone to shit and he bailed. He was smart."

Mark Andersen agreed. "It was just a matter of time before their fiery crash – or, alternatively, the un-glamorous, unceremonious grinding halt. It just seemed like the centre of the band was gone, it was coming unglued. There is almost a magic involved with a great band, [but] when it is gone, it is gone. Like Humpty Dumpty, it's so hard to put back together again."

However, there was a problem: Grohl hadn't told his Scream bandmates about his decision. Friedman was still shopping around the *Fumble* demos while trying to make the most out of the cash he'd invested in the band. He only got news of Grohl's departure second-hand and, even then, all he knew was that he was heading to Seattle "to help these guys out".

"Scream, meanwhile, were floundering. We didn't know what was going on – it was a tough time. And I wasn't with a label yet, I didn't have a corporation behind me; I was still trying to shop this demo into a record deal. I'd put some money into this, and I needed to know if Dave was leaving [the band]. Without their incredible drummer it'd be hard to get them a deal."

The unfortunate final act in the story of Dave Grohl and Scream, which dragged on for over a year after he left the band, has not been fully recounted before. Initially, it was purely a case of Friedman trying to reclaim his investment, which eventually played out as an abject lesson in the uncomfortable relationship between rock'n'roll, big business and loyalty.

Friedman became especially incensed when he found out that not only had Grohl signed with Nirvana, but the band had also inked a deal with Geffen a few months after, receiving a handy $300,000 advance. "I thought, 'What the fuck is that about?' It was huge news back then. I never actually had contracts with anyone before, but because of my experience with Suicidal Tendencies, I thought I should have a contract with these guys [Scream], if I am going to get them a major record deal.

"But for at least six months, maybe a year, all the guys from Scream were on their own not knowing for sure what Dave was doing with Nirvana. So Nirvana had signed this deal and Dave Grohl was in the band, although I was told he was *not* a signed member, *he was just a hired hand.* But he was signed to my contract with Scream."

Friedman then received a call from John Silva, his old acquaintance from LA, who was now managing Nirvana. "He asked did I want to take up my option on Dave, and if I did, I'd have to support him. I said, 'Look, I don't want to ruin the guy's career, I'm not that kind of guy, I'm not going to ask for a piece of the recording.' A year goes by then I saw Dave in the '[Smells Like] Teen Spirit' video, wearing a Scream T-shirt. I thought, 'This is fucking great. This is amazing.' I really liked it. Then all of a sudden Nirvana starts selling."

It was at this time that an acquaintance of Friedman's reminded him that he still had Grohl under contract; surely this was the opportunity to at least reclaim his seed money. "So I approached John," Friedman said, "who was now Mr Pseudo Big Shot, who was [also] managing Sonic Youth and the Beastie Boys – whose music I'd probably introduced him to – and he told me to fuck off, basically. 'Gee,' I thought, 'that's really cool.' I was put in touch with their lawyers, and I had to hire a lawyer, and my lawyer was afraid of theirs, and no one wanted to burn any bridges over $10,000.

"I learned some ugly stuff about lawyers," Friedman added. "All the lawyers were talking shit, saying, 'Fuck you, you don't have any rights to anything.' Even though I did have a contract with Dave, I had a pussy lawyer who worked at a big firm that didn't want to burn any bridges."

With negotiations ending in stalemate Friedman realised his money was as good as lost. It took several months before he changed tack, hiring "some hungry guys who work on contingency". They were no fools: by this time Nirvana's *Nevermind* was selling millions, and there was obviously serious money to be made, although Friedman insisted that this was never his intention.

Friedman's luck changed when he had a chance meeting with Silva at the Capitol Records building in LA. Friedman, who'd photographed the cover art for the Beastie Boys' album *Check Your Head*, and was there to oversee the final layout of his image, entered the building just as Silva was leaving. Friedman stopped him. "I said, 'Hey, you guys have known me for all these years, but you've told me to fuck off, you've ignored me, Dave hasn't returned any of my calls, and all I want to do is get back the $10,000 I put into these guys. And now I've had to spend more money on lawyers.' I wasn't asking for anything else, I wished the guy the best of luck. If you look at those contracts, [Grohl] was signed to me when he was in Nirvana. I thought it was only fair that I ask for a little more for my further legal fees and headaches.

"So I said, 'Hey man, guess what? I've hired some hungry lawyers and we're suing you for a million dollars – unless you get Dave to call me.' That's what it took to get a call."

Not long after, Grohl called Friedman, "And was the nice guy that he always was. I said, 'You could have called me a year ago. We're lucky that you called me on a good day when I'm in a good mood. But let me tell you this – your manager represents you, he speaks on your behalf. If he's an asshole, I only see you as being an asshole.'

"We talked for a few hours. I asked him to send me a cheque for this amount that I thought was fair and more than reasonable. At that time he hadn't received his first [Nirvana] royalty and told me that what I was asking for was more than a family member would make in a year. He didn't know anything [about the music business] – or pretended he didn't. I'm not free to disclose the amount – and it wasn't very much, relatively speaking – and I told him how I'd had all these fucking headaches.

"There's a point where people tell you to fuck off, and then you see them making millions of dollars, and it gets under your skin. What I was asking for wasn't even a tiny fraction of their advance. Obviously he'd called to take care of the business, because of the million-dollar threats, but towards the end of the conversation he said, 'My lawyer said that you really don't have that much of a case.' I told him that if he wanted to take that risk, it was up to him, but I was willing to say, 'Fuck all the lawyers, we'll do all this without them.' So I gave him a figure and said, 'You get me a cheque by the end of the week, we'll call it a done deal. I'll be fine with it.' So we cleared it up on very friendly terms."

Although years have passed since the conflict, it has obviously left a scar on Friedman. There is no love lost for John Silva. "Silva – could you believe it? He was this guy who totally owed me from the old days and didn't give a shit."

Like many others still close to Grohl, Pete Stahl is understandably guarded about the situation with Friedman. However, Stahl revealed that he was unaware of the $10,000 Friedman had sunk into the band, which seems unusual if not improbable. "He was supposedly shopping our demo around – which I paid for – when we broke up," Stahl told me via email.

John Silva and Gold Mountain refused to go on record about what they referred to as my "Glen Friedman question", despite several formal requests. Michael Meisel, responsible for the day-to-day management of Foo Fighters and with the firm since it signed Nirvana in 1991, was equally as guarded and protective as Stahl and Jones. "One of the things that I respect most about John Silva," Meisel wrote by way of a polite brush-off, "is his adamant refusal to ever give an interview. His point being that there is no shortage of managers who love to see their names in print – and [Silva doesn't want] to be one of those managers. I can there-fore promise that John will not want to give an interview."

Grohl's attorney, Jill Berliner, was unable or unwilling to shed any more light on the question of Glen E. Friedman, Scream and Dave Grohl, explaining that she only became involved with Grohl's career in 1994 and wasn't his attorney at the beginning of his time with Nirvana. "I do not have access to any relevant documents," she wrote to me, effectively closing any further correspondence.

Only once has Dave Grohl referred to this unpleasant situation. While speaking with *The Face* magazine in 2002, he obliquely mentioned how he "made serious mistakes when I was 22, signing contracts for shit. I didn't know what the hell I was doing."

Friedman's money arrived on time, effectively ending his relationship with Grohl, despite a mutual promise to keep in touch. "I heard from a friend that Courtney Love, whom I've never met, had something on her wall that said, 'Glen Friedman is the Devil'." By the time Friedman was finally compensated, Grohl had moved beyond DC – he was reaching Nirvana.

PART II

Seattle

CHAPTER SIX

The Odd Couple

"I did not see myself fitting into that picture at all when they first picked me up from the airport."

– Dave Grohl

WHEN Grohl's flight landed at Seattle's Sea-Tac Airport on a September afternoon in 1990, he really had no idea what to expect – all he knew was that the smouldering Scream mess was behind him. If Grohl took one thing away from the experience, it was the ability to travel lightly: when he arrived in Seattle, he had all his worldly possessions in two piles – a hefty box for his drum kit and a bag full of clothes.

His welcoming committee were a study in contrasts. Standing there was the basketball-player tall Chris Novoselic and the diminutive Kurt Cobain; the former dark and amiable, the latter blond and diffident. It was an impression that lodged in Grohl's memory. Long after, he remembered being greeted "by the biggest guy I'd ever seen and the scrawniest guy I'd ever seen". As the mismatched trio drove back to Tacoma in Nirvana's battered van, Grohl had the first of many uncomfortable moments with his new bandleader. As an icebreaker, Grohl offered Cobain an apple. "No thanks," he shot back. "It'll make my teeth bleed." Grohl smiled awkwardly and went back to looking out of the window.

During this uncomfortable teething period, Grohl perceived the six-foot-seven Novoselic as a "kind of a hippie pothead philosopher, hilariously funny", while Cobain was "tiny and reserved and . . . just quiet". To Grohl, they may as well have come from Mars. "I did not see myself fitting into that picture at all when they first picked me up from the airport," Grohl said.

Grohl also neglected to tell either that he wasn't exactly enamoured of

Nirvana. He'd heard their first album, *Bleach*, while drifting around Europe with Scream, and while Grohl could spot the Melvins' impact on their raw, guitar-powered sound, it didn't really distinguish Nirvana from the dozens of other northwest acts who'd fallen under the evil spell of Buzz Osborne. "I wasn't the biggest fan in the world," he freely admitted, "but I thought some of their songs were really great and some of Kurt's lyrics were really hilarious." Grohl, however, was disturbed by the appearance of the band: "They looked kind of nasty on the front [cover of *Bleach*], almost like a metal band, but with this retarded weirdness about them." As yet, he'd not seen the band play live.

Initially, Grohl roomed with Novoselic and his long-term girlfriend, Shelli. Soon after settling in, Cobain phoned Grohl for lengthy chats about musical tastes, as Grohl recalled in the *Nevermind* episode of the *Classic Albums* TV series. "I had a couple of conversations with Kurt where we talked about music and I listened to everything, from Public Enemy to Neil Young and the Bad Brains. We actually had a lot in common musically: we loved punk rock but we also loved Creedence Clearwater Revival; we loved Slayer as much as we loved Public Enemy." Grohl also mentioned that he was a big Beatles fan, which rang true with Cobain, a dedicated John Lennon admirer. Grohl discovered that his all-encompassing tastes were very much in synch with Cobain's, who was hoping to transform Nirvana into much more than just another amped-up Sub Pop bunch.

Grohl would also learn just how much he and Cobain shared in their pasts. A few years later, when Virginia Grohl met Cobain's mother Wendy, backstage at a *Saturday Night Live* appearance, they were stunned by the similarities in their sons. "We were just amazed at how much these two kids are alike," Wendy told Michael Azerrad. "They're like twins that got separated somehow."

Grohl vehemently downplayed this, but the facts spoke for themselves. While some of their similarities were the usual stuff of most suburban teenagers, others were undeniably peculiar. It was as if the pair had been living parallel lives.

Kurt Donald Cobain was born on February 20, 1967, at Grays Harbor Community Hospital in Aberdeen, Washington. His mother, Wendy, was a homemaker and his father, Don, a mechanic at a Chevron station in nearby Hoquiam, where the Cobains lived at 2830 Aberdeen Avenue. Just like Grohl, Cobain discovered music early in his life, singing pop standards such as the Beatles' 'Hey Jude' from the age of two. Kurt was a lively kid and, at the age of five, was prescribed Ritalin for his hyperactivity although, concerned by the way their son would sink into a Ritalin-induced stupor, his parents cut sugar out of his diet and ditched the medication, which seemed to work.

Dave Grohl's parents split when he was seven; Wendy and Don Cobain parted when their son was eight, but whereas the Grohls' divorce actually brought Grohl closer to his mother and sister, the opposite was the case with Cobain. His mother was granted custody, but when she remarried, her son bounced between his father's house in Montesano, Washington – Don Cobain had also remarried – as well as the homes of various uncles, aunts and grandparents, and later on his friends and classmates. Like Grohl, Cobain attended several different schools, without really settling at any.

Cobain reacted with hostility to the way he was treated as a seemingly surplus member of his own family, telling writer Jon Savage in 1993 that he "wanted to have the classic, you know, typical family. I resented my parents for quite a few years because of that."

Cobain was a drummer at heart, which explains the turnover of Nirvana timekeepers prior to Grohl's recruitment. Before Cobain's parents' split, they had bought their son a Mickey Mouse drum kit, which he gleefully beat the crap out of most days after school. Even better, he sometimes got the chance to lay into a real drum kit owned by his uncle, Chuck Fradenburg. Cobain's first "proper" instrument was a cheap guitar, a Sears model similar to Grohl's prized first guitar, a gift from the same Uncle Chuck. In Virginia, while Grohl strummed the chords to Led Zeppelin's 'Stairway To Heaven' in a perfect *Wayne's World* moment, Cobain did likewise in Aberdeen, also adding the Cars' 'My Best Friend's Girl', AC/DC's 'Back In Black' and Queen's 'Another One Bites The Dust' to his classic rock setlist.

Again like Grohl, Cobain had a major epiphany when seeing the B-52's 1980 appearance on *Saturday Night Live*. He and his pal Brendan sat in front of the television set transfixed, but whereas Grohl was able to buy the checkered Vans that were an essential component of the New Wave wardrobe, as worn by the B-52's, Cobain had to make do with drawing a checkerboard pattern on his battered sneakers.

Both Grohl and Cobain were teenage rock'n'roll dreamers. Grohl lied about his age to join Scream when only 17, while Cobain hung out with his mentors the Melvins even before he began ninth grade, in the summer of 1981. In the book *Never Fade Away: The Kurt Cobain Story*, Buzz Osborne described Cobain as looking "like a teenage runaway". Around the same time, Cobain became a dedicated pot smoker, getting high every day up until his senior year. Although a bright kid, his grades slipped and he eventually dropped out of Aberdeen High, without graduating, in 1985, although he soon returned – as a janitor.

Having been through the usual hard-rock rites of passage – his first "serious" rock show was a Sammy Hagar gig in 1979 – Osborne played a key role in turning Cobain onto punk rock. When hearing Osborne's mix tape, which opened with Black Flag's 'Damaged II', he became a true believer, another shared experience with Grohl. "It was like listening to something from a different planet," Cobain told Michael Azerrad. "[But] I sensed that it was speaking more clearly and more realistically than the average rock'n'roll lyric."

Along with his Aberdeen buddy Chris (Krist) Novoselic, who was born in Compton, California on May 16, 1965, but shifted north with his parents (who would also divorce) in 1979, and future Mudhoney bassist Matt Lukin, Cobain checked Black Flag out on September 25, 1984 at Seattle venue The Mountaineer. Cobain was obviously keen, because he bought his ticket with cash raised by selling off his record collection.

Bad Brains were another band to have a huge impact on the impressionable Cobain: he'd keep their *Rock For Light* album on repeat as he dropped acid during the day before cleaning the toilets at Aberdeen High by night. Bizarrely, in a move designed to appease his father, Cobain took the US Navy recruitment test around this time, but before he could sign up he left home again. En route to Olympia, Cobain spent a few nights sleeping under the bridge that spanned Aberdeen's Wishkah River. This period of rough living would be part of the inspiration for 'Something In The Way', the sombre closing track on Nirvana's *Nevermind*.

By the winter of 1985, Cobain was living in Olympia with some friends from Aberdeen, Steven and Eric Shillinger, and their family. He quickly connected with then bassist Dale Crover, who'd later drum for both the Melvins and Nirvana, and drummer Greg Hokanson. The trio recorded a raw demo tape, straight to a TEAC four-track, under the catchy moniker Fecal Matter. One of the tracks, 'Downer', later showed up on Nirvana's debut album, *Bleach*. The band actually picked up a few gigs, including an opening slot for the Melvins at the Spot Tavern in Moclips, Washington.

Hokanson was soon out of the picture, so Crover and Cobain recorded a second rough demo, which included another take on 'Downer', along with such tracks as 'Spank Thru', 'Suicide Samurai', 'Laminated Effect', 'Bambi Slaughter' and 'Buffy's Pregnant'. It was good enough to encourage Novoselic to form a "proper" band with his old pal from Aberdeen. As he admitted in the promo CD, *Nevermind: It's An Interview*, it was 'Spank Thru' that really clicked with Novoselic. "It got me excited, so I go, 'Hey man, let's start a band.'" With Cobain on drums, Novoselic attempting to sing and one Steve Newman on bass, this first ensemble was known as The Sellout, peddling Creedence Clearwater Revival covers to disinterested drunks. They then reinvented themselves as the Stiff Woodies, whose line-up, apart from Novoselic and Cobain, included, on a revolving-door basis, Buzz Osborne, Dale Crover and Matt Lukin.

During the next year, 1986, Cobain actually seemed busier away from music. He experimented with heroin, and was arrested for spray-painting "God Is Gay" and "Homo Sex Rules" on cars, receiving a $180 fine and six-month suspended sentence. Alongside Crover and Osborne, Cobain played one show under the name Brown Cow but '86 was more notable for the launch of Seattle's Sub Pop Records, the brainchild of two savvy operators, Jonathan Poneman and Bruce Pavitt.

Poneman, who's been described as a more youthful version of Reuben Kincaid, the fictional manager of TV pop group the Partridge Family, set up the label with a small inheritance but a grand vision – he wanted to create the Northwest's answer to Motown and Stax. His partner, Pavitt, was a long-time Northwest scenester who ran a fanzine *Subterranean Pop* (later abbreviated to Sub Pop), which began releasing cassette compilations, until it folded. Following this, Pavitt wrote a much-read music column in Seattle music freebie *The Rocket*.

The label debuted in autumn 1986 with the compilation *Sub Pop 100*, which included Sonic Youth, Steve Fisk, Skinny Puppy and Steve Albini. Naked Raygun, the same band who'd turned Dave Grohl onto punk a few years earlier in DC, also made the cut. It wasn't long before Sub Pop and Nirvana's paths crossed.

Cobain and Novoselic scored a handy rehearsal spot-cum-party-house – an empty apartment above Maria's Hair Design, where Novoselic's mother worked. In 1987, with Cobain on guitar and Novoselic playing bass, along with drummer Aaron Burckhard (whose inappropriate poodle perm and moustache stood out from his bandmates' appearance) who lived down the street from Cobain, the trio was variously known as Skid Row, Cap Chew, Windowpane and the award-winning Throat Oyster. Just like Grohl's early bands, the trio would play anywhere they were allowed to set up and plug in: community halls, house parties, and the like. While Cobain said little, Novoselic, who liked a drink, was every inch the party animal, sometimes stripping naked midway through shows and running amok, smashing up furniture and himself. Needless to say, they were rarely invited back for encores, let alone repeat performances.

By the time Grohl hit the road with Scream in spring 1987, Cobain, Novoselic and Burckhard had cut their first demo, essentially a live set recorded at Calvin Johnson's (the head of K Records) radio show on college station KAOS in Olympia. 'Love Buzz' (a cover of an obscure single by Dutch pop group Shocking Blue,* a big favourite of Novoselic's), 'Floyd The Barber' and 'Spank Thru' all made it on to a tape that would become among the most heavily bootlegged Nirvana recordings. In June 1987, Sub Pop released Green River's *Dry As A Bone* EP. Buried away in the promotional copy was the description of the EP as "ultra loose grunge". Soon after, UK *Melody Maker* writer Everett True latched onto the term and a whole new genre was given a name.

Not only did Burckhard have the wrong look but he wasn't prepared for the rigorous rehearsal schedule Cobain and Novoselic laid down. After he left the band in the latter part of 1987, Cobain and Novoselic ran an ad in Seattle music paper, *The Rocket*, which read: "SERIOUS DRUMMER WANTED. Underground attitude. Black Flag, Melvins, Zeppelin, Scratch Acid, Ethel Merman. [No seriously.] Versatile as heck. Kurdt 352-0992."†

In December, Cobain and Novoselic began practising with Dale

---

* They were best known for their 1970 hit 'Venus'.
† This was Cobain's home phone number in Olympia and the occasional spelling of his Christian name.

Crover, who drummed on the band's first "formal" demo tape, cut on January 23, 1988 at Reciprocal Recording with Jack Endino, who didn't so much "produce" records as hit the record button, telling the band to start playing. There were 10 songs on the tape, including 'Downer', 'Floyd The Barber', 'Aero Zeppelin', and a half-finished (they ran out of tape before it was completed) epic entitled 'Pen Cap Chew'. The session, known as the "Dale Demo", cost the band the grand sum of $152.44.

Endino passed a copy of the so-called "Dale Demo" to Jonathan Poneman, telling the Sub Pop co-owner that Cobain had an amazing voice, for a guy who "looked like a car mechanic". At the same time, Cobain was handing out the tape as if it was his business card (which in some ways it was). Early in 1988, Cobain met with Poneman at the Café Roma in Seattle, and the pair struck a deal to release a single on Sub Pop. With expert timing Dale Crover, a man that even Dave Grohl considered to be Nirvana's best drummer, left the band in March.

This time around, Cobain and Novoselic changed the wording of their ad in *The Rocket* to read: "DRUMMER WANTED: Play hard, sometimes light, underground, versatile, fast, medium, slow, versatile, serious, heavy, versatile, dorky, nirvana, hungry. Kurdt 352.0992." There was no mention of Ethel Merman this time but it was the first public mention of the trio's new name: Nirvana.

The next resident on the drum stool was Dave Foster, a man described by Cobain biographer Charles R. Cross as "a hard-pounding and hard-living Aberdeen drummer," whose first Nirvana show was at a house party in Olympia. Foster's T-shirt, stonewashed denims and moustache definitely stood him apart sartorially from his grungier bandmates (although, admittedly, Cobain was going through his bell-bottoms-and-platform-heels phase, more a sarcastic dig at stardom than some kind of glam statement). Their first "public" gig together was at Tacoma's Community World Theater on March 19, 1988. Chad Channing was also at the show; it was his first Nirvana experience.

Five weeks later, the band made their Seattle debut at the Vogue, as part of a weekly bill organised by Poneman and Pavitt known as Sub Pop Sunday. This led to a review in *The Rocket* from writer Dawn Anderson. "Kurt Cobain was so nervous that he was shaking in his flannels," she wrote. Other tastemakers, including *The Rocket*'s Managing Editor, Grant Alden, and soon-to-be legendary Seattle lensman Charles Peterson, were equally underwhelmed. Alden failed to see out their set, while Peterson didn't use a frame.

Novoselic and Cobain might well have run their *Rocket* ad every issue. Foster was thrown out of the band in May 1988 to be replaced (again) by Aaron Burckhard, who this time around didn't get beyond the rehearsal stage. Chad Channing had spoken with Novoselic and Cobain backstage at a show at Evergreen State College, who suggested he jammed with the band.

Speaking in *Nirvana: The Day By Day Eyewitness Chronicle*, Channing said that he thought "[they] seemed like straight-up, pretty normal guys." What Channing didn't know was that Cobain was a frustrated drummer, making him one tough bandleader.

Channing joined in late spring, sitting in on their initial photo session with Charles Peterson, at around the same time that Dave Grohl was recovering from his first European tour with Scream. Things slowly started to improve for Nirvana. Channing seemed to have the hands-of-thunder that sat well with Cobain's strange amalgam of the Melvins and the Beatles. They recorded their first single, another take of 'Love Buzz', on June 11 and 30, 1988. Endino was once again producer, so, typically, everything was cut live, apart from some rudimentary guitar double tracking.

Nirvana's first "serious" press coverage was in the August 1988 issue of *Backlash* magazine. Under the bold headline: "It May Be The Devil And It May Be The Lord . . . But It Sure As Hell Ain't Human", Dawn Anderson gushed, "I honestly believe that with enough practice, Nirvana could become . . . better than the Melvins." The first documented evidence of Cobain smashing a guitar, which would fast become a set-ending ritual, came at their August 29 gig at the Vogue. Cobain admitted that this was a result of his frustration with Channing's drumming (and some of his successors), made clear by his diving headfirst into the drum kit.

When the band returned to Reciprocal Studios in late September to mix the track 'Spank Thru' for a *Sub Pop 200* box set Endino was piecing together, Nirvana's inner chemistry became painfully clear to Channing. Speaking in *Nirvana: The Day By Day Eyewitness Chronicle*, he admitted that his only role in the band was playing drums, a state of affairs Dave Grohl would also come to recognise. "If [Sub Pop's] Bruce [Pavitt] and Poneman ever got together with the band and talked about important

110

stuff, you can bet it wasn't with me. It was always with Chris and Kurt. It was like any important decisions . . . regarding the band had nothing to do with me at all."

Released in November 1988, 'Love Buzz' appeared in a limited edition of 1,000. It was the first offering from the Sub Pop Single of the Month Club, a savvy marketing ploy from Pavitt and Poneman, whereby subscribers received one Sub Pop single per month for an upfront annual fee of $35. Sub Pop, whose main focus at the time was on Mudhoney, were as surprised as everyone else by the attention 'Love Buzz' received. "Sub Pop always treated Nirvana like they were not as big a deal [as Mudhoney]," said Charles R. Cross, then editor of *The Rocket*. "They were the B team."

Sub Pop got their "B team" back into the studio just before Christmas 1988, for the first of six sessions that generated their debut album, *Bleach*. The record cost, in total, $606.17, which was covered by Jason Everman, a long-time pal of Channing's. In exchange, he was given a guitarist credit on the record, even though he didn't actually record anything. (A few months later he briefly became a fourth member.)

When the band played their next show, at the release party for *Sub Pop 200*, on December 28 at Seattle venue the Underground, the buzz was tangible. John Peel, the revered English DJ, helped spread the word even further when he began playing *Sub Pop 200* on his radio show. A few months later, Everett True wrote his *Melody Maker* cover story on the Seattle scene, travelling on the Sub Pop dollar. Although Cross considered True's initial piece – and subsequent stories – "vastly overrated", the words 'Seattle', 'grunge' and 'Nirvana' were now spoken of with a certain reverence.

While word was starting to spread in hipper circles about Nirvana and 'Love Buzz', it was business as usual in the mainstream charts in 1988. Manufactured music for the masses ruled, thanks to the heinous touch of moguls Stock, Aitken and Waterman, typified by Australian soap starlet, Kylie Minogue, who had a transatlantic hit with yet another revival of Little Eva's 'The Locomotion'. Fake pop duo Milli Vanilli was exposed as the worst example yet of musical prefabrication, the unbearably smug former prog rock drummer Phil Collins revived 'A Groovy Kind Of Love', while U2 were in the midst of their pompous *Rattle And Hum* period. With Reagan in the White House, and Thatcher still residing at 10

Downing Street, some found the blind optimism of one-man-band Bobby McFerrin's 'Don't Worry, Be Happy' hard to swallow, although that didn't prevent it from becoming a worldwide hit. The symbols of the decade's avariciousness – Michael Jackson and Madonna – continued to dictate to the record business.

Rock veterans were still embarrassing themselves. The Beach Boys had a surprise number one in 'Kokomo', arguably the worst song of their lengthy career, Eric Clapton delivered albums and performances on auto-pilot, while the former voice of a generation, Bob Dylan, seemed in ter-minal decline – *Down In The Groove* was possibly the lowest point of his career. The Rolling Stones had nearly come apart thanks to Mick Jagger's ego preening in the form of two duff solo albums, until reconvening for a lucrative 1989/90 stadium tour with the added afterthought of a patchy album, *Steel Wheels*, to shift.

The contemporary scene that Nirvana was rebelling against was equally moribund. By the end of the Eighties it had reached its big-haired nadir, but the downward slide had begun during the Seventies when bands such as Grohl's heroes Led Zeppelin graduated from theatres to arenas. The bigger rock'n'roll's appeal grew, the more disconnected from reality its stars became. It didn't help that their audiences were too partisan or stoned to notice the difference.

Thanks to the advent of FM radio, slick record production, and non-stop touring, a clutch of AOR acts became money-making machines. Journey, Styx, Foreigner, Boston and the truly ludicrous REO Speedwagon all went supernova.* With MTV's debut in 1981, the music went into a further tailspin. High rotation on MTV was possibly even more commer-cially lucrative than saturation radio airplay, so rock videos had to be larger than life. Hair metal was the next tragic step.

The chosen form of skinny-legged, thin-hipped pretty boys with an unhealthy predilection for spandex, hair spray and eyeliner, "hair metal", in the form of such acts as Mötley Crüe, Bon Jovi, Warrant and Poison, had all the androgynous appeal of glam rock but favoured style over substance.

---

* Admittedly, many of these acts left some kind of mark on Grohl. During Foo Fighters' first tour, he brought Shudder To Think's Craig Wedren onstage for a cover of Journey's 'Lovin, Touchin', Squeezin''.

In 1989, as Sub Pop, Seattle and grunge started to make some kind of impression beyond the Pacific Northwest, the mainstream was so bland, particularly in America, that it was ripe for shaking up, as in 1976 when punks threatened the dismal status quo prevailing in Great Britain.

On January 21, Nirvana performed at Portland's Satyricon club. It was the night that Cobain first locked eyes on wild child Courtney Love, who was then living in Oregon. Her role in Cobain's – and by proxy Nirvana's – life would be filled with the same type of turgid melodrama that had marked her wayward life to that point. Speaking in Azerrad's *Come As You Are*, Cobain offered this unflattering sketch of his future partner: "I thought she looked like Nancy Spungen." Given that Spungen was the doomed partner of equally doomed Sex Pistol Sid Vicious, Cobain's words were particularly portentous.

Channing celebrated his 22nd birthday at the end of January and by then *Bleach* was in the can. "I think those were the best times," he said, looking back in *Eyewitness Nirvana*. "[They] may have been for them [Cobain and Novoselic] too, I don't know."

Nirvana played several shows during the early months of 1989, the most notorious being a double-bill with Treehouse. At the set's end, Novoselic decided to get in on the gear-trashing action that Cobain had instigated a short while back. In an act that Channing could have read as symbolic, Novoselic threw his bass high in the air and stepped aside as it fell on Channing's head, knocking him out cold.* The drummer was not amused.

Interest in the Seattle and Northwest scene was growing. Local writer Gillian G. Gaar, reporting in *Calendar* magazine, penned the somewhat facetious headline: "Screaming North: Seattle Bands Conquer The World". The magazine ran it virtually unchanged. "It's very true," Gaar told me, "except for the Screaming North part. They added that. If you have the article, at the end there are some listings as to when the bands were playing; they added something before it saying something along the lines of 'see these bands who may be the future of rock'." Neither Gaar, nor any of the Seattle bands including Nirvana, Mudhoney, Soundgarden, Tad and the rest, could have predicted how accurate her forecast was.

Around this time, Nirvana hit the road again, playing West Coast

---

* A shot taken of Novoselic's unsteady juggling act would appear on *Bleach*'s sleeve.

dates, first with the Melvins and then Mudhoney. Jason Everman made his Nirvana debut on February 25 at a University of Washington show, and the addition of a second guitarist, at least according to Jonathan Poneman, worked wonders. "I thought they were colossal," he said soon after.

With *Bleach* yet to be released, Nirvana became involved in some side projects, covering Kiss' 'Do You Love Me?' for a tribute album dedicated to the fire-breathing cartoon rockers, while Cobain recorded with Olympia's Go team, comprising his then girlfriend Tobi Vail and Calvin Johnson. When Nirvana shared a bill with acid-fried Okies the Flaming Lips on April 26, Lips leader Wayne Coyne observed, "I remember thinking Cobain looked like he should be in Lynyrd Skynyrd because he had really long hair and he kind of had a beard. We were like, 'God, this is fucked up.'" It was an observation that might have appealed to the southern rock lover in Dave Grohl.

On June 15, *Bleach* finally reached the stores. The first 1,000 copies were pressed on white vinyl, the following 2,000 packaged with a limited-edition poster. Sub Pop's expectations were low (as would be DGC's with *Nevermind*): they hoped to shift maybe 5,000 copies at most. Of course, this didn't prevent Sub Pop's spin department going into overdrive, with a press release mixing indie sarcasm with wishful thinking: "Hypnotic and righteous heaviness from these Olympia pop stars. They're young, they own their own van, and they're going to make us rich."

Squeezed into said vehicle – a white Dodge van – the four-piece Nirvana headed out on June 21 for their inaugural US tour, playing the first of 26 shows the following night at San Francisco's Covered Wagon. Just as Grohl had experienced with Scream, money was tight: sometimes the band would even announce a request for a bed for the night during their set. On a bad night Nirvana made $25, although they usually raked in $150, which was enough to cover food and gas to reach the next show.

Everman's tenure with Nirvana ended with a July 18 spot at New York's Pyramid Club, part of the New Music Seminar free-for-all. A love of obscure Scandinavian metal, along with his big hair and arena rock stage moves, ensured he and Cobain clashed. Everman had become increasingly withdrawn as the tour progressed; by the time they reached the East Coast, it was obvious that they couldn't continue playing together. In one of his last shows with the band, Everman played the entire gig wearing a Mickey

Mouse costume. Oddly, once the band blew out the few remaining tour dates, the four drove all the way back to Washington without mentioning Everman's imminent departure.*

Despite the low-key expectations, *Bleach* received some positive press. Tipster's bible the *CMJ New Music Report* announced that Nirvana "could be the coolest thing since toast", while long-time advocate Gillian G. Gaar, writing in *The Rocket*, paid dues to the band's refusal to slot easily into the Seattle stereotype. "Nirvana careens from one end of the thrash spectrum to the other," she wrote in July 1989, "giving a nod towards garage grunge, alternative noise, and hell-raising metal, without swearing allegiance to any of them."

Yet in spite of the increased attention that Nirvana and most of their Seattle brethren were receiving, *Bleach* only sold moderately. Just like DC's Dischord Records, Sub Pop was a regional label, miles – literally and philosophically – from the music biz capitals of New York and LA, without any of the marketing or distribution muscle of a major label. With the Internet not yet established as a reliable bastion of information, actually finding *Bleach* in record stores was a challenge.† Despite Sub Pop's claim that "They're going to make us rich," the label didn't really support the album. Cobain later realised that the band had done no more than a handful of interviews to promote the record.

The truth of the matter was that Sub Pop had a few internal problems to deal with. They'd lost a serious amount of money thanks to a wayward distribution venture, and that, combined with the dual financial strain of trying to release a record per week and also keep their roster on the road, was draining already limited resources. Matters weren't improved by members of various Sub Pop bands helping themselves to product out of the label's office.

Just as Grohl found an escape route from Scream, Cobain and Novoselic had insisted on a clause in their contract with Sub Pop, which they were now prepared to invoke. With indie heroes such as Sonic Youth and Dinosaur Jr signing to major labels (the former to Geffen, the latter to Sire), what until recently had been deemed the biggest of all

---

* In a dramatic career change, Everman later became a paratrooper.
† The album would only begin to sell in serious numbers after the phenomenal success of *Nevermind* in 1992.

cop-outs was now a perfectly acceptable move in reaching a wider audience. With attention now firmly fixed on such Seattle up-and-comers as Soundgarden, Nirvana knew that they had better seize the moment, or they'd end up spending the rest of their lives living out of the van.

Poneman and Pavitt knew that they couldn't compete with the multinationals, but battled to keep Nirvana on Sub Pop. When Cobain refused to return their calls, Pavitt turned up at his front door in Olympia, imploring him to sign a new contract. Although they talked for all of five hours, the band turned Sub Pop down a few days later. Significantly, it was Novoselic who made the call to the label; confrontation wasn't one of Cobain's stronger points.

While their unsteady relationship with Sub Pop stumbled to an unfortunate conclusion, Nirvana kept working. In August 1989, with Steve Fisk at the desk, they attempted to record five tracks – 'Polly', 'Token Eastern Song', 'Even In His Youth', 'Stain' and 'Been A Son' – at Music Source in Seattle. Only the latter two would make the *Blew* EP, the other songs were still very much works-in-progress. Between September 9 and 22, they played some mid-Western dates, documenting events, both on stage and off, on a $100 Pixel Vision camera. On October 20, they undertook their first European tour, co-headlining with heavyweight rockers Tad.

The two bands, plus their small crew and their gear, squeezed into a nine-seater mini van; an extremely tight fit, given that Tad frontman Tad Doyle tipped the scales at a notch over 300 pounds. Money was as tight as ever – somewhere around $100 per show – although their per diem now ran to a generous $10 a man. The tour started in Newcastle, on October 23 and rolled through Manchester, Leeds, London, Portsmouth and Birmingham, before heading to the continent, playing shows in Holland and West Germany, performing while the Berlin Wall came down.

Novoselic, whose interest in his Croatian background made him more politically aware than most punk rockers, admitted that this defining moment was lost on the Seattle roadshow. "We didn't know what was going on until a little before we got to the border and there were all these little cars crammed full of people offering us fruit," he reported to *The Rocket*.

The tour kept on through Austria, Switzerland, Belgium, Hungary and Italy, where Sub Pop's Poneman and Pavitt, who briefly joined the roadshow, watched while a tired and emotional Cobain climbed a rafter during Nirvana's set and threatened to jump, only to be pulled down by bouncers. The two-headed grunge beast hooked up with Mudhoney to end the tour at the Sub Pop Lame Fest in London on December 3, where Cobain and Novoselic spent part of Nirvana's set playing baseball with their gear, while Tad Doyle struck terror into the moshpit when feigning a stage dive. As drained as he was, Novoselic ended 1989 on an upbeat note, marrying his long-time girlfriend Shelli on December 30, in their Tacoma apartment.

CHAPTER SEVEN

Reaching Nirvana

"Even after the greatest show you've ever been to in your whole entire life, we'd get backstage and go, 'Oh, I'm going to get a beer.' Never, ever did I get one compliment in the four years I was in that band."

– Dave Grohl

IN April 1990, at roughly the same time that Scream undertook their final European tour, Nirvana went into Smart Studios in Madison, Wisconsin, for sessions with little known producer Butch Vig. Apart from a short West Coast tour in February, opening for Dinosaur Jr, they had spent the first few months of the year fine-tuning the songs, as well as recording an early version of the oft-recorded 'Sappy' (a.k.a. 'Verse Chorus Verse') with Jack Endino in Seattle. Cobain would return to the song several times in the studio over the years, without quite nailing it.

Vig was a smart choice as producer, having worked with dozens of indie and alternative acts. Crucially for Cobain (and later, Dave Grohl), Vig was a drummer, so he understood the type of rhythmic pulse Cobain was trying to capture. Based in his own Smart Studios in Madison, Wisconsin, Vig had worked with such bands as Killdozer, the Smashing Pumpkins, the Laughing Hyenas and Fluid, in the process becoming a surrogate in-house producer for labels Twin/Tone, Touch & Go and Mammoth. He'd also worked for Sub Pop, producing Tad's *8 Way Santa*. Despite the rock dude shades that became an integral part of his wardrobe, especially when he became renowned for his work on *Nevermind*, Vig seemed relatively unaffected.*

When they reached Madison, Nirvana's plan was ambitious: they

---

* When I spoke to him in LA in 2001, he had a serene, almost Zen-like air, despite a recent bout of hepatitis that had forced him to stop drumming temporarily with his band Garbage.

wanted to record their entire second album in five days, even though Cobain hadn't penned much in the way of lyrics. Still, the trio was well prepared, having just spent time jamming in a Seattle warehouse space they shared with Mudhoney. Early sketches of future *Nevermind* tracks, including 'In Bloom' and 'Lithium', came out of these warehouse jams.

Speaking with Gillian G. Gaar for a comprehensive *Goldmine* article about Nirvana's recorded history, Vig recalled, "I didn't really have to do too much fine tuning in terms of what they were doing. They had been playing most of the songs, the arrangements were pretty solid. I could tell that Kurt wasn't too pleased with Chad's drumming, because he kept going and getting behind the kit showing him how to play things." Vig found the band "funny and charming", although even then Cobain fluctuated between cheerfulness and sudden dark turns. "He would get really moody and sit in the corner and not talk for 45 minutes," Vig recalled.

Their stated ambition of cutting an entire album proved too ambitious, but the band did manage to record serviceable versions of 'In Bloom', 'Polly' and 'Lithium', plus 'Pay To Play' (later renamed 'Stay Away') and 'Imodium' (an antidiarrhoeal medicine), eventually re-titled 'Breed'. While at Smart, Nirvana also attempted a cover of the Velvet Underground's 'Here She Comes Now'.*

Vig didn't rate Nirvana too highly at the start of the sessions – he "wasn't too crazy" about *Bleach* – but he warmed to the band over the five days at Smart. "I thought they were totally amazing," Vig told Gaar. "They still had the punk attitude, but they were really, really hooky songs. And Kurt's lyric writing was becoming even more enigmatic. You weren't quite sure what he was singing about, but you knew it was really intense." Vig was sufficiently intrigued to check out Nirvana's sonic assault live at a double-bill with Tad on April 6, straight after the last day of recording. He could see that Nirvana had the ability to transcend their grungey punk roots, if only they could sort out their drummer problem.

Cobain and Novoselic's problems with Channing were increasing. "They said I was burning out on shows [and my timing] was off and stuff," Channing said in *Eyewitness Nirvana*, "and it's true. I was. I just wasn't getting into it any more."

---

* The Smart Studio sessions would effectively become well-polished demos for *Nevermind*. (In fact, the album version of 'Polly' is from Smart, although it was subsequently remixed.)

Chris Novoselic (left) and Grohl in the studio, 1991, recording *Nevermind* with producer Butch Vig.
'We were dying to go down and make the album, we really couldn't wait,' Grohl later said. 'We'd rehearsed
so much that we could have recorded it live.' *(Michel Linssen/Redferns)*

Grohl found bonding with Novoselic much easier than with Cobain, even though he shared an apartment with the Nirvana leader for many months. Novoselic would be the first bassist Grohl approached when forming the Foo Fighters, but he politely passed on the offer. *(Michel Linssen/Redferns)*

Working on *Nevermind* in 1991 was a totally new sensation for Grohl. 'I'd never made an album as serious as I'd imagined this to be,' he said. 'It was, "Oh, we're going pro, this is a real record".' *(Michel Linssen/Redferns)*

Novoselic, Grohl and Cobain (from left), in 1992, the year Nirvana-mania kicked into overdrive. 'Everything's fucking crazy!,' Grohl said, as *Nevermind* exploded. 'They're making a mistake; this is not supposed to happen to some stupid kid from Nowheresville.' *(Sipa Press/Rex Features)*

Grohl (left) and Novoselic share some rare downtime in 1992. When Novoselic first witnessed Grohl's powerhouse drumming with Scream, he turned to Cobain and said: 'Wish he'd be in our band.' *(Steve Eichner/Retna)*

Grohl, Cobain and Novoselic (from left), backstage at the MTV Video Music Awards, September 9, 1992.
On the same night, Cobain and Courtney Love jokingly asked Axl Rose to be the godfather of their baby Frances.
Rose suggested that Cobain 'shut his bitch up'. *(LFI)*

Novoselic, Cobain and Grohl (from left), July 1992, soon after Cobain allegedly OD'd in Belfast. 'All I do is walk up on stage and I play drums,' Grohl said of his role in the band. 'And then I go home. There's just so much that goes on that I don't even know about.' *(Steve Double/Retna)*

Jennifer Youngblood, who married Grohl in 1994. Grohl wrote the Foo Fighters' 'Big Me' as a valentine for Youngblood, and she took the controversial cover shot for the first Foo Fighters album. They divorced in 1997, when Grohl began an affair with Louise Post. *(Lisa Johnson)*

Cobain leads the Nirvana charge at the Big Day Out, Hordern Pavilion, Sydney, January 26, 1992. The band weren't headliners; they were stuck between indigenous pop act Yothu Yindi and ageing college rockers the Violent Femmes. *(Tony Mott/LFI)*

Grohl flails away during a 'secret' Nirvana gig, opening for Mudhoney at the Crocodile Café, Seattle, October 4, 1992. Afterwards, Grohl and Novoselic drank until closing time, but Cobain disappeared as soon as their set ended. Soon after, Grohl and Novoselic joined forces in alt-rock 'supergroup', Melvana. *(Charles Peterson/Retna)*

Chili Pepper Anthony Kiedis, Grohl, Novoselic and Peppers bassist Flea (from left). Cross-dressing was never a problem for Grohl. Even as a child, he staged 'little shows' for his family, usually wearing 'something as outlandish and ridiculous as possible.' *(LFI)*

'In Bloom' director Kevin Kerslake, Frances Bean, Cobain, Grohl and Novoselic (from left), MTV Video Music Awards, September 2, 1993, Universal City, California. Although personally invited by Cobain, Kerslake had just lost the gig of directing the band's next clip. *(LFI)*

Grohl thumps the tubs during the Scream reunion tour, New York, July 1993. 'I think this will throw everything back into perspective for me,' Grohl said prior to the tour. '[Playing with Nirvana] is not the same as playing on a small stage with guys who are basically my brothers.' *(LFI)*

Kurt Cobain onstage with Nirvana, February 1994, during the band's final European tour. He killed himself two months later. While Grohl admitted that Cobain often 'played dumb' for the media, he insisted that he could also be 'the most hilarious person you've ever met.' *(LFI)*

Grohl with Novoselic at the MTV Video Music Awards, September 8, 1994. 'Heart-Shaped Box' would win the band a posthumous Best Alternative Video award, although they were beaten by Aerosmith in the Video of the Year category. It was as though the alt-rock revolution had never happened. *(Maiman Rick/Corbis)*

After Nirvana rolled out of Madison, Vig's phone remained silent for several months. Despite their affinity, it seemed as though their working relationship had ended before it had begun. Bootleg tapes of the Smart sessions started to circulate among music biz tastemakers. The word was out. Standing at the back of the moshpit at Nirvana's New York show on April 26, alongside Iggy Pop and members of the bands Helmet and Sonic Youth, was Gary Gersh, head of A&R at Geffen, who'd liked what he heard on the bootleg.

Back in Seattle, two weeks after Chad Channing played his last Nirvana gig at Boise, Idaho, on May 17, Cobain and Novoselic took a ferry ride out to Channing's home on Bainbridge Island to break the inevitable news that he was out of the band. While Novoselic did the bulk of the talking, Cobain experienced the most guilt, apparently confessing afterwards that he felt as though he'd "just killed somebody". Speaking in *Come As You Are*, Channing insisted that he walked before he was fired, stating that his departure "was strictly along the musical line that it just wasn't working any more". In a statement that would strongly echo Grohl's subsequent confessions about life in Nirvana, Channing said that he felt like an extra wheel alongside Cobain and Novoselic. "I never felt like I was totally in the band," Channing said. "I was thinking, 'Why don't they get a drum machine?' Then they could programme it and do anything they damn well wanted."

Channing looks back on his time in Nirvana with mixed emotions: while he was never allowed creative input by Cobain or Novoselic, he did bond with the pair offstage. They'd often share the same bed while on the road, or sleep together in the back of the van. "We'd gone through hell together," he told Charles R. Cross. Although Channing went on to play with such bands as East Of The Equator and The Methodists, who recorded with Jack Endino, he's still regarded as "the Pete Best of Nirvana", the guy who missed out.[*]

Unfortunately, "Does anyone really care about Chad Channing?" seems to be the general sentiment on most Nirvana internet chat rooms nowadays.

Just prior to taking Novoselic's call, Grohl put in a few more sessions at Barrett Jones' Laundry Room. Alongside Jones and Bruce Merkle of the

---

[*] Although he continues to collect royalties from his work on *Bleach* and the bits-and-pieces collection *Incesticide*.

band 9353 was Tos Nieuwenhuizen from Dutch band God, whom Grohl had met and toured with while in Scream. He was now living in DC, spending most of his time propping up the bar at DC Space. Grohl's motley crew cut five tracks under the name Harlingtox Angel Divine (a.k.a. Harlingtox AD). At the same time, Grohl and Jones began tinkering with tracks that would end up on Grohl's highly collectible *Pocketwatch* tape.

"How did this occur?" read the liner notes to the Harlingtox CD. "The Harlingtox story was hatched in Washington, DC in the spring and summer of 1990. It's very 1990-like. It reeks of Bush/Quayle annoyances and growing pains in general. Harlingtox was never a band, there has never been a Harlingtox show. It was musically arranged by Dave and Tos, probably first conceptualised in Europe during a Scream/God tour the previous year."

The tone of the Harlingtox project was well represented by the tracks they recorded. Opening with 'Treason Daddy Brother In Crime Real Patriots Type Stuff', the openly surreal Divines worked their way through 'Orbiting Prisons In Space', the Motörhead-flavoured 'Recycled Children Never To Be Grown', and 'Obtaining A Bachelors Degree', finishing with 'Open Straightedge Arms'. The final track suggested that despite Grohl's love of the DC hardcore community, he didn't necessarily embrace the drug-less lifestyle choice. Grohl's fast-developing skills as a musical everyman were evident; he arranged each track with Nieuwenhuizen, played bass, guitar and drums on the opener and contributed guitar licks on 'Recycled Children'. Although this bizarre record wouldn't receive a formal release until 1996, and even then only on Jones' boutique Laundry Room Records, it proved that Grohl's time in Jones' studio had been well spent, laying the foundation for Grohl's future project, Probot.

During the summer of 1990, music biz whispers heated up about Nirvana and, in particular, who would replace Chad Channing. It was even rumoured that Dinosaur Jr's J Mascis would switch from guitar back to his original role as a drummer in joining Cobain and Novoselic. Instead the pair decided to temporarily "borrow" Dan Peters, from Mudhoney (who were on hold while guitarist Steve Turner finished college). With Peters on drums, and using gear borrowed from Tad, they recorded the single 'Sliver' on July 11, in Reciprocal Studios with Jack Endino.

While officially toeing the punk party line, disdaining the business side of music whenever asked, Cobain and Novoselic consulted attorney Alan Mintz, of the LA-based Ziffen, Brittenham & Branca, while being wined and dined by reps from virtually every major label. Novoselic finally got back in touch with Butch Vig and asked him how he'd feel about producing a major label album for the band (although they hadn't yet signed with one!). Vig couldn't agree quickly enough.

The Melvins' Dale Crover was hired as drummer when Nirvana headed out on August 13 for eight West Coast dates with Sonic Youth, the New York art noise band who would play a key role in advising Nirvana which label to sign with.

A few weeks later, when Grohl arrived in Seattle on September 21, Nirvana's musical chairs continued. Dan Peters was back in the fold and seriously considering formally applying for the drummer's gig. He even sat in on a September 23 interview for the British music weekly *Sounds*. As the band were using his grungy rehearsal space in south Seattle, Cobain and Novoselic bought Peters a hefty kit to replace his small-but-solid set-up.

Peters played the sum total of just one Nirvana gig at Seattle's Motor Sports International and Garage on September 22, 1990, with the Melvins and the Dwarves on the bill. Playing a set that included 'Imodium', 'Pay To Play' and 'In Bloom', the band pulled a crowd of 1,500 including, ironically, Dave Grohl. The night was a turning point for Nirvana; it was by far their largest hometown gig to date, suddenly making them bigger than Mudhoney, Soundgarden and many other Northwest contenders.

Grohl was impressed but noticed how different the Seattle audience was to DC. "It didn't seem like a punk rock scene to me," he said in 2000, "and that's all I had ever really known. The kids weren't punk rockers, they were dirty little burnouts. And I'd never seen anything like that before. I thought it was pretty hilarious."

As condescending as Grohl's comments might seem, he was spot on. The burgeoning Seattle scene was vastly different to the hardcore underground he'd experienced with Scream. For one thing, many of the Seattle bands had their eyes on the prize of a major label – the purist ideology of DC and Dischord didn't bear much weight. Achieving some degree of success was a valid goal, especially if you'd done time in a decrepit van in the back of beyond. Cobain and Novoselic typified this approach; while they desired creative control and still viewed their music as non-negotiable, they were willing to court the major labels in LA and New York that were hoping to sign them.

When asked to describe the differences between the scenes from both coasts, Charles R. Cross told me, "Both of those scenes were insular and clearly influenced greatly by Black Flag, but Seattle also had New Wave elements, artier bands, and more hardcore metal. The DC scene, in my observation, was far more intellectual than the metal heads that were in many Seattle bands." Curiously, Grohl would be painted a "rocker" by the hipper than thou members of the Seattle music scene, although this didn't prevent him being bombarded with questions about the DC hardcore world.

Speaking in the *Classic Albums* TV special, Jonathan Poneman commented, "There was a tremendous amount of coherence in the Seattle music scene. Everybody was going to the same parties, taking the same drugs, listening to the same music. A lot of cross-pollination was happening."

Cross downplays any suggestion that the Seattle bands were driven by a lust for recognition. Just like Poneman, he believes they shared a communal spirit similar to the ideology of the noise-makers hanging out in the Dischord basement. "The fellowship between [Seattle] musicians was key in my opinion. More bands were playing to impress their friends and musician buddies than they were playing for an audience or wealth or success. They helped create a cohesion that was a big part of the scene." This may have been the case during the early Nineties, but once A&R departments started waving chequebooks in the wake of *Nevermind*, that original sense of camaraderie would soon dissipate.

Three days after the Motor Sports gig, Grohl officially auditioned for Cobain and Novoselic at the Dutchman, the rehearsal space that Peters supplied for the band. If Grohl had learned one key thing about drumming from his time with Scream, it was the majesty of power. When he tried out for Nirvana, he simply flayed away, playing with the same force and speed he'd used when backing the Stahl brothers.

"I hit the drums as hard as I could; I had these really big drums," he said in the *Classic Albums* show. "Scream was a fast hardcore punk rock band, but we also played sort-of rock songs. It was the most powerhouse drumming I could produce; every night I'd play until I collapsed." As soon as Grohl counted the band in, Novoselic, for one, could sense the difference. "Once Dave joined, Nirvana was like a tight machine," he admitted during the same *Classic Albums* episode. "I don't know if it was providence or not, but something guided us to get together. You could feel the impact right away."

Grohl's serviceable singing voice also helped to win him acceptance, although he would soon learn that Cobain and Novoselic were not overly generous with their praise. "Nirvana was never a band that complimented each other," Grohl would admit. "Even after the greatest show you've ever been to in your whole entire life, we'd get backstage and go, 'Oh, I'm going to get a beer.' Never, ever did I get one compliment in the four years I was in that band."

A few weeks after the 'Sliver' single, Nirvana's last release for Sub Pop, appeared in US stores, Grohl's formal induction took place on October 11 at the North Shore Surf Club in Olympia, a bar with a capacity of about 300. The show had sold out so quickly that an impressed Grohl called his mother and sister to pass along the news. The signs were positive from their first soundcheck. Whereas previously, Cobain, in typically frustrated drummer style, would take over the kit for a few songs, now he let Grohl blaze away uninterrupted. The gig was a technical disaster; the power repeatedly blew out and the band had to shut down half their gear to avoid further blackouts. However, the set was still a triumph for Grohl, who thumped the tubs with such raw animal ferocity that he actually broke his snare drum. At the show's conclusion, Cobain proudly held the wrecked snare above his head like a trophy. Grohl had officially passed the audition.

Cross noted the immediate difference in Nirvana's sound when Grohl joined. "Dave played a huge role [in Nirvana's success] if only because he added that kind of drumming sound that worked on the charts. Mudhoney's Dan Peters was a great drummer himself, but not a monster drummer like Grohl."

Cobain's way of handling the sacking of Dan Peters was one of the less admirable moves in his short life. A few days prior to Grohl's debut, Cobain played an acoustic set on Calvin Johnson's KAOS radio show, broadcast from Olympia's Evergreen College, during which Cobain broke the news about Nirvana's latest drummer. "His name is Dave," Cobain told Johnson, "and he's a baby Dale Crover and within a few years' practice, he may even give him a run for his money." Cobain admitted to feeling slight remorse about Peters' rapid-fire departure, but he had no reservations in calling Grohl "the drummer of our dreams".

Cobain's dream became a nightmare for Peters. Nirvana had a European tour booked through late October, sharing bills with she-rockers L7, and with Mudhoney still on an extended hiatus and Nirvana's star in the ascendancy, Peters was keen to be involved. When Cobain called Peters, he sidestepped the issue, instead choosing to speak about the band's likely major label deal. When Peters ran out of patience and asked about the tour and his spot in the band, Cobain finally came clean and admitted that he'd hired Grohl.

Peters put on a brave front when speaking with Michael Azerrad for *Come As You Are*. "I wasn't bummed at all," he insisted. "I kind of half-assed expected it and I was like, 'Oh, that's cool.'" However, Peters stated that Cobain's communication skills at the time "were kind of not happening". As for Grohl's recruitment, Peters was incredibly generous, admitting that the former Scream-er's style was far better suited to Cobain's songs than his own. "He's got the heavy shit right there," he said. "He beats the fuck out of those drums."

Novoselic offered the excuse that he and Cobain didn't want to derail Mudhoney's future by stealing their drummer, even if the band weren't actually together at that time.* In the final analysis, Peters had almost as much claim as Chad Channing to the unfortunate tag of "Nirvana's Pete Best".

Novoselic, Cobain and Grohl hired a rehearsal space, a converted barn in Tacoma. The décor was a Seventies fashion disaster – brown shag carpet being the house speciality – and the PA was barely serviceable, but it was a step up from the room above the hair salon of Novoselic's mother. The trio worked hard, rehearsing almost every night, from 10 pm to one in the morning. Notably, the tension that so tangibly existed between Cobain and previous drummers was conspicuous by its absence. Grohl may have had some trouble connecting personally with Cobain, but he felt very much at home during these explorative jam sessions. "We'd always start

---

* Peters did eventually return to the Seattle power-riffers, after a short stint with the much-lauded Screaming Trees.

off the practice just jamming," Grohl told Azerrad. "We'd set up and plug in and jam for 20 minutes on nothing at all."*

Like Charles R. Cross, those close to Nirvana could spot the obvious difference once Grohl joined. According to soundman Craig Montgomery, "Dave . . . was like the perfect drummer with the band. Everything really came together." Another impressed onlooker was Cobain sidekick, fellow musician and Kill Rock Stars label founder Matthew "Slim" Moon (who'd once shared a bill with Nirvana in a band dubbed Nisqually Delta Podunk Nightmare). "Something happened after Dave Grohl joined Nirvana," Moon opined in *Eyewitness Nirvana*. "Suddenly they were much bigger."

Barely a month passed between Grohl's debut at the North Shore Surf Club and the European tour but the trio was definitely ready. Grohl was particularly excited because he was dating Jennifer Finch, the bassist for L7, so the tour would be part grunge roadshow, part love-in. Finch was another long-time associate of Nirvana's, having played host to the band in LA when Chad Channing manned the kit. She'd also booked an LA show for Scream, in a double-bill with Bad Religion.

Nirvana's first UK stop, a John Peel session on October 21, was conducted in typically contrary style: rather than push the new songs they had cut with Vig, they played cover versions, including rough takes on Devo's 'Turnaround', the Vaselines' 'Molly's Lips' and the Wipers' 'D7'. The tour became a blur as the bands swept through Birmingham, Leeds, London, Edinburgh and Nottingham, playing to crowds of 1,000 or more each night. Not only had Nirvana found the right drummer, but their road crew was now falling into place. Among them was Craig Montgomery, who was in charge of sound, and tour manager Alex MacLeod, whom Grohl had previously met – and clashed with – during a Scream tour. Anton Brookes signed on as their UK publicist – all would become key Nirvana backroom players.

Amid the UK press response were some incisive observations. Journalist Kevan Roberts, who was at the Nottingham show on October 27, noticed a key improvement. "I remember Dave singing, and thinking how good it sounded," he stated in *Eyewitness Nirvana*. "I was almost surprised by it,

---

* Grohl has claimed that dozens of tunes came out of these jams, but the band simply didn't have the gear to record them, so the songs were lost.

how it worked between the two of them [Grohl and Cobain]. It seemed to make a big difference in their sound."

When Nirvana returned to Tacoma in early November, Grohl shifted his few possessions out of the house Novoselic and his wife Shelli shared and moved into an apartment with Cobain on Pear Street, Olympia.

Grohl had lifestyle adjustments to make when he moved to Olympia; he quickly discovered how the relentlessly bleak, soggy Seattle weather could damage one's psyche. It didn't take him long to understand why Seattle-ites were dependent on caffeine and alcohol to lift their spirits. Olympia, Grohl recalled, "was the first place I'd ever been where it would rain for, like, two whole weeks. Olympia, Washington, is depressing enough – and I was living with this person that I didn't know."

Virtually from the day that Cobain met Grohl at Seattle Airport, Cobain had been in a dark funk, rarely bothering to talk or even acknowledge the new boy. At one stage, Cobain stopped talking completely and Grohl began to wonder whether he'd made the right move in leaving Scream behind. This may have been attributable to Cobain's recent split with Tobi Vail. Finally, on another long ride back from Tacoma to Olympia, Cobain broke the uncomfortable silence. He turned to Grohl and admitted, "I'm not always like this." Grohl felt enormously relieved. Speaking in *Come As You Are*, he recalled saying to Cobain, " 'Oh, that's cool.' But I was thinking to myself, 'Oh, thank God!' "

While Cobain may have explained away his surliness, he still kept mainly to himself, sketching out lyrics and song ideas in his journal each night behind his bedroom's closed door. "He would retire to his room and write for hours and hours before turning out his light and going to sleep," Grohl said in 2003.

The six-foot-tall Grohl had to squeeze onto a five-foot-long couch, and the incessant clicking noise from Cobain's pet turtles kept him awake at night. Corn dog sticks* littered the floor, prompting Cobain to admit, "It was the most filthy pigsty I'd ever lived in." There wasn't even a television, so during the long, grey afternoons the two would tinker with a four-track machine, one of Cobain's few luxuries, and play guitars. This early, getting acquainted period with Cobain would be documented in

---

* For non-Americans, a corn dog is a hot dog coated in cornbread batter, fried in hot oil, and placed on a stick.

the Foo Fighters' track 'Friend Of A Friend', which, although it didn't appear officially until 2005, was actually written by Grohl during the slow months of 1990. "They [Cobain and Novoselic] were friends of a friend of mine [Buzz Osborne]," Grohl explained, "which is how I joined the band."*

Grohl also wrote 'Marigold', a future Nirvana B-side, during his time in Olympia, a song hugely inspired by *The Winding Sheet*, the solo album from Screaming Trees singer Mark Lanegan, which was on repeat play in the Grohl/Cobain crash pad. "[That] LP really reminds me of my first few months there," he said in 1997, "[when I was] getting used to things."

During his time living with Cobain, Grohl learnt a useful lesson about songwriting. "Through Kurt, I saw the beauty of minimalism and the importance of music that's stripped down. That's more powerful," Grohl added, "because it's just so . . . desperate." Admittedly, Grohl was somewhat hamstrung by the fact that Cobain played guitar left-handed, and Grohl didn't own a six-string. He dealt with that by simply flipping his housemate's guitar over and playing it upside down.

Life in Olympia wasn't all doom and gloom. According to one insider who spoke with Charles R. Cross for his Cobain study *Heavier Than Heaven*, Grohl's extroverted nature improved Cobain's state of mind. "The house [they shared] became boy-land," Cross wrote. "Now Kurt had someone to hang out with all the time. It kind of had this husband-and-wife feel to it."†

Cobain was pretty much hopeless at everything in life bar music, so Grohl took over most of the house's domestic duties, even washing Cobain's clothes. Those years on the road with Scream had obviously bred a steely sense of self-reliance, a view corroborated by then-girlfriend Jennifer Finch. "Dave was raised in a van by wolves," she told Cross.

Grohl introduced Cobain to the cheap thrills of handmade tattoos, after Cobain had commented favourably on Grohl's self-inflicted Black Flag inkwork. Cobain's first attempt was a simple K inside a shield, the logo of Calvin Johnson's K Records. Cobain jabbed repeatedly at his arm with a

---

* The song also appeared on Grohl's hard-to-find *Pocketwatch* cassette.
† It's significant that when Grohl eventually moved out in June 1991 to set up house with Barrett Jones in west Seattle, Cobain's on-again, off-again flirtation with heroin went into overdrive.

sharp needle and then poured India ink into the wound. As DIY tattoos went, it worked well enough. While Cobain couldn't match Grohl's voracious appetite for women – after Finch, Grohl dated Kathleen Hanna of Bikini Kill, and others – they did share more juvenile interests, whiling away the hours by firing a BB gun, knocking out the windows of the State Lottery Building that was situated directly across the street from their apartment.

"There wasn't a lot to do," Grohl explained to Azerrad. "There was a lot of time just spent sitting in the room totally silent, reading or just totally silent doing nothing, staring at the walls or going downtown and seeing a 99 cent movie or shooting BB guns in the backyard."

When not playing amateur sniper with Grohl, Cobain, along with Novoselic, was attempting to take care of business. The pair had two key role models for almost every key decision they would make – in the studio, the question would be: "What would John Lennon do?" In the business world, they'd ask: "What would Sonic Youth do?" According to Cross, Cobain, especially, placed Sonic Youth's Thurston Moore and Kim Gordon "just short of royalty". Although they hadn't yet decided on the right label, Nirvana found the perfect management team in Gold Mountain, whom they signed with in November 1990, after a recommendation from Moore and Gordon. As well as Sonic Youth, Gold Mountain's client roster included Belinda Carlisle, former Go Go turned solo pop star.

During their recent tour, Cobain and Novoselic had seen the rewards that good management could provide. While Nirvana spluttered from town to town in their clunky Dodge van, selling T-shirts for gas money, Sonic Youth cruised in the comfort zone on a deluxe tour bus. Surely *they* were doing something right.

Until his departure in 1992, Gold Mountain was run by Danny Goldberg, whose staff included John Silva, the man who'd cause Glen E. Friedman much pain in his attempts to recover his Scream money, plus Michael Meisel and Janet Billig. Although Cobain and Novoselic almost always conducted Nirvana's business affairs, there was a special bond between Grohl and Goldberg: Gold Mountain's boss had been Led Zeppelin's publicist. Whenever they met, the fan in Grohl would ply Goldberg with questions about his rock'n'roll heroes. Goldberg, meanwhile, advised Nirvana that A&R man Gary Gersh and DGC/Geffen were definitely the best team for the band; after all, they had signed Sonic Youth, whose most recent album, *Goo*, had been their first commercial *and* critical success, having sold more than 250,000 copies.

Even with the Gold Mountain deal locked in, progress was slow for Nirvana as 1990 ended. After a show at Seattle's Off Ramp on November 25, before a full house positively heaving with A&R scouts, Grohl headed back to Virginia for some R&R (rest and recording) with Barrett Jones – the first of what would become known as the *Pocketwatch* sessions.

The six tracks they recorded on December 23 at Upland Studios in Arlington were ample proof of Grohl's fast-improving songwriting skills. 'Pokey The Little Puppy', the cut that opens the *Pocketwatch* tape, was basically a fuzzy-guitar-powered instrumental workout, a chance for Grohl to experiment with his swiftly developing multi-instrumentalist chops. Although clearly a loosener, 'Pokey' was still an edgy, dynamic track laden with choppy guitar riffs, brawny yet restrained drumming and no-nonsense bass playing. It forged a rock-steady template for the type of direction Grohl would eventually head with Foo Fighters – even if the song had a truly crap title.

The next track, 'Petrol CB', was far more interesting. Here, Grohl dabbled in more metallic waters; the song was introduced by a serrated guitar riff sharp enough to cut through steel, accompanied by a frustratingly inaudible vocal – it seemed as though Grohl was singing through a bucket on his head. 'Petrol CB' took an unexpectedly sweet right-turn when a more emphatic vocal melody kicked in, demonstrating the type of deep melodicism that Grohl would return to frequently. (Jones helped out here with backing vocals, the only non-Grohl contribution during the two sessions, apart from some last-minute lyrics supplied by Geoff Turner.) The haunting, reverb-laden refrain: "There's that song again", drifts in and out like the voice of a ghost. It's easily the most accomplished cut on this first *Pocketwatch* session but, of course, it's not as bizarrely funny as 'Just Another Story About Skeeter Thompson'.

Similar in form (and perversity) to the Velvet Underground's genuinely disturbing track 'The Gift', the sonic backdrop of 'Just Another Story' was a relatively direct, punked-up guitar/bass/drums drone. It was designed for no other reason than to provide some kind of setting for Grohl's increasingly demented soliloquy about Thompson's colourful love life, typified by the song's deadpan closing line, "Does this look like pus to you?"

Just like 'Pokey The Little Puppy', 'Throwing Needles' was a warp-speed riffathon, another chance for Grohl to flex some six-string muscle, with a serviceable vocal and a subtle surf rock twist – the type of jam that Grohl revisited when commissioned to provide the soundtrack to the film *Touch* a few years later.

The surreally titled 'Color Pictures Of A Marigold' – subsequently re-cut by Nirvana as 'Marigold' – showed off Grohl's less-is-more aesthetic, picked up from Cobain during those wet Olympia afternoons. Still unsure about the strength or merit of his voice, Grohl's vocal barely rose above a whisper but it carried a beautiful, stark simplicity that echoed such John Lennon tracks as 'Julia' or 'My Mummy's Dead'. "I have the stupidest voice," Grohl complained when asked about his vocals. "I was totally embarrassed and scared that anyone would hear them [the *Pocketwatch* demos]."

'Friend Of A Friend', the album's obvious standout (and the original sketch of a track that would eventually be re-recorded for Foo Fighters' album *In Your Honor*) was written at the Olympia flat. The lyric, as direct and uncluttered as the song's acoustic base, offered up several evocative insights into Grohl's early days with Nirvana. This was especially true in the following lines, which were clearly his observations on Cobain, although Grohl continues to deny this: "He needs a quiet room / With a lock to keep him" / "He says never mind / No one speaks / When he plays". Grohl then turned his attention to his taller, more gregarious bandmate: "He thinks he drinks too much / Cause when he tells his two best friends / No one speaks."

The song's uncluttered structure and the clarity and candour of the lyrics provided evidence of Grohl's increasing abilities as a craftsman. Jenny Toomey, who'd eventually release the *Pocketwatch* tape on her Simple Machines label, clearly agreed, describing Grohl's lyrics to *Alternative Press* in 1996 as "just heartbreaking". She even felt that Grohl had a "great" voice, despite his frequent protests to the contrary.

In the latter months of 1990, Nirvana were finally about to commit themselves to a record label. Again it was Sonic Youth who played a key role by influencing Cobain and Novoselic's decision to get back into the studio with Butch Vig. It seemed as though Charisma had snared the band, having offered an advance of $200,000. However just before signing,

Sonic Youth advised the band that DGC was the better option. They also spoke highly of Gary Gersh, while DGC's Mark Kates and Ray Farrell clearly weren't corporate hacks, having spent years working with indie labels before moving to the mighty Geffen. Gersh, who officially signed the band, insisted that his intentions were honourable, even though it was obvious that the alt-rock world was inching closer to the mainstream, a trend that every major label had spotted. "It wasn't because I thought this is going to change the face of popular music," he said on the *Classic Albums* documentary. "I thought there was something special between Dave and Chris and Kurt when they got on stage."

Nirvana signed to DGC for a $287,000 advance, one of the largest figures offered to a Northwest band at that time. However the money didn't go far, as they soon found out. Taxes, legal fees, Gold Mountain's commission and Glen E. Friedman's Scream investment swallowed much of the sum and there was also the matter of the band's contract with Sub Pop. A further $37,500 was paid out to buy Nirvana from the struggling indie. It may have hurt to lose their most exciting band, but the sale saved the label's bacon in both a commercial and critical sense. Pavitt and Poneman picked up a useful two per cent of sales on Nirvana's next two albums – what was to be a significant amount – with the Sub Pop imprint appearing on the rear sleeve of *Nevermind*. As Poneman told Azerrad, "Had we not had that agreement, Bruce and I would probably be washing dishes at this moment." Sub Pop was also allowed to release one more Nirvana single, a molten cover of the Vaselines' 'Molly's Lips', which appeared in April 1991.

Still, Nirvana had made the right move. They could easily have gone with one of the numerous other labels offering them the world, and accepted a far higher advance. This, of course, would have meant that they would not have reaped quite the same rewards when their record sales increased dramatically.

While awaiting their advance and the opportunity to finally get back in the studio, Cobain, Novoselic and Grohl got by on roughly $1,000 a month, supplied by Gold Mountain, at a time when the Glen E. Friedman/ Grohl situation was finally being settled. Grohl was still resorting to selling T-shirts at Olympia's Positively 4th Street record store to keep him in cigarette money. "You get $35 bucks and you're so happy," Grohl told Azerrad, "because you don't have to eat corn dogs that night – you can have a Hungry Man Dinner." Grohl wryly noted the differences between the perception and the reality of signing with a multi-national, telling *Spin*, "We're snubbed by people who think we're big rock stars. They think that when you get signed to a major label that you get all this cash to spend."

When Grohl joined Nirvana, he was under the impression that their next album would be on Sub Pop – obviously Cobain and Novoselic hadn't filled him in on their plans. Years later, he admitted to feeling uneasy about moving on. "There was definitely some guilt," Grohl said in 1999, "because we had just made that step from being on Sub Pop – a cool independent label – and then all of a sudden we were joining up with this corporate beast we had always disagreed with."

It was around this time, thanks to Novoselic letting it slip, that Grohl discovered that Cobain was using heroin. After much searching, Cobain had found a dealer in Olympia and despite the intimacy of their shared apartment he had somehow kept his habit a secret from Grohl.

When Grohl returned from LA, where he'd been sitting in with L7 at a Rock For Choice benefit, Cobain admitted to his drug misdemeanours. "Kurt said he wouldn't do it again and I believed him," a somewhat naïve Grohl admitted in *Come As You Are*. "It seemed so innocent . . . like a kid sticking a firecracker in a cat's butt and lighting it off for the hell of it. It didn't seem like anything at all."

On New Year's Day 1991, two weeks before Grohl's 22nd birthday, Nirvana cut tracks at Music Source in Seattle, with soundman Craig Montgomery producing. The session, gratis thanks to Montgomery's pal Brian Nelson who worked at the studio, was Grohl's first with the band, and memorable for the wrong reasons. Not only did Montgomery fail to capture the band's energy on tape but "the drums were falling apart". Nonetheless, two of the tracks, 'Aneurysm' and 'Even In His Youth', would be used as the B-side for the 'Smells Like Teen Spirit' single.

Nirvana also played a number of shows between the start of the year and late April. On January 16 there was a hometown gig at Olympia's Evergreen State College, while in March they undertook a short Canadian tour, playing gigs in Edmonton, Calgary, Victoria and Vancouver. At the latter show, photographer Charles Peterson snapped Cobain during the seemingly impossible act of playing guitar while balancing on his head.

This gymnast-worthy shot turned up on the sleeve of one of several versions of the 'Teen Spirit' single.

One key show on April 17 at Seattle's OK Hotel demonstrated both the propulsive power that Grohl added to the band, and the dazzling potential of a certain new tune they were road-testing. Cobain walked on stage, introducing Nirvana by mumbling, "Hello, we're major label corporate rock sell-outs." The band then roared into a skeletal version of 'Smells Like Teen Spirit'. Cobain might not have finalised the song's lyrics, nor did he have much of a voice with which to sing it, but as the band lurched between the song's restrained verses and its powder keg chorus, the place completely erupted, with crowd surfers and stage divers falling left, right and centre, like flannel-clad lemmings.* If "anger is an energy," as John Lydon once suggested in song, then the incendiary 'Smells Like Teen Spirit' embodied that wholeheartedly.

"It was funny and clever," Grohl agreed, when asked about the song's potent connection with a young, alienated audience. "[But] just to see Kurt write the lyrics . . . five minutes before he sings them, you just kind of find it a little bit hard to believe that the song has a lot to say about something."

Sub Pop's publicist Nils Bernstein was at the OK Hotel show, as he recalled on the *Classic Albums* doc. "I remember . . . thinking, 'Now it's all over, now they're actually writing huge, amazing songs.' "

The task of getting those "huge, amazing songs" on tape was down to three possible candidates. David Briggs, the veteran producer of Neil Young, had been under consideration for a time, as had REM producer Don Dixon. But Butch Vig had worked with the band and won their trust, and he finally got the nod. The sessions were set down for late April at Sound City Studios in Van Nuys, California, even though Vig would have preferred to resume working with the band in Madison. Before starting *Nevermind* – which at one stage had the working title of *Sheep* – on May 2, the band put in three days of pre-production at a location in North Hollywood, sharing rehearsal space with Lenny Kravitz and Belinda Carlisle.

---

* The display was captured on a roughly shot video and turned up on the DVD segment of Nirvana's *With The Lights Out* box set.

"We were dying to go down and make the album, we really couldn't wait," Grohl told *Classic Albums*. "We'd rehearsed so much that we could have recorded it live and it would have sounded similar to the way it does on the album."

Pre-production was something of a novelty for Grohl, whose previous recordings had been done on a shoestring. "I'd never made an album as serious as I'd imagined this to be," he said. "It was, 'Oh, we're going pro, this is a real record.'"

To get to the studio, Grohl and Cobain set off from Olympia in Cobain's dodgy Datsun B210, a gift, as Grohl recalled, from "some little old woman". Despite her generosity, there was simply no way the car could handle the lengthy drive from Seattle to LA, a fact that Cobain and Grohl discovered after only a few miles on the I5; within 20 minutes the temperature gauge was way in the red. Grohl and Cobain pulled off the road and let the engine cool down before setting out again – the pattern for a start-stop odyssey which took them a marathon five hours just to reach Oregon.

According to Grohl, "We thought, 'Fuck, man, this is torture.'" He found a pay phone and put in a mercy call to Novoselic. "[I] told him, 'This car – we can't do it.' So we headed back to Tacoma, to jump in [Novoselic's] van, but it took us another five hours, because the thing kept boiling over every 20 minutes." Rolling into a quarry near Novoselic's house, they proceeded to stone the crap out of the B210, the target for all their pent-up frustrations. "[Then] we dumped it out of the front of Chris' house," Grohl said, "and went down in the van."

When the band arrived at Sound City, Grohl was underwhelmed by the location: he'd been expecting some glossy, upscale LA setting. Instead he was stuck in a Californian suburban wasteland. What did impress him, however, was Sound City's track record, noting, as he walked through the studio's corridors, the numerous gold and platinum records of such acts as Fleetwood Mac and Tom Petty who'd recorded there.

Grohl opted to rent a kit for the *Nevermind* sessions; there was simply no way his drums, as rudimentary as they were, would fit into Cobain's disagreeable Datsun. Grohl visited the Drum Doctor, paying the sum of $1,542 on a rental kit that he used for the next 10 days. Among his rentals was a brass snare drum, the loudest snare that the Drum Doctor could supply, promptly nicknamed "The Terminator", a tag that proved well deserved.

As a fellow drummer, Vig was hugely impressed by Grohl's playing during pre-production and, like so many others, could immediately spot the difference it made to the band's sound. "The drums were punishing; it was incredible," Vig said to *Classic Albums*. Even without close miking Grohl's kit, 'Smells Like Teen Spirit', in particular, positively exploded. Vig was so impressed, in fact, that he started to break into a sweat and found that he had trouble speaking. He simply turned to the band at the end of the song and said, "That was good, guys, can you play it again?"

The first song recorded at Sound City was 'In Bloom', a track with almost the same melodic tug as 'Teen Spirit'. Grohl's usefulness was immediately evident when adding the high backing vocals to Cobain's lines, at Vig's suggestion. The producer thought that Cobain and Grohl's voices "sounded cool together" and, although Cobain wasn't wildly enthused by the idea, Vig won Cobain over by reminding him that "John Lennon did it". Vig then double-tracked their harmonies and the blend meshed perfectly.

"I didn't throw a bunch of drum fills in there ['In Bloom'], I tried to keep it as simple as possible," Grohl told *Classic Albums*. "That was kind of an unspoken rule." This ideology also extended to Cobain's songwriting. "We almost wanted them to be like children's songs," Grohl said of the album. "We'd tell people that the songs were intended to be as simple as possible."

Grohl had very little to add to 'Polly', a dark, brooding ballad inspired by a story Cobain had read in the local Tacoma paper outlining the kidnapping and torture of a teenage girl after a show at the Community World Theater. In a typically perverse move, and perhaps inspired by Hüsker Dü's 'Diane',* which shared a similar theme, Cobain adopted the point of view of the abductor, a stance that was certain to raise controversy. This would not be the last time that Nirvana deliberately unsettled their label by refusing to play the corporate game.

Grohl was more involved in the recording of the equally sombre 'Something In The Way', the album's closing track. Cobain had gone

* This melodic hardcore trio from Minneapolis were an admitted major influence on Nirvana. 'Diane' appeared on *Metal Circus*, Hüsker Dü's debut release for SST, in 1983.

through some epic hassles trying to get the right vibe for this mournfully downbeat ballad. Eventually, Vig coaxed him into the control room, where he recorded the song, almost whispering the lyrics to the accompaniment of his battered five-string acoustic. "[I] literally held my breath for three minutes while he sang," said Vig. "It was that powerful. And that was the core of the track."

Standing at the back of the control room while Grohl overdubbed drums onto the track, Cobain found it impossible to restrain his inner drummer, mouthing "quieter, quieter" to the naturally hard-hitting Grohl. Eventually, Grohl nailed it. In Vig's words, he "played it very mellow, very understated".

Grohl compensated by belting the daylights out of the kit during 'Smells Like Teen Spirit', while 'Drain You' was probably the best time he had during the making of *Nevermind*. "I guess the middle section of 'Drain You' would be the 'Bohemian Rhapsody' of *Nevermind*, because there's more than one guitar going on," he chuckled during the *Classic Albums* interview. "It was all about atmospherics, dynamics and some kind of chaotic crescendo that would happen in the middle of the song." Cobain called it their 'Won't Get Fooled Again' moment, as Vig added squeaky toys and other unexpected sound effects to the mix.

The band seemed satisfied with the results but, to a man, Nirvana had no idea how the record would eventually explode and break down the barrier that had, up until then, separated the indie/alternative world from the mainstream. According to Grohl, "We weren't on a mission. We just wanted to make a great record. Kurt probably wanted to sell 20 million records and be the biggest band in the world but I'm sure he didn't want the baggage that came along with that. I didn't."

If Cobain was impressed with Grohl's abilities – before the sessions, an excited Cobain had put in a call to Vig saying, "I've found the greatest drummer in the world" – he wasn't dispensing such compliments during the making of *Nevermind*. Cobain's frequent mood swings often affected the atmosphere in the studio. Grohl would back off whenever a situation turned ugly, reminding himself that he was "just the drummer in the band". It proved to be a handy defence mechanism.

During the first week of June, as the album was being mixed by Andy Wallace, Cobain, Grohl and Novoselic would frequently drive around the

Hollywood Hills, a tape of the mixes-in-progress blaring out of their rented car stereo. "That was something else," Grohl remembered.

In spite of Cobain's future rejection of *Nevermind* – he moaned about it being overproduced, too polished, not sufficiently punk-sounding – he couldn't deny that Vig had worked wonders in the studio. The relatively fresh producer had transformed poor-sounding boom box demos into a hard rock masterpiece.* As Grohl recalled, "All of a sudden, you have Butch Vig making it sound like *Led Zeppelin IV*." He was especially impressed when first hearing 'Smells Like Teen Spirit' blasting from the studio's speakers. It was a reaction soon to be shared by several million others.

"[*Nevermind*] was the great experience of my life," Grohl told *Rolling Stone* in 2001. "I celebrate it every now and then."

Grohl and the band also had a blast filming the iconic 'Smells Like Teen Spirit' clip, in which Grohl sported his Scream T-shirt – either an affectionate nod to his old band or an admission of guilt for deserting them, depending on whom you speak with. Cobain's concept for the video could be described in two words: teen spirit. Directly inspired by two of his favourite films – *Over The Edge*, an obscure cult flick starring Matt Dillon, and *Rock 'n' Roll High School*, a Roger Corman-produced B-movie vehicle for the Ramones – Cobain wanted to see a lot of young kids running amok. He got way more than he bargained for.

The director, Sam Bayer, knew nothing of Nirvana beforehand, but had been flogging his promo reel among the various LA record labels, trying to hustle work. He figured that Nirvana hired him because his reel "was so bad".† Bayer also worked cheaply; the entire shoot came in under $50,000, with most of the youthful extras – many of them Nirvana fans – working for free. "They weren't from central casting," Bayer said to *Classic Albums*. "That was real."

'Teen Spirit' was shot at GMT Studios in Culver City, California, beginning at 11.30 am and continuing for the entire day, with only a break

---

* Vig was paid $100,000 for his efforts – bumped up from the original offer of $65,000.

† The 'Teen Spirit' video launched the career of Sam Bayer who went on to direct clips for the Smashing Pumpkins, the Offspring, Sheryl Crow, Blink-182, David Bowie and the Cranberries, as well as working on feature films. True to form, Cobain would publicly reject Bayer's clip for 'Teen Spirit', and they never worked together again.

for lunch.* The filming was both physically and mentally draining. Towards the end of the day, Bayer says that he threw his arms up in the air and told the extras to destroy the set, which led to the carnage taking place in the latter half of the clip. Grohl had a slightly different take on events, telling *Newsweek* magazine about Bayer's ineffectual attempts at crowd control. Initially, the director had instructed the extras to look bored and generally unhappy, but not to leave their seats. "[But] when they got to the first chorus, the crowd was completely out of control, and the director was screaming at the top of his lungs for everybody to fucking calm down and be cool, or they'll get kicked out. So it was pretty hilarious, actually, seeing this man trying to control these children who just wanted to destroy." Grohl cheerfully played on as the ensuing mayhem was unleashed around him.

Cobain characteristically downplayed any possible suggestions of being a rock hero. During the song's instrumental passage, he asked Bayer not to focus on his hands, as most video directors would do. When Bayer's camera did aim towards Cobain's hands, he made sure that his fingers were in the wrong place for the notes – yet another raised middle finger from the stubborn frontman.

By the end of the shoot, Cobain had also reached the end of his tether. There was nothing faked about the blood-curdling scream that he summoned at the song's finale – and it was Cobain who insisted that Mayer's camera get a severe facial close-up for the final shot that made the viewer feel like they could see inside the pores of his skin.

One of the video's extras, a Nirvana fan called Drunk Ted, told *Flipside* magazine that the smoke permeating the shoot was actually chalk dust, so the kids were bored, restless *and* also had trouble breathing. According to Drunk Ted, Novoselic readily mixed with the faithful between shoots, but Cobain moodily sat by Grohl's drum kit in a no-go zone set aside for the band.

While Nirvana and Vig were working on *Nevermind* in Van Nuys, such fluff as Amy Grant's 'Baby Baby', Roxette's 'Joyride' and Mariah Carey's 'I Don't Wanna Cry' were riding high in the US charts. Rock'n'roll was

---

* The cast was familiar enough with 'Teen Spirit' by their lunch break to sing, "Hold the mayo! And the pickles!" instead of the correct lyrics, "An albino! A mosquito!"

being represented by such misogynistic bands as Warrant, Poison and Queensryche. Elektra had dropped somewhere near $40 million in re-signing the ridiculous Mötley Crüe, Columbia spent the same amount on renegotiations with ageing rockers Aerosmith, and Guns N' Roses were about to release their bloated double set of *Use Your Illusion* albums. Nirvana's entrance couldn't have been more timely – if there was ever a moment when the mainstream needed shaking out of its complacency, it was the early Nineties.

But there were signs that the public's tastes were expanding, which would assist Nirvana's climb. REM, who had started life in the early Eighties as arty pop outsiders from Athens, Georgia, scored their biggest hit with the haunting 'Losing My Religion', which scaled the US Top 5 in June 1991. Soon after, REM bagged a record six MTV awards. Singer Michael Stipe's ability to remain experimental and still shift serious units had a profound impact on Kurt Cobain.

On June 30, Dave Grohl helped Barrett Jones shift the Laundry Room into a new HQ in west Seattle – the basement of Grohl's house. After Jones' landlady in Virginia had walked in on him practising with a band in his rented house and asked him to move out, Jones moved in with Grohl, "for around three years," he told me. Having survived a 1987 tour as soundman/roadie for Scream, thanks to Grohl, Jones secured the job of Nirvana's drum tech.

After Nirvana completed a West Coast tour with Dinosaur Jr, Grohl got back to work on the second set of *Pocketwatch* recordings at WGNS Studios in DC with Geoff Turner, who had been briefly involved with the first session for *Pocketwatch*.

Almost matching the work rate Jones and Grohl had set several months earlier, the pair cut four tracks in a day, though none of them quite had the sweet melodicism of 'Petrol CB' or the no-holds-barred weirdness of 'Just Another Story About Skeeter Thompson'. The pick of the bunch was 'Milk', which came on like a slowed-down version of Grohl's much-loved Hüsker Dü. A madly insinuating guitar riff carried the track, with Grohl whispering his vocal as if it was some kind of profound mantra.

Of the other tracks cut with Turner, 'Bruce', a titanium-strength slab of dark metal, was the biggest departure from the brisk, melodic numbers that dominated *Pocketwatch*. 'Hell's Garden' was another straightforward hard rock jam, punctuated by the type of full-throated roar that Cobain used to profound effect on 'Smells Like Teen Spirit' and, later, 'Heart-Shaped Box'.

The jerky rhythms of the last track, 'Winnebago', resembled a punkier version of New Wave outfit the Cars, with Grohl's melodious strengths being fully displayed. He'd also nailed the hard rock dynamics that would come to play such a key part in Foo Fighters' attack; the interplay between guitar, bass and drums was impressive, especially when the track built to its drum thrashing close. However, 'Winnebago' also revealed that Grohl, just like Cobain, lacked inspiration when it came to song titles. Naming a track after the senior citizen's vehicle of choice was about as inspired as Cobain stealing the name of a diarrhoea medicine ('Imodium'), or a cheap fragrance ('Teen Spirit').

During the *Pocketwatch* sessions, Jenny Toomey dropped by the studio on business of her own. She was impressed by what she was hearing; so impressed, in fact, that she hung about WGNS long after her business was through, even though she couldn't recall being asked to stay. Toomey ran an Arlington-based label called Simple Machines that released music from many of the region's hardcore bands.* Although the songs Grohl was recording didn't quite fit with Simple Machines' genre of choice, she still liked what she heard.

Toomey approached Grohl about a possible release but he was unsure; he still lacked confidence in his voice and songwriting. At first, Grohl and Jones simply produced a cassette of the songs and passed them among their friends. As small-scale releases went, they couldn't get any more grassroots. However Toomey was persistent, and eventually convinced Grohl to grant her a limited release of the *Pocketwatch* tape. It was one of eight cassettes released by Simple Machines as part of their Tool Set series, available for $5 by mail order.

"Late orders nearly broke the label in half when Dave became famous," Toomey said in *Eyewitness Nirvana*. "It took endless hours to dub the things, our profit was tiny, and after years of use, the master cassette ultimately sounded like it had been recorded on a boom-box wrapped in cotton, set on a concrete floor, duct-taped under an oil drum."†

---

* A passionate supporter of independent music, Toomey would go on to write and record her own songs, and also become heavily involved with the Future of Music Coalition.
† Despite demand for the tape, Simple Machines eventually had to delete it because Grohl held the master.

When the tracks were officially released, Grohl had to come up with a name for a one-off band. "I called the band Late," he revealed in 2005, "because I always thought it'd be cool to be on stage and say, 'Hi, we're Late,' which is so stupid." When the *Pocketwatch* standout 'Petrol CB', retitled 'There's That Song', was used on Simple Machines' 1992 box set *Neapolitan Metropolitan*, Grohl got into the ice-cream-themed mood of the release and renamed himself Alex "Vanilla" McCloud, while his sidekick became Barrett "Peanut Butter Cup" Jones.

With hindsight, Grohl could look back upon the *Pocketwatch* sessions as a welcome release from the madness that was starting to build around Nirvana.

CHAPTER EIGHT

Whatever, Nevermind

"We knocked Michael Jackson off the top of the charts? This is fucking ridiculous!
Everything's fucking crazy! They're making a mistake; this is not supposed to
happen to some stupid kid from Nowheresville."

– Dave Grohl

B Y the summer of 1991, the grunge revolution was in full flannel-
shirted swing. Hole, featuring the future Mrs. Kurt Cobain, Courtney
Love, had unleashed their scorching debut LP, *Pretty On The Inside*, while
Sub Pop released *The Grunge Years*, a compilation featuring Nirvana's
'Dive', plus songs from Tad, L7, Screaming Trees, Babes In Toyland and
others. In mid August, Boston alt-rock station WFNX started to play
'Smells Like Teen Spirit'. The station's music director, Kurt St Thomas,
gushed to Ted Volk, DGC's Northeast radio rep, that the song had the
potential to "change the face of music".

Grohl and Nirvana returned to Europe on August 19, again with their
mentors Sonic Youth; the first date being in Cork, Ireland on August 20.
At many of the summer festivals that they played, Nirvana were placed
down the bill among the early opening acts (sometimes as early as 11 am),
but it was their set on August 23 at the Reading Festival that proved to
UK punters that there might well be some legitimacy in Everett True's
claims as to Nirvana's greatness. Grohl spotted a frenzied communal
response in the crowd when pounding through 'Smells Like Teen Spirit';
it was just like the carnage they'd witnessed at the OK Hotel a few months
before. Cobain was in a rare good mood at Reading, bringing the
Vaselines' Eugene Kelly onstage to help him through their cover of
'Molly's Lips'. Nirvana then jammed on the Doors' 'The End', before
Cobain threw himself into Grohl's drum kit with such force that he

145

dislocated his shoulder. However, this time it appeared as though his act of wilful destruction was enacted out of joy, rather than rage.

Unlike Novoselic or Cobain, Grohl wasn't inclined to wreck his gear wilfully, being more an onlooker than participator. The hard years spent with Scream, scraping by on $7 a day meant that he placed a high value on his equipment. It was only after *Nevermind* broke, and the big dollars started rolling in, that Grohl would get physical at the end of a set. "I remember shows where Chris and Kurt spent three or four moments destroying their gear," Grohl recalled on *Classic Albums*. "[And] I'm just sitting at my drums watching them. There's no music, just thousands of people watching them smash their guitars."

The atmosphere on the European roadshow was especially buoyant, thanks to the festival gigs being more like all-day parties, fuelled by good weather and loads of free booze. His relationship with Jennifer Finch now over, Grohl was falling deeply for Detroit photographer Jennifer Youngblood, their romance soundtracked by the Pixies' album *Trompe le Monde*, released just after Nirvana started touring *Nevermind*.

"I met the woman who I married while listening to that record," Grohl said in 1999. "I remember driving around in our tiny van going from show to show as our lives became more insane by the minute and all I could do was put on the headphones, listen to the Pixies and think about the woman who stole my heart." Nirvana's own 'Come As You Are' was another key song in their relationship. Whenever the couple were apart, Youngblood couldn't bear to hear it. "If that song comes on the radio," Grohl once said on her behalf, "she can't listen to it."

Over the years, Grohl has developed a reputation as a ladies' man. "I fall in love so very easily," he'd admit. "I think I might have an over abundance of whatever that endorphin is in my system."

Grohl had things other than romance on his mind when he returned to the USA in early September. 'Smells Like Teen Spirit' was set to be more than the brand name of a cheap deodorant; it was about to become the touchstone for a new movement. Grohl was unconvinced at first, even though Donita Sparks, of L7, in whom Grohl had great faith, assured him that *Nevermind* was going to be huge. "I didn't believe her. I was going, 'There's absolutely no way.' "

The feverish response at Reading to 'Teen Spirit' was only the first sign of what was to follow. While Nirvana and Sonic Youth rampaged through

Europe, DGC staffers sat down for their weekly marketing meeting. Most had been present at Nirvana's memorable LA show at the Roxy on August 15, which had obviously left its mark. It was agreed that the initial pressing of *Nevermind* should be doubled from 40,000 to 80,000. Of course, this was nowhere near enough, as events would prove.

On August 27, 'Teen Spirit', backed by 'Drain You', was sent to US radio stations. Initially, 'Teen Spirit' wasn't expected to be the serious chart contender (DGC plumped for 'Come As You Are'), merely an introduction for the band and the album to college radio. DGC were hoping that around 15 stations would pick up the song during that first week – instead, virtually every rock station was playing 'Teen Spirit'. Commercial radio in Middle America also started to embrace the song even though it contained enough lyrical putdowns for an entire thesis on self-loathing.

Another key indicator to the album's unforeseen success came on August 29, when Boston alternative station WFNX played *Nevermind* from start to finish – an accolade only granted to the upper echelons of rock acts.

When 'Teen Spirit' was delivered to record stores on September 10, there were, of course, the usual naysayers. Although a fan of the song, Dave Navarro, sometime guitarist for Jane's Addiction and Red Hot Chili Peppers, thought 'Teen Spirit' was essentially an angry remake of Boston's 'More Than A Feeling'.*

Although MTV hadn't yet picked up the 'Teen Spirit' clip, more than 300 punters squeezed into Seattle's Beehive Records on September 16 for an in-store appearance that included Nirvana's jam on Kiss' 'Love Gun'. Many kids again watched from outside the store, as members of Soundgarden walked away from the gathering, unable to get even a glimpse of their Seattle peers. Five days later, 'Smells Like Teen Spirit' debuted at number 27 on the *Billboard* Modern Rock Tracks chart.

Nirvana's first North American tour promoting *Nevermind*, which was released on September 24, kicked off at Toronto's Opera House. It was an enjoyable trek with even Cobain in good spirits. The band packed clubs in New England and New York, before tearing through Pennsylvania,

---

* 'Teen Spirit' didn't escape the clutches of arch satirist "Weird" Al Yankovic, who reinvented Cobain's anger as 'Smells Like Nirvana'.

Philadelphia and DC, playing Grohl's old hardcore haunt, the 9.30 Club, while Virginia Grohl proudly looked on, holding her own among the frenetic stage divers and moshers. Afterwards, she shared pizza with her son and his bandmates backstage.

Grohl later described the *Nevermind* club tour as "insane", comparing it to Foo Fighters' first US tour in 1995* where "the spirit, the atmosphere" were almost identical. "There were so many great things that happened," he said, "and it was so much fun."

When the tour reached Detroit, media attention took notice of Grohl's prowess. "It was like, yeah, now they got it, now they got a guy who kicks ass on the drum kit," noted the *Detroit Free Press'* Gary Graff, who had seen the band in 1990 with Channing. The *Chicago Tribune's* Greg Kot noted how Grohl "transformed the band into this incredible power-house", while the *Seattle Times* were also quick to praise Nirvana's powerful drummer.

During the October 12 show at Chicago's Cabaret Metro, Grohl's kit didn't survive the obligatory set-ending carnage – it was completely destroyed. The band had plenty to get excited about; *Nevermind* had debuted in the *Billboard* Top 200 at number 144. This was also the night that Cobain consummated his relationship with Courtney Love.

October 14 was a banner day for Nirvana. MTV put the 'Teen Spirit' clip into their Buzz Bin, a spot reserved for videos with serious commercial potential. It would remain there for nine weeks running. But Grohl had some regrets. "It would have been interesting to wait six months before we put the 'Teen Spirit' video on MTV," Grohl told *Rolling Stone* in 2001. "I would have rather had everyone listen to the record and get into the music before they had this four-minute teenage-rebellion commercial. [And] the bigger the shows got, the farther we got from our ideal."

As the tour continued, *Nevermind* kept on selling. By the end of October, it had achieved the seemingly unachievable and gone gold, as it lodged in the *Billboard* Top 40. "If you looked at the Top 10 in the year before *Nevermind*," Grohl theorised in *Come As You Are*, "there was rarely any rock music in it except for bad heavy metal shit that no one could relate to. When our music came out, I think it was a combination of stoners, skaters [and] derelict kids who saw a group of derelict kids playing

---

* The Foos played many of the same venues that Nirvana had trashed a few years previously.

music that sounded like we were pissed [off]. And I think a lot of people related to that."

Grohl later described this "whirlwind" period as "the best and worst times of my life". Up until then, Grohl hadn't even owned a credit card.* In 2001, *Rolling Stone* asked whether the change to his financial situation had come as a shock. "Fuck, yeah," Grohl replied. "It was unbelievable. We went from selling amp heads and 'Love Buzz' singles for food to having millions of dollars. Coming from Springfield, Virginia, I went from having no money at all and working at Tower Records to being set up for life."

When Grohl received his first substantial cheque, he bought a Nintendo and a BB gun to replace the dodgy firearm he and Cobain played with at their Olympia apartment. "[These were] the things I wanted as a kid," Grohl explained.

Grohl's crash course in fame came one night on the road, when sharing a room with Cobain. A lifelong smoker, Grohl found himself out of cigarettes and was just about to go and buy some, when Cobain stopped him. "No," Cobain laughingly told his bandmate, "we can call and have somebody do that now."

Chris Novoselic also found it hard to adjust to this upward mobility. He and his wife Shelli had spotted a modest home that they liked and were about to put down an equally modest deposit when the royalty cheques started flooding in. The pair paid for the house outright with $265,000 in cash. It was unlikely that anyone in Nirvana would again resort to flogging T-shirts to survive.

With *Nevermind* selling by the truckload, DGC was intent on gaining as much exposure as possible. Nirvana naïvely thought they could sidestep the usual demands that came with being on a major label but as Reuben Radding, Grohl's former Dain Bramage bandmate, pointed out to me, playing music now occupied only a small part of Grohl's time; the rest was filled up with media calls, photo shoots and meet and greets.

Grohl continued to develop his songwriting which acted as a useful winding down from his physical performances on stage. "While Nirvana

* Nirvana's accountants sent Grohl his first credit card during downtime in Hawaii, with a note reading: "You might need this." Grohl went out and bought a fancy pair of sunglasses, which he duly lost.

was on tour, I'd bring a guitar with me, so in hotel rooms, late at night, I'd have something to do." At the end of each tour leg, Grohl reconvened with Barrett Jones in the basement of their west Seattle house. As Grohl explained, "These songs just started coming out."

Whereas Cobain began to disappear into his twin foils of heroin and Courtney Love, and Novoselic hit the bottle, the pressure took its toll on Grohl in more unusual ways. He suddenly developed a fear of flying and suffered his first bout of claustrophobia. He also endured chronic panic attacks, usually setting in just before going on stage, which would continue throughout the band's short, manic sets.

"I was out of my fucking mind," Grohl told Michael Azerrad. "While we're playing, I will just get freaked out that I'm going to get freaked out and go insane and puke and vomit and faint and then a hundred thousand people will have to go home and I'll be personally responsible . . . Everything was so completely insane, everything was just going at a hundred miles an hour and it was intensified tenfold."*

Grohl has repeatedly referred to these times as a "blur" and a "tornado", even though the amount of shows the band was playing was no greater than his days with Scream. Of course, the size of the shows and the off-stage pressures were unlike anything he'd ever experienced.

"I'm most proud that I've remained close to my family and friends," he said in 2003, "and none of this [success] has ever made me feel alienated from them. [And] I've never got fucked up on drugs or got into such a bad place [that] I felt trapped and couldn't get out."

Thanks to the breakout success of the 'Teen Spirit' single and video, *Nevermind* rapidly ascended the charts, muscling aside such pop behemoths as Prince (*Diamonds And Pearls*), Mariah Carey (*Emotions*) and Michael Jackson (*Dangerous*). Nirvana headed back to Europe in November for a six week tour but their absence failed to hinder its progress. *Nevermind* cracked the *Billboard* Top 20 on November 9, racing from 35 to 17, in the same week that 'Teen Spirit' reached 27 on *Billboard*'s Mainstream Rock Tracks chart.† When asked how Nirvana was reacting to this turn of

---

* Interestingly, Grohl has only ever had to call off one show mid-set, when a nasty bout of food poisoning caught up with him onstage with Foo Fighters in Japan.
† *Nevermind* would stay in the Top 20 for 30 weeks – 20 of those in the Top 10. In just two months, the album shifted 1.2 million copies in the US alone.

events, Grohl replied: "We don't jump around and laugh or jump for joy. We just sort of say, 'Oh.' But when someone says, 'Rush want you to tour with them,' we burst out laughing."

As Nirvana played a manic show in Belgium (where Grohl shifted to bass for their take on Leadbelly's 'Where Did You Sleep Last Night?'), 'Smells Like Teen Spirit' reached the top of *Billboard*'s Modern Rock Tracks chart. A few days later, in London, the band toasted their success with a *Top Of The Pops* TV appearance, in which they deliberately didn't bother trying to mime "the hit".

Looking back in 2001, Grohl told *Rolling Stone*. "[*Nevermind*] was the great experience of my life. I celebrate it every now and then."

Nirvana was back in America by early December, having blown out the last few dates of their European tour due to a mixture of stress, excessive boozing and Cobain's raging stomach problems (which wasn't helped by him using heroin again when the tour reached Amsterdam). Novoselic spent Christmas with his mother in Aberdeen, Grohl retreated to his new west Seattle home, while Cobain and Love set up house in LA. It had been the strangest year of their lives.

Grohl began to spend more time with Novoselic in early 1992, as Cobain sank ever deeper into his deadly twilight world. The pair drank together until closing time at Seattle's Crocodile Café on January 2, and a week later in New York they took in a taping of *The Late Show With David Letterman*, during a break in filming Nirvana's first *Saturday Night Live* spot.* The performances of 'Teen Spirit' and 'Territorial Pissings' offered up the usual chaos, closing with Novoselic French kissing both his bandmates.

That week, *Nevermind* achieved the seemingly unachievable, selling 373,520 copies, outstripping Michael Jackson's *Dangerous*, U2's *Achtung Baby* and MC Hammer's *Too Legit To Quit*. The album was also number one on the *Billboard* Top 200 and also topped charts in France, Ireland, Australia, Canada, Belgium and elsewhere.

Dave Grohl's first reaction was to laugh out loud when he got the news. "It was like, 'Wait a second, my band's at number one?' " he recalled in

---

* While in New York, Grohl and Novoselic were interviewed, albeit separately, for the promo CD *Nevermind: It's An Interview*. Cobain was absent.

1997. "We knocked Michael Jackson off the top of the charts? This is fucking ridiculous! Everything's fucking crazy! They're making a mistake; this is not supposed to happen to some stupid kid from Nowheresville." Even the *New York Times* business section ran a profile on the success of the band and their album – a true sign of their acceptance into the mainstream.

In the same week that corporate cowboy Garth Brooks' album *Ropin' The Wind* temporarily unseated *Nevermind* at the top of the album charts, Grohl and Novoselic joined forces in the first of many side projects. Along with the Melvins' Buzz Osborne, an alt-rock Zelig during the Eighties and Nineties, they formed Melvana, opening for the little-known Bliss and Barrett Jones' band Churn at the Crocodile Café, with a two-song set of 'Sacrifice' and 'Way Of The World', both Flipper covers.

The audience had been tipped off about this supposedly unannounced jam thanks to an anonymous call to local station KNDD. During the soundcheck, Jones asked the venue's sound crew if they had an extra snare drum, or possibly a spare drum head, knowing what Grohl was capable of. (Nirvana sets usually ended with a pile of sawdust on the drum riser.) As soon as the three started playing, Grohl put his stick straight through a skin. Jones simply shook his head, mumbled "I told you so" and set about repairing the damage.

Under the pseudonym Dale Nixon*, Grohl also drummed on Osborne's *King Buzzo* EP, released in July 1992, calling their collaboration "an honour". The four tracks included a remix of 'Just Another Story About Skeeter Thompson', simply re-titled 'Skeeter'. During a few days of Nirvana downtime, Grohl and Jones got together at the Laundry Room to record skeletal versions of the Grohl-penned tracks 'Good Grief' and 'Exhausted', which eventually reached the first Foo Fighters album.

While Nirvana toured Australia as part of the inaugural Big Day Out festival, 'Teen Spirit' was certified gold, having sold more than 500,000 copies. Just days later it reached the top spot on *Billboard*'s Hot 100 Singles Sales chart. However, there wasn't a great deal of celebrating. While locked away at the band's hotel in Sydney, Cobain hung a sign on his door reading: Please Burn Down My Room. He failed to show up at a reception

* The same *nom de plume* Black Flag guitarist Greg Ginn used on their *My War* album.

at DGC's Sydney office to celebrate *Nevermind*'s mind-boggling success. Grohl and Novoselic dutifully turned up to press the flesh but behind the strained smiles both must have been wondering what was happening to their strung-out leader who they rarely saw outside of soundchecks and gigs.

On February 1, *Nevermind* returned to the top position in *Billboard* as the media saturation continued unabated. Glaring from the cover of *Spin*, at a time when the mag was trying hard to establish itself as the alternative *Rolling Stone*, Cobain took the time to diss his Seattle peers Pearl Jam as "corporate" and "cock rock" during the accompanying interview. Elsewhere, ex-Sex Pistol John Lydon heaped praise on Nirvana, while Guns N' Roses' mouthpiece Axl Rose asked the band to play at his 30th birthday bash, having sported a Nirvana cap in GN'R's 'Don't Cry' video. With *Nevermind* having sold three million copies, the band could afford to tell Rose where he could stick his birthday party.

On February 24, with the album's second single, 'Come As You Are', enjoying healthy sales, Cobain married Courtney Love in his pyjamas at Waikiki Beach. Grohl and Barrett Jones were among the small gathering – an offended Novoselic and his wife Shelli were absent. (Shelli had dared to voice her disapproval of the union. Novoselic, to his credit, stood by his wife.) Grohl, had played a strong, if inadvertent role in the early days of Cobain and Love's romance, acting as a go-between, frequently relaying messages from Love to Cobain (while he and Cobain roomed together on the road). By the time the pair married, he realised they were in the midst of a heavy downward spiral, despite Love's recently discovered pregnancy, and was keeping his distance.

Speaking in *Come As You Are*, Grohl remembered walking in on the couple in New York. "They were . . . nodding out in bed, just wasted. It was disgusting and gross . . . It makes me angry that they would be so pathetic as to do something like that." Despite his exposure to a wide variety of drugs, Grohl claims he did not realise the extent of Cobain's drug use until this incident, putting it down to a mixture of naivety and denial on his part.

The gradual fractures developing within Nirvana weren't anything new. An endless procession of groups, from the Beatles on down, had slowly come apart as their success increased. In Nirvana's case, it was the usual pressures of fame, money, and a lead singer being tagged the "voice of a generation" – something he didn't ask for. Combined with Cobain's addiction and his increasingly erratic behaviour, it was surprising that Nirvana lasted as long as they did. Speaking in *Come As You Are*, which was written prior to Cobain's death, Grohl was incredibly pragmatic. Admittedly, many of Grohl's comments were tainted by his recent discovery of Cobain's smack habit, but the distinct impression emerged that Nirvana was no love-in and Grohl understood his place in the band.

When asked in 1994 about the inter-band dynamic, Grohl admitted in *Come As You Are*, "For the most part, we're really removed from each other; far removed . . . It's not like bosom buddies." He described his bandmates as "friends, but we're not best friends". Grohl rationalised his place in Nirvana simply. "All I do is walk up on stage and I play drums," he said on different occasions. "And then afterward, I go home. There's just so much that goes on that I don't even know about." When asked why he didn't intervene to stop Cobain's drug use, particularly when he could see how much damage it was causing, Grohl said he didn't feel it was his role to pass judgement. "The first thing you want to do is tell them, 'Look – stop.' [But] you don't feel like it's your place."

Tellingly, when looking at virtually every Nirvana photo shoot, Grohl can usually be found lurking in the background behind his two bandmates, a slightly uncomfortable presence. Cobain's actions ensured life wasn't going to be made any easier. In spring 1992, he insisted that the band's publishing royalties be redistributed. Up until that point, all monies had been split equally between each band member, although there was no doubting that Cobain was principal songwriter.* After a heated discussion and, at one point, a total volte-face by Cobain who agreed to continue his even split with Novoselic and Grohl, it was decided that Cobain would take 90 per cent of publishing royalties, backdated to the release of *Nevermind*. In arguing his case, Cobain claimed he only asked his partners' opinions of his songs "just to make them feel part of the band". In short, it was a massive "fuck you", an action most likely encouraged by Courtney Love.

Grohl, for one, was incensed, telling Azerrad, "Chris and I were just like, 'If this is any indication of how much of a dick Kurt is going to be

---

* The sleeve for *Nevermind* reads: "All songs [sic] lyrics by Kurt Cobain/Music by Nirvana", which suggested Grohl and Novoselic's input was not inconsiderable.

then I don't want to be in a band with someone like that.' " While the deal was being thrashed out, a fiery phone discussion took place between Cobain and Grohl. Cobain said that Grohl and Novoselic were "greedy". "Whatever," Grohl snapped back, slamming the phone down in Cobain's ear. Eventually, Cobain accepted a 75 per cent retroactive royalty split but the damage had been done.

While Grohl and Novoselic simmered, Cobain checked into a rehab facility, for the first but not the last time. He failed to complete the treatment, opting to detox at home, as if cold turkey was akin to finishing an antibiotics prescription. As Cobain half-heartedly tried to kick his habit, sales of *Nevermind* cruised past the four million mark, and A&R scouts were descending on Seattle, desperately in search of "the next Nirvana".

This spelled the kiss of death for new, original music in the Northwest, as groups swiftly formed, grew their hair and adopted the necessary flannel wardrobe (not always in that order), in the hope of being signed by a major. The look extended beyond America – English Nirvana clones like Rumpelstiltskin and Bush cashed in, as did Australian teen grungers Silverchair.

Although band relations were poor during 1992, Nirvana agreed to play one big show, after being offered an irresistible $250,000 to headline the annual Reading Festival on August 30. Of course, there were problems: the band had barely rehearsed all year, and there was a not wholly un-reliable whisper circulating that Nirvana was as good as over. "Will they make it? Are they in rehab? Are they dead?" was Grohl's summation of affairs.

At one stage such a strong rumour arose about Nirvana pulling out of the show that even those close to Grohl began calling, asking for con-firmation. It was hardly the perfect lead-up to a gig in front of 40,000 punters. Grohl, meanwhile, had his inner demons to confront. When finally meeting his Nirvana predecessor, Dan Peters, Grohl inquired about the biggest audience he'd ever fronted. Peters told him that Mudhoney had once played to a crowd of 35,000. Grohl suffered another panic attack at the thought of such a large-scale gig. "I almost shit my pants," Grohl admitted.

"It was a bad time for the band," Grohl understated. "And then we had to step up in front of 40,000 people. [But] luckily, something special happened. We expected it to be the biggest disaster of the year, but it turned into one of the greatest things in my life."

While his personal life may have been immersed in turmoil, Cobain hadn't totally lost his sense of mischief; making his entrance by being pushed on stage in a wheelchair, clad in a hospital gown, an ironic comment on his supposed catatonic state. After mumbling the first line from the theme to *The Rose*⋆ he comically fell out of the chair, as if terminally flaked out on stage. With the pantomime part of the show over, the band roared into a triple volley of raw punk rock with 'Breed', 'Drain You' and 'Aneurysm'. Unlike their typical 45-minute grand slams, over 20 songs were performed, including a snatch of 'More Than A Feeling', as a retort to Dave Navarro's jibe, leading into a venomous 'Smells Like Teen Spirit'.

Clearly enjoying themselves, the trio indulged in some rare mid-set banter, most of which dealt with those "end of Nirvana" rumours. When Cobain stepped up to the mic and announced, "I'd like to officially and publicly announce that this is our last show," Novoselic quipped on cue, "For today." Grohl introduced 'Tourette's' with, "This is a new song and we don't feel like actually going through the trouble of putting it out ourselves, so . . . all of you bootleggers . . . go ahead." What made the set even more memorable for Grohl was the moment when, at Cobain's prompting, the audience broke into 'Happy Birthday' for Virginia, who was seated at the side of the stage. A beaming Grohl declared, "I love my sister and I love my mommy, too."

Nirvana closed their set with a punk rock rendition of Jimi Hendrix's famous interpretation of 'The Star Spangled Banner'. At one point the three of them exchanged instruments, which gave Grohl the chance to trash Cobain's guitar, while Novoselic flailed away at Grohl's drum kit.

It was one of the rare occasions during Grohl's time in Nirvana that he came away satisfied from an important show. "It proved that the three of us had a chemistry that went beyond a rehearsal room or a magazine cover," he summed up. Virginia Grohl knew it, too; when her son came up to her after the show, she was in tears. Grohl summed up the scene as "pretty emotional".

★   ★   ★

⋆ A 1980 film, starring Bette Midler and Alan Bates, loosely based on the late Janis Joplin's life.

After returning from Europe, Nirvana went their separate ways. Cobain holed up with Love and their baby daughter, Frances Bean, in LA; Grohl spent some R&R back in Virginia, while Novoselic and his wife stayed in Seattle. Even though there was talk about a new Nirvana album – and they'd actually briefly got together at Barrett Jones' Laundry Room, to record a couple of throwaway tracks – they were in no shape to think about a follow-up to a record as successful and influential as *Nevermind*.

Grohl was becoming increasingly isolated from Novoselic and Cobain, and felt that key band decisions were being made without his input. "I was really bummed out," he later said. Then Grohl received an unexpected letter from Cobain. "It was all, 'I love you like a brother,'" Grohl revealed in 1999. "It said, 'I can't wait to get back in the studio and make a record so we can whittle ourselves back down to a comfortable level,' which, of course, never really happened."

Grohl was choked up by Cobain's honesty, and to this day considers the letter to be "absolutely irreplaceable". For so long he'd felt like an outsider, but now Grohl actually felt he belonged in Nirvana.

Despite the high of Reading, much of 1992 was taken up by a seemingly endless procession of tabloid headlines involving Cobain and Love – the worst being "Rock Star's Baby Is Born A Junkie", which ran in supermarket rag *The Globe* towards the end of the year. Cobain and Love were also fighting a running battle with LA authorities, who briefly took their baby into custody, fearing for the child's safety. Cobain estimated that he spent almost a quarter of a million dollars in legal bills during the year. It must have been a massive relief to get back in the studio towards the end of February 1993.

If Kurt Cobain was looking for a producer who could "whittle Nirvana back down to a comfortable level", he found the right ally in Steve Albini, whose style was totally different to Butch Vig and Andy Wallace, who mixed *Nevermind*. Albini's records were characterised by an abrasive, almost corrosive quality that had a polarising effect on listeners.

Albini initially led the Chicago band Big Black, before recording with the offensively named Rapeman,* but it was as a producer that he left the biggest impression on Cobain. Albini's "whack it down" style was

---

* The name brought Albini accusations of misogyny, which didn't seem to offend Cobain's feminist sensibilities.

exemplified in his production of such indie acts as PJ Harvey, Helmet, Superchunk, and Jesus Lizard. Two Albini produced albums were particular favourites of Cobain's: the Pixies' *Surfer Rosa* and the Breeders' *Pod*. Perversely, Albini wasn't a Nirvana fan – previously dismissing them as "REM with a fuzzbox" – but the money and kudos proved impossible to resist.

Albini and the band convened at Pachyderm Studios, just outside Minnesota, where Albini had recorded such bands as Killing Joke and the Wedding Present. To avoid being detected, Nirvana booked into the studio as the Simon Ritchie Group, the real name of the Sex Pistols' doomed bassist Sid Vicious. The sessions ran for just two weeks, costing DGC $24,000 in studio time, with Albini receiving $100,000 for his services.*

Despite the low budget and Cobain's insistence on getting back to their punk roots, there were some rock star trappings. The band had their gear shipped in, which blew three days out of the schedule. At one stage Cobain threw a tantrum and considered flying in his guitar tech to help with tuning his guitars, but when the band began working on Cobain's new songs, the basic tracks were laid down in a mere six days. Albini devoted a great deal of time into getting Grohl's drum sound just right by placing microphones at different parts of the room, using very little in the way of digital-age effects.

The songs that Cobain had written reflected his desire to strip back the commercial sheen of *Nevermind*. Such tracks as the dubious 'Rape Me' and the more melodic 'Pennyroyal Tea' were pared to the bone, while the album's lead single and standout track, 'Heart-Shaped Box', packed a punch that physically hurt. When asked by Azerrad about Cobain's songs, Grohl replied: "They're so simple and so to the point and so right. Something that would take me an hour to explain, Kurt would sum up in two words. That's something he has that I've never seen in anyone else."

Albini insisted on keeping proceedings in the studio as minimalistic as possible. The songs were virtually recorded live, with very little discarded – possibly to the album's detriment. There was only the band, some studio staff and Albini working together, but after a week Mrs. Cobain breezed in

---

* The mixing board was the same set-up as used for AC/DC's *Back In Black* album – a fact that Grohl must have appreciated.

and altered the mood. According to Azerrad, she and Grohl had a heated clash (although neither would reveal specifically what caused it), while Love's opinions got under the mercurial Albini's skin. When the album was completed, he referred to her as "a psycho hose beast". Love responded by stating that the only way Albini would accept her was "if I was from the East Coast, played the cello, had big tits and small hoop earrings . . . and never said a word."

Like Butch Vig before him, Albini had nothing but praise for Grohl, both as a drummer and as an emollient presence. "Probably the easiest guy to deal with of them all was Dave Grohl," he told Azerrad. "For one, he's an excellent drummer, so there's never any worry whether he's going to be able to play. He's also a very pleasant, very goofy guy to be around." Albini said that watching Grohl play and recording the results was "the highlight of my appreciation of the band". Coming from someone as hard to please as Albini, this was high praise indeed.

Apart from Courtney Love's intrusion, making what would become *In Utero* had been a relatively fruitful experience. However the remainder of 1993 had its troughs. Just prior to recording the album, Nirvana played two massive South American shows, the first in Sao Paulo, Brazil, before a crowd of 80,000, the second to around 70,000 at the Apotoese Stadium, Rio. While the attendances were staggering, the shows weren't quite so impressive.

Despite the usual hijinks – Grohl wore a bra during the second show, Flea from Red Hot Chili Peppers jammed during 'Teen Spirit', playing trumpet – Grohl described both shows as "pretty horrible" sets that turned into "weird little jam sessions that were ridiculously bad". Grohl contributed to the chaos by taking lead vocals for a cover of Duran Duran's 'Rio', while Cobain earnestly croaked his way through Jacques Brel's 'Seasons In The Sun', a maudlin one-hit-wonder for Terry Jacks in 1974. (Cobain revealed, half tongue-in-cheek, that it was a favourite song from his childhood, which would reduce him to a blubbing mess.)

Further Nirvana concerts were sporadic between the recording of *In Utero* and its release in early September, 1993. At Novoselic's urging, they played a benefit for Bosnian rape victims in San Francisco on April 9, helping to raise $50,000. (Gaining a political awareness, Novoselic helped organise the event.) Soon after, a story ran in the *Chicago Tribune* in which

Steve Albini claimed that DGC and Gold Mountain "hated" the finished tapes of *In Utero*. "I have no faith this record will be released," he told writer Greg Kot. Although no one from DGC would go on record, Bill Bennett, the label's GM at the time, later confirmed their uncertainty regarding the record's commercial potential.

Cobain's problems ran deeper. On May 2, he overdosed and ended up in Seattle's Harborview Medical Center. A few weeks later he was hauled into the Seattle Police Department (Cobain, Love and their baby Frances Bean had recently relocated back to Seattle from LA), in relation to a domestic assault. Love didn't lay any charges, but it was yet another scene played out in a real-life soap opera which was inexorably heading towards a tragic denouement.

After Pete Stahl discovered that Dischord was planning to release the Scream back catalogue, he called Grohl and floated the suggestion of a reunion. With Nirvana's activities at a minimum, Grohl agreed, revealing to the *Washington Post* (June 30) that several club shows had been booked, insisting that the Scream reunion "right now is the most important thing happening to me." Almost three years had passed since Grohl's hasty departure from Scream. If there was any bad blood between Grohl and the Stahls, it had since been forgotten.*

"I think this will throw everything back into perspective for me," he declared. "We'll play these clubs, and maybe sleep on people's floors like we always did, then in the fall I go out with Nirvana . . . and play in front of 10 or 15,000 people, go to the nice hotel and watch TV till I fall asleep. It's not the same as playing on a small stage with guys who are basically my brothers." Novoselic and Cobain would surely have agreed with Grohl's desire to get back to playing clubs and simpler concerns but his frank remarks about brotherhood must have felt like a slap in the face.

Appropriately, the first Scream show took place in DC on July 4 at the annual Smoke Out Bash On The Mall. Over the next two nights they played the 9.30 Club – the place where Grohl first set eyes on the band from Bailey's Crossing. The *Washington Post* was fulsome in its praise, noting that Scream "played with passion and precision". The reunion tour then swung through New York, Boston, Detroit, Minneapolis,

---

* Pete Stahl certainly didn't mention it during our few email exchanges.

Seattle and San Francisco before ending, somewhat symbolically, at the Whiskey in LA, the city where the band had crashed and burned in 1990.

The *Los Angeles Times* review zeroed in on the long-haired tornado behind the Stahl brothers and Skeeter Thompson, reporting, "Drummer Dave Grohl supercharged the usual punk-rock polka stuff with an extraordinary array of back-beat flams and paradiddles." Grohl couldn't avoid the spotlight, even when trying to get back to basics.

'Heart-Shaped Box', the first official taste of *In Utero*, was released during August. The single was backed by Grohl's 'Marigold', an unexpected vote of confidence for the budding songwriter, who also sang lead vocal. *In Utero* was released in the UK on September 13, with a US CD release following on the 21st. Chain store Wal-Mart refused to stock the record because of the images of foetuses that appeared on the back cover, and the dubious sensibilities of 'Rape Me'. K-Mart also rejected the album.

This may have hurt DGC's commercial plans for *In Utero*, but the band was more concerned about the media response. The reviews turned out to be uncertain, at best. This ambivalence was warranted, because the album simply didn't have *Nevermind*'s sonic force or bounty of great songs. Cobain's pop smarts occasionally got a look in, most noticeably on 'Heart-Shaped Box' and 'All Apologies' but these two tracks had been polished prior to release by REM producer Scott Litt, once DGC recognised the commercial appeal in both. In trying to return to a less commercial sound, Cobain had undermined his ability to write smart, melodic rock songs. Much of *In Utero* sounds forced and unconvincing, and despite Albini's respect for Grohl's abilities, the production doesn't do the drummer any favours; at times it sounds as if he were slapping away on a soggy cardboard box.*

Cobain was inviting attention with the album's opening salvo, growling that "teenage angst has paid off well / now I'm bored and old". As maxims went, this ranked with Pete Townshend's ill-advised wish that he hoped he'd die before he got old. Self-loathing such as Cobain's certainly wasn't endemic in the punk songbook: one of the key philosophies of underground legends Fugazi and Black Flag, bands deeply admired by Nirvana, was all-inclusiveness, especially in their lyrics. John Mulvey in

---

* Grohl's work was singled out for praise by most of the album's reviewers.

NME (September 4) took Cobain's taunt at face value, casting Cobain as "rock's most compulsive fuck up", a confused singer/songwriter whose new songs were deeply affected by his recent "births, marriages and rumoured deaths".

Mulvey was on the money when describing *In Utero* as "a profoundly confused record. It's neither a self-destructive squall of hardcore nihilism as originally rumoured, nor . . . *Nevermind II*. [But] it's not, unlike its predecessor, a revolutionary record, either . . . As a follow-up to one of the best records of the past 10 years it just isn't quite there."

The American response to the album was more positive. In his *Rolling Stone* (September 16) review, David Fricke precisely summed up the personal dilemma that haunted Cobain throughout the album. "Never in the history of rock'n'roll overnight sensations has an artist, with the possible exception of John Lennon, been so emotionally overwhelmed by his sudden good fortune, despised it with such devilish vigour and exorcised his discontent with such bristling, bull's-eye candour." In short, this was Cobain's very own *John Lennon/Plastic Ono Band*, rock music as exorcism.

Cobain would have loved the John Lennon comparisons, which Fricke repeated later in the same review when he cast Cobain as the Nineties answer to the troubled but often brilliant former Beatle. "If Generation Hex is ever going to have its own Lennon," Fricke wrote, "someone who genuinely believes in rock'n'roll salvation but doesn't confuse mere catharsis with true deliverance, Cobain is damn near it."

With underground hero Pat Smear, formerly of infamous LA punks the Germs, on second guitar, Nirvana premiered 'Heart-Shaped Box' and 'Rape Me' on *Saturday Night Live* during the week of *In Utero*'s release, before setting out on their first US tour in two years on October 18. Grohl's prediction during Scream's reunion tour – that there would be an uncomfortable gulf between band and crowd, both literally and figuratively – proved to be self-fulfilling. After a sea of cigarette lighters sparked into life during the opening night in Phoenix, Novoselic told MTV that he "felt like we were doing Aerosmith's 'Dream On' or something." This wasn't what Cobain had envisaged. Nirvana had become part of the rock'n'roll machine – touring with an album to push, performing before unquestioning crowds who chose to overlook such taunts as "teenage angst has paid off well".

A rare light-hearted moment occurred when the band reached Chicago on October 23. Gary Graff of the *Detroit Free Press* thought he was conducting a phone interview with Grohl, but it turned out that he was actually speaking with comic Bobcat Goldthwait, who pulled off a convincing Grohl impersonation.* "I was totally convinced that I had interviewed Dave Grohl," Graff admitted only after the real thing got on the line and put him straight.

If the tour was a disillusioning affair for Cobain there was no situation that his wife could not make worse. On December 9, during an interview with notorious radio shock jock Howard Stern, Courtney Love revealed that her husband "hated [Grohl's] guts" because he had become "such a dick". Love also criticised Grohl for refusing to take Cobain's calls in the midst of his recent drug crisis, conveniently overlooking the fact that much of Grohl's antipathy towards Cobain stemmed from his selfish publishing redistribution decision, not to mention Grohl's general uneasiness around heroin users. Grohl showed admirable restraint in not rising to the bait, preferring to later reply through various Foo Fighters' songs, the scathing 'Stacked Actors' in particular.

In the face of this disharmony, Grohl and Novoselic were still managing to maintain unity, recording basic tracks in the North Seattle studio of producer Robert Lang, in late January 1994, for the proposed Nirvana album that never was. (The posthumously released 'You Know You're Right' would emerge from these sessions.) When arriving in Europe during the first week of February for what would be Nirvana's final tour, Grohl, Novoselic and their partners rode together in one bus, while Cobain, Smear and tour manager Alex MacLeod travelled separately. What was taking place on the other bus has never been revealed, but one crew member, who was about to board with Cobain and co, was warned off by Jennifer Youngblood with "Don't go there, it's evil . . ."

In spite of the clear division within the band, the European trip was a personally memorable time for Grohl and Youngblood who, having recently wed, honeymooned in Ireland. When asked about his honeymoon, Grohl responded with, "Fucking Duran Duran! That song ['Ordinary World'] haunts me. We were going around Ireland and that song was playing and it was beautiful." Grohl admitted it wasn't the hippest song to have forever etched in your memory; if he had his time again he would

---

* Goldthwait would MC Nirvana's New Year's Eve show at Oakland Coliseum.

have preferred something from Goldie or James Brown. "But it's true," he confessed. "I'm a sucker for crap, I really am."

While on honeymoon, Grohl brought along his guitar and wrote two future Foo Fighters' tunes – 'This Is A Call' and 'Watershed'. Another early Foo Fighters' song with a strong Youngblood connection was 'Big Me', a track Grohl has stated was an "out-and-out love song" written for his first wife.

Grohl also detoured to Germany to work on the soundtrack for *Backbeat*, a biopic of early Beatles' bassist Stuart Sutcliffe and the group's early days in Hamburg. Grohl played as part of the Backbeat band, alongside Sonic Youth's Thurston Moore, Soul Asylum's Dave Pirner and numerous other indie rock luminaries. By this time, the last two dates of the Nirvana tour had been cancelled and, on March 4 in Rome, Cobain made a suicide attempt – washing down somewhere between 50 and 60 Rohypnol tablets with champagne (a suicide note was found in his hotel room). He remained in a coma for 20 hours.

When Cobain was well enough to return home, his life fell apart. Love filed a report with Seattle police on March 18, when Cobain locked himself in a room with a gun, threatening to kill himself. A week later those closest to Cobain – including Novoselic, Pat Smear, Gary Gersh, but notably excluding Grohl – staged an intervention. Cobain agreed to detox at the Exodus Recovery Centre in Marina del Rey, California. After a false start, he checked in on March 30, but only after buying a 20-gauge shotgun and a box of bullets.

The last couple of days in Kurt Cobain's life have been the subject of much speculation, and, frankly, they are beyond the scope of this book. The cold, hard facts are that he was found dead, of a shotgun blast, in the greenhouse of his Seattle home on the morning of April 8. His wallet lay on the floor nearby, open at his driver's licence to aid in identification, along with a suicide note that would become the subject of much scrutiny.

To his credit, Grohl has never revealed where he was when Cobain killed himself, or how he dealt with such a tragic situation. "Think about it: if you lost your good friend, you would still be hurting," became Grohl's standard, slightly irritable response.

Grohl rarely kept still over the next few months, dividing time between his base in Seattle and his mother's home in Virginia, occasionally checking in on his equally shell-shocked friend, Chris Novoselic. For the second time in his life, Grohl went into therapy, in an attempt to get his head around Cobain's action and the emotional repercussions it obviously had.

Despite their sometimes rocky relationship Grohl frequently defended Cobain, often reminding journalists that Cobain wasn't just some brooding punk poet constantly under a black cloud. "He could also be the most hilarious person you've ever met," Grohl insisted, fondly recalling Cobain's strange cackle of a laugh. Even though Cobain sometimes "played dumb", Grohl considered him one of the most brilliant men he'd ever met.

When the dust eventually settled, Grohl was finally able to isolate the best times in Nirvana, the moments when he genuinely felt part of the band. Not surprisingly, most of these occurred before *Nevermind* was released. His favourite tour with Nirvana was that first UK visit in October 1990. Although he complained that with him being the new boy Cobain and Novoselic weren't big on communicating, there was a key moment where Cobain went out of his way to make Grohl feel welcome. Grohl couldn't remember the name of the bar or the city the band was in, but they were in a state of post-gig euphoria, boozing it up while Ride and My Bloody Valentine rang through the PA. A drunken grinning Cobain ambled over, as Grohl recalled, "He said, 'Man, I'm so glad you're in this band; you have no idea. We really feel like you're a brother to us and we're so happy and thankful that you joined the band and made us what we are.' That was great," Grohl said. "It was the only time he ever said anything like that."

Grohl has revealed that for years after, he found himself thinking at least once a day about his troubled bandmate who frequently appeared in his dreams. Not long after Cobain's death, Grohl reluctantly checked out the *Backbeat* movie. He had a suspicion that he'd break down at the moment of the film's tragic end – and he was right. The feeling of loss was way too close. "I knew that when [former Beatle] Stu Sutcliffe died, I wouldn't be able to handle it. I knew."

On another level, Grohl said that his "soul went dead to music" for some time after. As he explained in 1994, music was his entire world – it formed the basis of his relationship with most people. "So when something like Kurt dying happens," Grohl said, "the music reminds you of everything and you've just gotta turn it off." It would take some months before he discovered that music also had the power to heal.

PART III

The World

CHAPTER NINE

Learning To Fly

"To continue almost seemed in vain – I was always going to be 'that guy from Kurt Cobain's band'."

– Dave Grohl

IN the months immediately following Cobain's suicide, Dave Grohl seriously considered getting out of the music business altogether. "I was about as confused as I've ever been," he admitted. "To continue almost seemed in vain – I was always going to be 'that guy from Kurt Cobain's band' and I knew that. I wasn't even sure if I had the desire to make music any more."

To Grohl, Cobain's death was a tragic waste – if this was what rock'n' roll glory brought, he was unsure he wanted any part of it. But what else could he do?

It was a postcard from Seattle band Seven Year Bitch that convinced Grohl to reconsider. Unlike Nirvana, they had suffered two devastating losses. Guitarist Stefanie Sargent OD'd and died in 1992, while vocalist Mia Zapata had been brutally raped and murdered outside a Seattle music venue in July 1993. But yet they kept going, recording the *Viva! Zapata!* album as a tribute to their singer.

The message on the postcard, sent by the band's remaining members to Grohl, was simple but heartfelt, reading, "We know what you're going through. The desire to play music is gone for now, but it will return. Don't worry." That postcard, Grohl admitted, was crucial. "I knew that there was only one thing that I was truly cut out to do and that was music." He decided to book studio time and see what he could make out of the bounty of songs he'd written over the past few years.

During the summer of 1993, Grohl had spoken with a Detroit label about releasing some of his solo work, although nothing came of this. This time around, Grohl had a lot more to prove. As determined as he was to move out of the shadow of Nirvana, Grohl opted to ease himself back into the spotlight gradually.

Before Cobain's death, Nirvana had allegedly been offered a hefty $9 million to headline the Lollapalooza 1994 event. Grohl attended the roadshow – which featured the Smashing Pumpkins, the Beastie Boys, the Flaming Lips and the Verve – when it rolled through Clarkston, Michigan, a relatively nondescript Detroit suburb. Hiding beneath a black Sepultura cap, Grohl blended in with the locals, although he was spotted by writer Wes Orshoski, who'd previously met him with Nirvana. Recalling the encounter in a story for *Harp* magazine, Orshoski asked Grohl how he'd been – not the smartest question given recent events. Grohl genially replied that he was fine, before disappearing back into the crowd. Just then, Nirvana's 'All Apologies' spilled out of the PA – and the crowd erupted.

Eleven years later, Orshoski had the chance to remind Grohl of that poignant moment. Grohl responded, "I totally remember that. When the audience started cheering, I got really choked up, because I thought, 'Whoa, we were supposed to be here, doing this.' What happened?" Grohl humbly stated that it was one of the first times he realised to what extent Nirvana's music had reached.

Although he had resolved to return to the studio, Grohl first undertook some outside work. In late May, he and Pat Smear cut tracks with Mike Watt for his *Ball-Hog Or Tug Boat?* album. A key member of underground heroes the Minutemen and fIREHOSE, Watt ranked with the Melvins' Buzz Osborne among Grohl's inspirations. Grohl drummed on two tracks – 'Big Train' and 'Against The 70's' – while Smear sang on 'Forever' and 'One Reporter's Opinion'.

It was during the Watt sessions that Grohl met Eddie Vedder, the austere lead singer for Pearl Jam. Clearly not harbouring any of the animosity Cobain had felt towards Vedder, Grohl gave him a cassette of two recently recorded tracks, an original called 'Exhausted', and 'Gas Chamber', a cover of a song by punk band, the Angry Samoans. 'Exhausted' was one of several songs Grohl recorded during Nirvana downtime in 1992, as he shuttled between Seattle and DC. The song reflected Grohl's growing interest in harmonies and arrangements; he was learning that there was way more to music than beating the skins off his drums.

A few weeks later, on July 12, Grohl reunited with Chris Novoselic, who had, since Cobain's death, been maintaining a low profile on his farm in the wilds of Washington State. He had developed a love of flying and devoted much of his time and money into securing his pilot's licence. Instead of a questionable "tribute to Kurt" concert before a potential MTV audience of millions, in commendably low-key fashion the pair played Olympia's Yo Yo A Go Go Festival backing up 10-year-old Simon Timony as part of pre-teen San Francisco cult group the Stinky Puffs, who'd been an eccentric obsession of Cobain's. During their 45-minute set, the briefly renamed Super Stinky Puffs pulled off a fair take on 'I'll Love You Anyway', Timony's broken-hearted swansong to his pal Cobain.

In the wake of Nirvana's demise, Grohl's sudden availability had not gone unnoticed. He passed on the offer of drumming for black metallers Danzig while a hot rumour circulated that he'd also been asked to join Pearl Jam. When the question was raised by one of her students, Virginia Grohl quizzed her son. "I don't know where the fuck those rumours came from," was the terse response.

Grohl did respond to an offer from an unlikely quarter. Tom Petty had recently lost the services of long-time Heartbreaker, Stan Lynch, and his search for a drummer became more urgent when the band was booked for a *Saturday Night Live* spot on November 19. Petty had caught Nirvana's *MTV Unplugged* set and, despite their age difference, he was impressed enough to contact Grohl, who took up Petty's offer, strictly for the *SNL* taping, performing 'You Don't Know How It Feels' and 'Queen Bee'. "That was a gas, playing with Dave," he said in his biography, *Conversations With Tom Petty*.

"It was so much fun," Grohl confirmed. "When we rehearsed, they treated me like I was in the band. It was such an honour."

In fact, Petty was so impressed that he floated the idea of Grohl signing on as a full-time Heartbreaker. Even though he already had vague solo plans, Grohl was sorely tempted. However he eventually passed on Petty's offer for two reasons: he had his own music to record, and he didn't especially relish the idea of becoming a drummer-for-hire at the age of 26. "I thought I might as well try something new while I'm young," he decided.

Grohl opted to connect again with sonic sidekick Barrett Jones, this time at the prosaically named Robert Lang's Studio, in Seattle, where Nirvana had cut their final haphazard sessions.

Between October 17 and 23, Grohl and Jones – with slight assistance from Greg Dulli, of Afghan Whigs, on the track 'X-Static' – recorded the *Foo Fighters* album. Even though he knew that any product would be under close scrutiny, simply because he was "that guy from Nirvana", Grohl had no master plan apart from seeing how many songs he could record, with as little assistance as possible, and ideally in as little time. (This haste was due, in part, to economics in that Lang's was a "proper" 24-track studio.)

Jones had confidence that the *Foo Fighters* album was capable of being more than a mere solo indulgence. He understood Grohl's name would receive attention, but he also recognised the accessibility of the songs. "Dave wrote great songs, was a great performer and was in the biggest band in the world at that time," Jones told me. "How could it not be huge?"

Grohl, however, was less interested in kudos and more interested in setting himself disciplines. He was so meticulous in his approach to the songs that he recorded them in the same order that they eventually appeared on the album. The opener, 'This Is A Call', took Grohl all of 45 minutes to nail. According to Grohl, "It [then] became this little game." He would literally run from room to room in Lang's studio, "still sweating and shaking from playing drums and [then] pick up the guitar and put down a track, do the bass, maybe another guitar part, have a sip of coffee and then go in and do the next song." Although he has never expressed it, Grohl's need for economy might have been a reaction to the frustration of those final, incomplete Nirvana sessions, when more time was spent waiting for Cobain to show.

As one of the few people there to witness Grohl's working techniques, Dulli was astounded by his proficiency. "He'd do a whole song in about 40 minutes. I was completely fascinated by it. [And] he could do it because he has perfect time." Dulli didn't even have to leave his chair to add his part to 'X-Static' – Grohl handed him his guitar and Dulli played while sitting down.

Grohl clearly stated his intentions for these songs – only three of which ('I'll Stick Around', 'Oh, George' and 'This Is A Call') were written in the months after Cobain's death. He wasn't looking for a major record deal – he just wanted to see what he could accomplish in the studio. In fact, when the album was completed, only 100 copies were pressed on vinyl. More revealingly, Grohl still didn't have much confidence in his voice; he wasn't sure if he had what it took to front a live band.

With 'This Is A Call', the start of Grohl's first "official" solo career, he immediately established the sonic template for Foo Fighters – a more commercially palatable version of the soft-loud dynamics that powered such Nirvana hits as 'Smells Like Teen Spirit' and 'Heart-Shaped Box'. When pushed about the song's meaning, Grohl explained that 'This Is A Call' was a (loud) greeting, of sorts, to anyone who had played a key role in his life, be they family, lovers or friends. "It's a hello," he explained, "and a thank you." The sentiment made a change from the "fuck you" which seemed to be at the black heart of many of Cobain's songs. As with so many of the songs that would make up the first Foo Fighters album, Grohl frequently had to clarify the lyric's intention: it wasn't some kind of message beamed to Cobain in the afterlife. "I knew there were certain things that people were going to read into," Grohl would concede. "A lot of fuss was made about 'This Is A Call' and the line about it being a 'call to arms'. But it's supposed to be uplifting and happy." It wouldn't be the first time a Grohl lyric was misread.

Grohl evidently valued 'I'll Stick Around' above the other tracks because it actually required two run-throughs before he was satisfied with the cut. As ever, he downplayed any significant meaning behind his roared chant of "I'll stick around." "It's just a very negative song about feeling you were violated or deprived," he stated. The song seemed to infer that Grohl had no plans to follow Cobain into a downward spiral.

"As I was singing, 'I don't owe you anything', I realised people might think it was about Kurt," he admitted to *Rolling Stone*, soon after the album's release, in order to clarify the songs' meaning. "[But] it would fucking break my heart to think that people are under that impression." Yet whatever Grohl *was* singing about, he was keeping mum, only adding to the song's ambiguity. "I knew while I was recording it that it was probably the strongest song I've ever written, because it was the one song that I actually meant and felt emotionally." The closest Grohl would come to any form of disclosure was by begrudgingly admitting that it was hard to deny "that the personal experiences of the last four or five years haven't made their way into any of these songs." Although he didn't mention her by name – and, shrewd operator that he was, never would – it was hard not to think that Grohl had grunge widow and serial stirrer Courtney Love in mind. Video director Gerald Casale certainly thought so, as he would later reveal to me.

The gentle 'Big Me', revealing Grohl's growing interest in music beyond the grunge/flannel straitjacket, was a valentine to Youngblood, even though Grohl defined the song as "girl meets boy, boy falls in love, girl tells him to fuck off". This was also the song chosen by Grohl for the video that would create a whole new persona for the band: chronic piss-takers. In what has now become a benchmark clip, the band put their own spin on the Mentos' candy ad, renaming their sweet Footos. The song, to Grohl's relief, would become as well known as the clip. Dante Ferrando, who'd become Grohl's partner in the DC club the Black Cat, recalled hearing it one day while strolling through an Atlantic City casino. "That's when I realised how huge Dave had gotten."

Throughout the rest of the album, Grohl maintained a steady balance between melodic rockers and more subdued moments. 'Alone + Easy Target' and 'Good Grief' were both high-energy fillers while 'Floaty' required some unobtrusive vocal effects from Jones because of Grohl's concerns about the lack of oomph in his voice. All of these tracks were written by Grohl during his Nirvana break in summer 1992. It was a time Grohl would recall as a "blast".

'Weenie Beanie', a grunged-up guitar workout with a distorted, Tom Waits-style vocal, was another song subjected to extra scrutiny, primarily due to the line "one shot nothing". Grohl would go to some lengths to explain, yet again, that the song had absolutely nothing to do with Cobain biting the bullet. "I've taken heat for a lot of lyrics I wrote four years ago," Grohl shrugged. He should have perhaps considered an instrumental album because, no matter how deeply buried in the mix, his words were examined and dissected in a search for clues to his true feelings about certain individuals. Grohl played it smart, denying there was any connections to his recent past.*

'Oh, George' was the album's one genuine throwaway, described by its creator as a song that he wished he'd never written. His comment that the

* 'Weenie Beanie' was actually written in 1991.

track, just like the album, was made so quickly that "it doesn't really count", was strangely defensive given that the song is actually an inoffensive, radio-friendly slice of guitar pop. Elsewhere on the album, Grohl was by turns playful (as on the rueful strum of 'For All The Cows', a distant relation of Neil Young's 'For The Turnstiles'), reverential ('Watershed' is a nod to his love of hardcore and old-school punk via Mike Watt), frank ('X-Static') and melancholy on album closer 'Exhausted', a clear indicator of the broader musical scope Grohl would aim for. "It's sad but it makes you feel good," Grohl would explain, "and it fades out in the end, so in a way it continues in your head."

For an album conceived as a personal challenge, there was a lot to like about *Foo Fighters*; by turns melodic, heartfelt, diverse and urgent. Grohl may have had misgivings about his voice and the influence of Nirvana's soft/loud dynamics was still tangible but there was enough quality material to make it a promising debut.

When the sessions were completed at the end of October 1994, Grohl remained firm in his conviction that there would only be a limited number of copies pressed. These were only handed out to such close confidantes as Novoselic, Nirvana's tour manager, Alex MacLeod and – possibly to Grohl's regret – Gary Gersh, who had moved to Capitol Records, and Mark Kates, Gersh's A&R replacement at Geffen/DGC.*

The bootleg tape of the sessions began to circulate ("like the Ebola virus," according to Grohl) among other key music biz players, and soon enough Grohl's answering machine was clogged with offers.

A wariness of contracts was something Grohl had learned the hard way from past experience. The unfulfilled contract with Glen Friedman, along with the royalty dispute which almost derailed Nirvana, were enough to make Grohl tread warily after deciding that his album was more than a post-Nirvana dalliance.

Grohl was, by this time, sufficiently savvy to realise that a P&D deal (production and distribution) was what he needed in order to find the album a home while retaining control. This required forming his own company which he called Roswell Records. Grohl took the name from

---

* Inevitably, bootlegs of the album reached LA and Seattle radio stations a full two months before the album's release, leading to a "cease and desist" order from Capitol.

the mysterious New Mexico site where, allegedly, the wreckage of alien spaceships was stored by the US government and their contents were probed by scientists sworn to secrecy. If there really was a cabinet somewhere in America bursting with X Files, as many believers insisted, then most were probably stored at Roswell.*

Grohl's solo work was officially dubbed *Foo Fighters*, named for the term used by Allied pilots in World War II to describe UFOs and other reported aerial sightings. Grohl also liked the anonymity that a band name provided. "I wanted to call it Foo Fighters so it would sound like a band," he explained, "and everyone would go, 'Wow, who is this band from Seattle? I've never seen a picture of them. I've never heard of them.'" As 1994 drew to a close, Grohl accepted that he should tour to promote *Foo Fighters*. "I [still] couldn't imagine the Foo Fighters becoming a band at that point," he admitted, "just because I hadn't met any musicians that I thought would make it work." Grohl didn't realise that he already had the one guy who could "make it work".

Pat Smear was born Georg Ruthenberg in Los Angeles on August 5, 1959; his father was German and his mother a Cherokee Indian. From the beginning Smear was an outsider; he ran away to join a religious sect when he was 13 and after being brought back home his parents enrolled him in The Innovative Program School, a Santa Monica institute for troubled kids, based on the campus of University High. His classmates included Kira Roessler, a future member of Black Flag, while former students included Sonic Youth's Kim Gordon, along with LA scenester Kim Fowley and Frank Sinatra, Jr.

While at the School, Smear met Jan Paul Beahm – they shared the same speed dealer – who was in the act of reinventing himself as Darby Crash. After graduation, Smear and Crash tried and failed to fit in with various bands before forming the Germs, a fabled LA outfit influenced by the Stooges and the Sex Pistols. Crash only recorded one album with the band – 1979's *GI* – before dying from a heroin overdose.† However that

---

* Grohl's passing interest in alien life and UFOs would soon be picked apart with the same diligence and curiosity as his lyrics. He responded by insisting "that UFO stuff is all overblown."

† His death – on December 7, 1980 – was overshadowed by the loss of John Lennon the following day.

one album, along with the band's wild reputation, was enough to make Crash a punk rock martyr and the Germs the heroes of numerous hopefuls. Among these was Kurt Cobain, Dave Grohl, and various members of Hollywood punk/funk upstarts, Red Hot Chili Peppers, who'd later try to lure Smear into the band when their guitarist, John Frusciante, went off the rails.*

Smear was a kind of Hollywood Zelig – not only had he played guitar in one of LA's most revered punk bands, and released several solo albums, but he also scored bit parts in such films as Ridley Scott's *Blade Runner*, George Lucas' disastrous *Howard The Duck* and Penelope Spheeris' rockumentary, *The Decline Of Western Civilisation*. He made a cameo appearance (draped in dreadlocks) in the video for Prince's 'Raspberry Beret' and scored TV parts in the motorcycle cops hit *CHiPS* and TV detective *Quincy*, the show that introduced a young Dave Grohl to the Hollywood version of punk rockers.

Just like Grohl, Cobain's suicide left its mark on Smear. He spent the following months holed up in LA, strumming a guitar, thinking about his next move. According to Smear, "I sat on the couch with the remote control in my hand for a year." He wasn't even sure if he wanted to play in another band, because of the needle and the damage done to Crash and Cobain.

Grohl had kept in touch with Smear after Nirvana's split, and gave him a copy of the Foo Fighters tape one night in a club. Smear knew about the bootleg, which was fast becoming the worst kept secret in LA, but had no idea what to expect. "I knew that the band would need two guitars," said Grohl, "but I didn't think that Pat would want to commit to anything, or that he would even like my music. To my surprise, not only did he like the tape, he expressed interest in joining up."

Grohl needed a sidekick, someone who could handle his share of the spotlight, easing Grohl's uncertainty about his abilities as a band leader and singer. As well as his punk pedigree and confident charisma, Smear's choppy riffs would help beef up the band's live sound, just as he had done with Nirvana.

---

* The Germs' legend and influence was so large that in 2006, *What We Do Is Secret*, a feature film documenting their fast life and short times, was released, along with a tribute album entitled *A Small Circle Of Friends*.

By the time Smear agreed to become a Foo Fighter, Grohl had recruited bassist Nate Mendel, whose fiancée was a close friend of Jennifer Youngblood. They met at a Thanksgiving party hosted by the Grohls; the pair allegedly bonded over shared musical tastes and the discovery that Grohl's Seattle home was haunted.

Mendel was born near the desert in the remote eastern part of Washington State in 1968. There was just one industry in his hometown which involved servicing the nearby military base where nuclear devices were tested. "It wasn't," he deadpanned, "one of the most cosmopolitan places you could imagine." Mendel may have been living in the boondocks but it was there that his path first intersected with Grohl's when seeing the peripatetic Scream play in 1986. Mendel's strongest recollection of the night was the sheer terror he experienced when cutting in front of Skeeter Thompson in the toilet queue. "He looked like an angry bastard," Mendel recalled, "but it was a brilliant gig."

Mendel moved to Seattle when he was 18 and immersed himself in the pre-grunge music scene. Mendel had not intended on a career in music, attending college with the aim of becoming a historian, until he joined his first band, the trashy Product Of Rape. His next band, Diddly Squat, lived up to their name, but Christ On A Crutch made some inroads, touring and releasing a handful of singles before imploding in 1993. Mendel's next move was the straight-edge outfit Brotherhood but his time with them demonstrated that the straight-edge lifestyle wasn't necessarily for him.

Continuing in a series of bands with improbable names, Mendel's next outfit was dubbed Chewbacca Kaboom, who, apart from their peculiar *Star Wars* fixation, included a drummer by the name of William Goldsmith. Chewbacca Kaboom morphed into Sunny Day Real Estate, a group led by singer Jeremy Enigk, who had briefly played with Mendel in Reason For Hate.

After a few well-received singles, Sunny Day Real Estate signed to Sub Pop and delivered their 1994 album, *Diary*, which many pundits consider the ground zero of the emo-core movement,* with one critic later tagging it "the emo *OK Computer*". Despite the kudos, and the fact that the album was for a time Sub Pop's second-biggest seller behind Nirvana's *Bleach*, the

---

* Emo-core is a nebulous term for emotional punk rock music with more melodic content than standard punk but expressing the same sensibility and attitude.

band began to crumble when Enigk said hello to God and goodbye to reality. Enigk was a true eccentric: he named songs after numbers, refused to tour California or participate in interviews and released only one publicity photo. Enigk's born-again conversion seemed the next illogical step.

"Yes, sir, I have given my life to Christ," he wrote in a letter to a curious fan. "For a long time I dwelt on a lot of pain in my life. I took a shot on calling upon God. He answered me. My pain was gone." When Enigk insisted to his bandmates that his saviour would make for some great lyrical subject matter, the end was nigh for Sunny Day Real Estate. Mendel, for one, took an un-Christian approach. "I wanted to fucking murder him," he said.

Mendel and Grohl met backstage at one of SDRE's final Seattle shows. Mendel was more impressed by Grohl's hardcore past than his recent Nirvana fame. "I'd never really met someone in a famous band before," Mendel said. "But he seemed cool and friendly and I knew, because of his DC hardcore roots, he'd probably be OK." When Chris Novoselic politely passed on Grohl's offer to join his band, Mendel was in.

Via Mendel, Grohl also found a drummer in William Goldsmith, which came about, in part, because Goldsmith and Mendel had made a "play together, stay together" pact after the blessed demise of Sunny Day Real Estate. "Play together or not at all," Goldsmith said when asked about their agreement, "[because] we like each other."

Goldsmith (born July 4, 1972) had a curious family history – a distant relative, 18th century Dubliner Oliver Goldsmith, was a legendary man of letters, whose most renowned work was *She Stoops To Conquer*. Goldsmith acquired a fondness for a tipple from his uncle many times removed. He started drumming in the fifth grade, coping with the usual school orchestra gigs until developing a taste for the Who's Keith Moon and Led Zep's John Bonham. Prior to hooking up with Mendel in Sunny Day Real Estate, Goldsmith played in an 11-piece ensemble called Screaming Hormones and spent several years studying musical theory.

Goldsmith realised Grohl's offer to join Foo Fighters was enticing, but it came with a considerable caveat. No matter how solid a player, he'd still be drumming for a band fronted by the hugely admired drummer from one of the most famous bands of the Nineties. "I really didn't feel comfortable playing drums for Dave," he declared early on in his Foos tenure.

179

"I felt really weird and inadequate." Goldsmith decided to share these reservations with Grohl who rashly promised Goldsmith that if he quit, Grohl would end the band.

Goldsmith wasn't the first drummer Grohl had earmarked for his band. Among the many that auditioned for the role was Josh Freese, who'd eventually go on to become the punk drummer-for-hire in bands including the Vandals and A Perfect Circle, along with more than 100 recording credits. According to a friend of Freese's, who preferred to remain anonymous, not only did Freese audition for the job, but was told by Grohl that he "100% got the gig as Foo Fighters drummer when they first began". However, Grohl continued auditioning drummers, without telling Freese – some hopefuls even used Freese's kit during their try-outs. Once again proving that confrontation wasn't his strongest suit, Grohl failed to inform Freese that he'd decided to go with Goldsmith. Freese found out the hard way. When arriving at the rehearsal space to pack up his gear for the first tour he was expecting to undertake with the band, Goldsmith discovered that the others had left without him.

To all outward appearances, Grohl had put together the perfect rock'n'roll beast – a tight-knit outfit, far removed from Nirvana's tensions, with both respected names (himself and Pat Smear) and a competent rhythm section in William Goldsmith and Nate Mendel.

Grohl often stated that their collective "dysfunctional band experiences" helped draw himself, Mendel, Goldsmith and Smear closer together. During a "meet the band" piece in *Blender* magazine in 1995, Goldsmith described life in the Foos as "kind of a snugly-kittens-in-a-box type feeling", which he further illustrated by hugging Mendel and planting a wet one on Smear's cheek.

Grohl's love of therapy also helped the band to open up to each other. "We talked about that when we first got together," he said. "From day one we didn't want any secrets, any skeletons." For the first few months of the Foos' existence this policy of full disclosure worked to the band's advantage – they couldn't have been any tighter.

The only setback in those early months was an injury to Goldsmith, during the band's second formal rehearsal. In an overzealous effort to impress Grohl, Goldsmith was drumming so hard that a stick snapped in half, spun upwards and embedded itself between his eye and nose. When a dazed Goldsmith asked Grohl to describe the extent of his injury, Grohl advised him not to look in the mirror. Following an urgent visit to the emergency room, their rehearsals continued.

The words Grohl bandied about were "grassroots" and "low key", being wary of exposing his new outfit to premature hype. Also, the Scream reunion, playing modest venues, had been fun. An influence at the time was an obscure project by Police drummer Stewart Copeland called *Klark Kent* that Grohl had recently discovered.* Much like Kent's Superman alter-ego, Copeland kept his identity secret, creating a fake bio to further muddy the waters.

In keeping with this mindset, the Foos were launched via a keg party at a friend's house in Seattle. Grohl wasn't so sure this was the right move. Who was going to have the balls to inform him that his band sucked if he was paying for the drinks? "It was the wrong idea to play your first show in front of all your good friends," Grohl later admitted. "[You should] just do it in front of strangers."

Foo Fighters official baptism of fire came at the Jambalaya Club in Arcata, California, on February 23, 1995, during a break in the album's mixing.† They opened, unannounced, for the Unseen, a group of teen upstarts who, Grohl recalled, "dressed like the Jam and could play any song you asked for". Earlier that day, Grohl and co. raided a local thrift shop for T-shirts (including a tasty number promoting the local Hooters chain). They created a Foo Fighters stencil, sprayed it on to the shirts, and sold them for a few dollars at the merchandise stall before the gig. The show was as big a hit as the trade in Foos T-shirts. "We just drank and danced," said Grohl. "It was so fun . . . there were no rules and no expectations."

Two more gigs followed, in Portland on March 3 and at the Velvet Elvis club in Seattle the day after. For Goldsmith, the Seattle gig was tough; Sunny Day Real Estate gigs there had invariably been train-wrecks. "I absolutely despise playing in Seattle," Goldsmith said. "You're on the

---

* Recorded just before the Police's commercial breakthrough, a single, 'Don't Care', was first released in 1978 and a mini-album (on 10″ green Kryptonite vinyl), *Klark Kent*, appeared in 1980.

† A few weeks earlier, on January 8, Eddie Vedder had played the two-track tape Grohl had given him on his *Self-Pollution Radio Show*. Vedder announced the songs simply as being by "Dave Grohl".

spot, all these people sitting and staring." Grohl and Smear had no such concerns. Fifteen minutes after the show, with the sweat still drying, they looked at each other excitedly and declared: "Let's go play somewhere else!"

There was a break in the schedule when Grohl flew to Australia in March on the excuse of using up accumulated Frequent Flyer points. Pearl Jam was touring the country at the time and, having vehemently denied the rumours linking them, Grohl sat in on a few songs during several of their shows. In particular, during their set at Melbourne's Flinders Park Tennis Centre on March 17, Grohl helped the band tear a hole in Neil Young's anthemic 'Rocking In The Free World'. This blast of raw power was caught on the Pearl Jam promo disc, *Rarified And Live*. A 29-date, six-week Foo Fighters tour, supporting Mike Watt, awaited Grohl on his return, beginning in Phoenix on April 12 and then swinging through Albuquerque, New Mexico, Denver, Colorado, Nashville, Tennessee, Atlanta, Georgia and numerous other middling cities, then hitting the music biz centres of New York – where they put in a two-night stand at downtown venue Tramps – and Los Angeles, before ending with a final date in San Diego, California.

If Grohl was serious about getting back to basics, Watt was the perfect example. During his time playing bass with San Pedro punks the Minutemen and fIREHOSE, Watt had turned Black Flag's idea of low-rent touring into a design for life. His bands lugged their own gear, slept on friends' floors, recorded only during graveyard shifts when rates were dirt cheap, and kept their van on the road at all times. He even invented his own punk lexicon while with the Minutemen: they "jammed econo", which basically equated to total self-sufficiency. "You have to be econo," Watt explained, "so maybe when the hard times hit, you can weather them."

Although Grohl's panic attacks would reappear – sometimes mid-set during those first Foos shows – the Watt tour was an early peak for the band. "It was so incredibly refreshing to do something where you're frightened, really scared to do it," Grohl said. "Every once in a while, in the middle of a set, my stomach would turn and I'd have a little panic attack." The Foos were living some of the concepts of "jamming econo", travelling together in one van at minimum cost and with a skeleton crew. For a band that would eventually become a stadium monster, this was as grounded as Foo Fighters would ever be. The action in the van was divided roughly between Mendel's obsession with *Harper's* magazine and the *Jesus Christ Superstar* soundtrack, and Goldsmith's mysterious need to steal Grohl's camera – which he did on no less than three occasions – to take photos of his own dick. This must have shocked Grohl when he had the film developed. "I see pictures of Hootie & The Blowfish playing golf on tour," Grohl told one writer who visited the Foo van, "and I realise that we're a little different."

Grohl was pragmatic concerning the sea of Nirvana and Kurt Cobain T-shirts that greeted him at each gig. "You could take it two ways, you could think that all these people are here just because they liked Nirvana – or they want to support us. I thought it was great that there was a committed family vibe."

Just before the Watt tour, Grohl signed a "P&D" deal with Capitol, shrewdly inserting a "key man" clause, which basically meant that if Gary Gersh – who was the label president and whom Grohl referred to as a "father figure" – jumped ship, the Foos and Roswell Records could default too. "I'm not signed to the label," Grohl explained. "That means I'm not their employee. The records are out on Roswell Records and I sign all the cheques."*

Two weeks before the release of debut single, 'This Is A Call', Foo Fighters played another guerrilla support slot, at Capitol's suggestion, opening for Teenage Fanclub at King's College in London. Grohl initially baulked at the idea of flying to the UK on a Wednesday, playing on Friday and heading home two days later. He was also wary of the reaction from the fickle UK press.

"We were sort of waiting for the English press to tear us to shreds, because they usually do," he admitted. "Sometimes they love you at first and then they knock you down." Grohl needn't have worried, because both press and public were equal in their support. When released on June 19 and without the aid of a promotional video, 'This Is A Call' bolted into the UK Top 10, peaking at number five.

The low-key approach was further accentuated by the sleeve of *Foo Fighters*, released on July 4. The stark image, taken by Jennifer Youngblood,

---

* Grohl's initial plan of also using Roswell as a label to release music from up-and-comers never came to fruition.

showing only a toy gun used by action hero Buck Rogers, was designed to fit in with the sci-fi theme and the band's enigmatic origins.* Grohl could not have expected the minor controversy which was stirred up when some observers decided that this was his ironic comment on Cobain's gun fixation. As recently as 2005, he was still defending the cover shot. "People kind of freaked out on that," he said, "[but] you know, honestly, that never came to mind once. Obviously it didn't, because if I thought people would associate that with [Cobain's suicide], I would never have done it."

Foo Fighters was rapturously received on both sides of the Atlantic, even though references to "Cobain", "Nirvana" and "grunge" were used throughout virtually every review. Nirvana scored no less than five mentions in Alec Foege's four-star review in *Rolling Stone* (August 10). Foege showed great perception in noting that Grohl's influences extended further than Seattle, comparing 'Oh, George' to Steve Miller, 'Good Grief' (Cheap Trick) and 'Exhausted' (the Beach Boys).

"Dave Grohl could turn out to be the Nineties punk equivalent of Tom Petty," Foege continued, observing how Grohl's "good-natured humility" and his ability to transform the "average rock cliché" into something more emotionally potent gave him the potential to achieve similar success. For Grohl, this was the ultimate compliment – he'd become a big Petty fan after their *Saturday Night Live* bonding session.

Foo Fighters made *Spin*'s Top 20 of 1995 and the *New York Times*' Top 10 Albums of that year. It ranked twelfth in *NME*'s Top 50 Albums of the Year, sixth in the *Village Voice*'s annual Pazz & Jop Critics' Poll, and came second in *Rolling Stone*'s 1996 Reader's Poll.† Highly regarded critic, Jon Pareles, cut to the chase in his *New York Times* review. "[Grohl's] songs stare down misgivings with cryptic lyrics, memorable tunes and a willingness to bash ahead."

While some reviews touched a negative note – *Spin* rated the album "flawed yet worthy", while *Q* condescendingly described it as "grunge-quite-lite" – they still praised Grohl's ability to render even the heavier songs on the album "accessible by [using] layers of melody, much of it

---

* Of course, Grohl's role in the Foos was very much public knowledge, and the inside band shots, placed at Capitol's insistence, removed any doubt about their identities.
† *Foo Fighters* was later included in the Top 20 of *Kerrang!*'s 100 Albums You Must Hear Before You Die poll.

The Foo Fighters, 1995: Pat Smear, Grohl, William Goldsmith and Nate Mendel (from left). Goldsmith would leave during sessions for *The Colour And The Shape*. Even now, producer Gil Norton has regrets about the handling of his dismissal. 'I still feel bad about that,' said Norton. *(Ian Tilton/Corbis)*

Pat Smear, former guitarist for the Germs and Nirvana, and, briefly, a Foo Fighter. When he very publicly left the band, on-stage at the MTV Awards in 1997, his farewell speech amounted to: 'I'd like to introduce Franz Stahl, who will be taking over. Rock on guys. Foo Fighters!' *(Ross Halfin/Idols)*

Forming a new band so soon after the end of Nirvana was never Grohl's original intention. 'To continue almost seemed in vain – I was always going to be "that guy from Kurt Cobain's band" and I knew that,' he said. *(Ross Halfin/Idols)*

Grohl, Taylor Hawkins, Smear and Mendel. During the brief time they shared as Foo Fighters, new kid Hawkins and punk icon Smear formed a special bond. Hawkins said that life with Smear was 'like having a big sister in the band'. *(Kevin Cummins/Idols)*

Grohl, Hawkins, Mendel and Franz Stahl (from left) at the Versus fashion show, March 28, 1998. Despite his long history with Grohl, Stahl was never a comfortable fit as a Foo Fighter. 'It just seemed like the three of us were moving in one direction and Franz wasn't,' Grohl admitted. *(Nick Elgar/Corbis)*

The Foo three, Hawkins, Grohl and Mendel (from left). The trio recorded *There Is Nothing Left To Lose* in the basement of Grohl's Virginia home over a four-month stretch. Hawkins later confessed he was in a 'fucked-up state of mind' for much of the time. *(Mick Hutson/Idols)*

(From left): Hawkins, Mendel and Grohl with new
Foo Chris Shiflett, who joined in 1999.
'There was no real interrogation process,' Shiflett said
of his audition for the band. 'We just shot the shit and
talked about tour stuff, band stuff and silly stories.'
(Ross Halfin/Idols)

Grohl's then girlfriend, former Hole and
Smashing Pumpkins bassist, Melissa Auf Der Maur,
offers him a birthday cake (and a wish)
on-stage at Rock In Rio, 2001. Grohl had just turned 32.
Like his relationship with Louise Post, their
affair wasn't built to last. *(LFI)*

Grohl (left) and Queen's Brian May tie their mothers down at the Rock and Roll Hall of Fame concert,
New York, March 2001. Grohl was thrilled by the experience; to him it was like 'living in a comic book, because you
always think of these people as super-heroes when you're a little kid.' *(Dave Allocca/Rex Features)*

Hawkins in the studio, laying down tracks for One By One, 2002. He was still recovering from a near-fatal OD in England the previous year. 'I'm not proud of what happened,' he said. 'The drummer of a rock band takes too many drugs, becomes ill, has to go into rehab; it's just so embarrassing.' *(Tony Wooliscroft/Idols)*

Grohl during the stop-start *One By One* sessions, which would subsequently become known as the 'Million Dollar Demos'. 'I'd get halfway through... and scrap the whole fucking song,' said Grohl, 'something we'd [just] spent a week on.' *(Tony Wooliscroft/Idols)*

Shiflett (and Mendel) were left to complete their work on *One By One* while Grohl was on the road with the Queens of the Stone Age. 'Guys, you're going to have to finish your parts by yourselves,' Grohl told them. 'Whatever it takes to make it work, shit, that's what it takes.' *(Tony Wooliscroft/Idols)*

Mendel, Hawkins, Grohl and Shiflett (from left), back together again, 2002.
'Let's just hope it doesn't take another near-death experience for their next album to be this good,'
one writer observed of *One By One*. (Mick Hutson/Idols)

Grohl with Queens Nick Oliveri and Josh Homme (from left), the men who almost stole him away from the Foos. 'I just said, "Fuck it, I'm going to go off and play with the Queens for a while and see how I feel when I get back",' Grohl said afterwards.
(Joe Giron/Corbis)

(Top Right) Grohl with Lemmy during the Probot project. Grohl was seriously impressed by the man from Motorhead; they bonded over booze and strippers. 'I realised that of all the rockers I'd met in my life, I'd never met a real rocker before. Lemmy is the fucking rocker – he is the one.'
(Annamaria DiSanto/WireImage)

Grohl at the 2003 Grammys – where the Foos won the trophy for 'Best Hard Rock Song' – with his mother. Grohl made a point of keeping his family and loved ones close at all times; so much so that he bought his mother a house so she could also live on the west coast. *(Theo Wargo/WireImage)*

Grohl and Jordyn Blum became parents on April 15, 2006, when their daughter Violet Maye was born in LA. Grohl delivered a press release that read: 'Father, mother and child are happy, healthy and up to [their] ears in green s–ts.' *(LFI)*

Dave Grohl, drummer, lover, father, multi-millionaire, bandleader. He once compared life in the Foo Fighters to the film Apocalypse Now. 'We're heading up the river and Chef – that's me – jumps off and gets spooked by that tiger. He gets back on, screaming "Never get off the boat!" Well, man, the Foo Fighters is the boat.'
(Martyn Goodacre/Retna)

descended directly from [Byrd] Roger McGuinn, if he'd had fewer strings."

Grohl needn't have been concerned about the UK press response. *Melody Maker* declared the album "bloody essential", declaring that the Foo Fighters were "almost as perfect as the Young Gods, the Swiss maestros weaned on Hüsker Dü and Anastasia Screamed. We're talking THAT breathtaking, that joyously gone."

NME traded superlatives with their opposition weekly, countering with a typically overstated view that the album was "massively important", full of "memorable songs, satisfyingly crunchy guitars and an unambiguously joyful spirit". *Foo Fighters* rated highly in *Musician* ("the album is packed with simple, forceful melodies, precise harmonies and inventive arrangements"), and even *Entertainment Weekly*, who mixed high praise with inaccurate comparison when saying "it's as if Lennon and McCartney had grown up in Seattle".

Foo Fighters peaked at three in the UK and number 23 in the *Billboard* Top 200, selling more than a million copies in the USA alone, charting highly in Sweden, Germany, Finland, Austria, Australia, New Zealand, and elsewhere. Four singles were eventually lifted from the album; of these, 'Big Me' made it to the number three position on *Billboard*'s Modern Rock Tracks chart, while 'This Is A Call' went one better.

The response was enough to convince Capitol that a video was necessary for the album's second single, 'I'll Stick Around'. Against his better judgement, Grohl caved in to their demands. His choice of director was ex-Devo bassist/singer and fellow Ohio native, Gerald Casale.*

Like Butch Vig and Steve Albini before him, Casale didn't rate Nirvana. "I felt the raw energy," he explained, "but the aesthetic was too earnest for me. I heard the pain of the beats but not the intelligence." 'I'll Stick Around' was the only Foo Fighters' track Casale had heard when he agreed to work on the video.

On first listen, Casale felt he understood precisely whom the song was directed at, despite Grohl's protestations to the contrary. "I knew it was about Courtney Love," Casale insisted. "I knew all about the justifiable rancour and I was on his [Grohl's] side. She is a vexing germ."

---

* When I asked Casale why he was hired, he attributed it to Devo's "anti-video" stance or, more precisely, the band's "pre-music-video videos".

Casale didn't hold back when it came to the video's theme. "The concept I submitted was similar to the one we shot but the 3D animated 'virus' was literally a bloated, charred, inflated girl representing Courtney." Grohl's management and label were naturally fearful of possible litigation – "weapon number one wielded by diseased 'talent'," according to Casale – and eventually altered Casale's original design to a "3D HIV virus based on medical models from *Scientific America* magazine".

During the video, the virus, which Casale christened the "Foo Ball", attacked the band. "I liked that idea," says Casale, "especially because the entomology of 'Foo Fighters' originated in World War II when soldiers would end up shooting at things that weren't there when flares lit up the landscape during night fighting. Very Jungian, don't you think?"

In keeping with Grohl's increasingly thwarted efforts to maintain virtually no image for his band, the clip was declared a "non-video video". Casale was comfortable with the term. "Non-video video is a compliment," he told me. "It only cost US $60K. I don't think Dave ever appreciated what I delivered for the money, considering their 'not-into-it' pose." Grohl had minimal creative input, as Casale explained. "They were not very involved because . . . Dave thought videos were a sell-out to 'the man'. He made it under pressure from the label. [But] he had the idea of eating all the chess pieces and then spitting them out. We had to shoot that with frame-by-frame stop-action animation. That took an inordinate portion of the shoot time which then severely impacted on the rest of the shoot because the band was over two hours late getting on set to begin with."

When the video was released, Casale accepted Grohl's decision to play down the Courtney connotation. "I have total sympathy for the intense anger in his vocals. The woman is a monster. [But] Dave is an astute businessman and a multi-millionaire. He would never come clean about such matters. Why should he?"

Not surprisingly, Grohl and Casale didn't renew their association. "As soon as the Foo Fighters were successful," Casale shrugs, "he went to huge budgets and A-list directors. He even made disparaging remarks about our video on MTV interviews. I'm used to this type of 'let no good deed go unpunished' backlash. You never want to be the teacher. The student will kill you."

★   ★   ★

For a project that began with such small-scale intentions, Foo Fighters maintained an outrageously high profile for the rest of 1995, playing almost 100 shows in support of their debut album. They swiftly gained a reputation as a great live band, playing fast, energetically and without the need to trash their gear as Nirvana had – a redundant spectacle taken up by lesser acts like Pearl Jam and The Vines.

During this time, Grohl reconnected with the Stahls who had formed a new band, Wool. Along with Sub Pop outfit Shudder To Think, Wool opened for Foo Fighters during a month-long North American tour, which kicked off on July 20 at Vancouver's Commodore Ballroom. In quick succession, the three bands blitzed Seattle – where the Foos staged an impromptu gig on top of a dumpster behind the Weathered Wall – Portland, San Francisco, LA, and San Diego, before heading east. On August 14, Foo Fighters made the first of many *Late Night With Letterman* appearances, blasting through 'This Is A Call', before the tour finally wound down in Nashville, Tennessee, on August 22, having played 25 shows in little over a month.

This was just the beginning of the long haul, for the band had signed on to play numerous European summer free-for-alls, including the Lowlands Festival in Holland and Belgium's Pukkelpop Festival. The most crucial date – and the most challenging for Grohl – was his return after three years to the Reading Festival on August 26.

Grohl insisted that the band played on the secondary *Melody Maker* stage, away from the main action, in a further effort to keep things low key. That didn't stop several thousand punters spilling out of the small tent where the *MM* stage was located. The main stage was virtually deserted while the Foos played their brief set, which staggered from song to song with frequent stoppages as security pulled hundreds of punters down from the wobbly scaffolding supporting the tent. Grohl looked back at the gig with mixed feelings.

"It was bad for those people being crushed and trampled, to say the least. I couldn't believe it was happening, that the security guards were passing out, or that there were so many people who wanted to squeeze into this little tent to see the big mess we were making onstage."

Grohl learned a lesson: from this time onwards, Foo Fighters would headline whenever they toured the UK. When they returned in November, they played two nights at the Brixton Academy, plus a gig at Leeds'

Town & Country Club. Like so many shows on the tour, the critical response was as fervent as the feedback from the crowd. As *Time Out* wrote of the Leeds' show, "It's a set of howling cathartic power." And Grohl's on-stage nerves were obviously fading fast, because he'd become something of a raconteur. Amidst the usual polite comments of "thank you" and "have a good night", Grohl even suggested that the crowd head home after the show and "have a nice hot bath", because that's what his mother always recommended he do after playing a show. Love – and cleanliness – were in abundance at Foos' gigs. The mania continued in other far-flung places, including Australia, where the band ended 1995 with the kind of welcome usually reserved for homecoming sports heroes at a New Year's Eve show at Sydney's Macquarie University.

The early months of 1996 were occupied by touring New Zealand and south-east Asia, before returning for yet another lap of the USA and Canada. In rare downtime they returned to Robert Lang's Seattle studio on January 24 for the first "proper" Foo Fighters band recording, cutting three tracks, including a cover of Gary Numan's 'Down In The Park', for the *Songs In The Key Of X* soundtrack. The seemingly never-ending tour wound up with more European dates throughout July, climaxing at the Phoenix Festival in genteel Stratford-upon-Avon on July 20.

Grohl said of that last show, "Of course we were burnt. We thought, 'OK, so this Phoenix show is the last show – after this we can go home. It's gonna be so great.' It could have been the most energetic, out-of-control performance we'd ever put on, or we could have just stood there and enjoyed the huge audience." A road-weary Foos chose the latter.

In 1996 alone, Foo Fighters had played an additional 70-odd dates, while sales of the album climbed to 1.9 million.

CHAPTER TEN

Nothing Left To Lose

"It was such a shame. I was 25, my wife was even younger. It would have been better had we not got married."

– Dave Grohl

BARELY a week had passed since Foo Fighters lacklustre finale at the Phoenix Festival and, while Goldsmith, Smear and Mendel were glad for some downtime after spending more than a year living in each other's pockets, workaholic Grohl entered Robert Lang's Studio with Barrett Jones. The man simply couldn't slow down. As he explained at the time, "I can't sit on my ass and do nothing." He was also experiencing some trouble at home, having spent so long away from Jennifer Youngblood, and he found the studio a useful retreat.

Grohl had been commissioned to write the soundtrack for *Touch* – a Paul Schrader-directed film noir B-grade thriller. Schrader was a well-respected man, having won a Golden Globe for his script to the chilling urban blues of *Taxi Driver*, and directing such arthouse flicks as *The Comfort Of Strangers* and *Light Sleeper*. The cast of *Touch* featured Christopher Walken, Skeet Ulrich and Paul Mazursky. Noir master Elmore Leonard wrote the potboiler upon which Schrader based his screenplay. The film's producers placed a call to Grohl, purely on spec, to establish whether he was interested in scoring the movie. Grohl viewed a rough cut and immediately agreed, although he forewarned them, "You realise I haven't done this before. I could really fuck it up." As it turned out, Grohl was the ideal man for the job, because the producers were looking for someone totally inexperienced in making film music. He was sent a copy of the rough cut, along with a checklist indicating where the incidental music (and occasional complete song) should go.

The last thing Grohl wanted was to make another *Reality Bites*, where the soundtrack dictated the onscreen action. "The songs had to stay in the background," he said. "I tried to come up with some music that would go with the images, without being too in-your-face."

Recorded over a two-week stretch, with guests including John Doe, ex-singer/bassist with legendary LA cowpunks X, Grohl's regular side-kick, Barrett Jones, who co-produced the album and played keyboards on one track, and Louise Post, from alt-poppers Veruca Salt, the resultant soundtrack admirably succeeded in marrying lightweight surf-punk instrumentals such as 'Bill Hill Theme' and 'Outrage', with more noir-ish pieces ('Scene 4') and the gently twangy 'Making Popcorn'. Doe sang a sterling, aching-hearted lead on 'This Love Thing', and Post also took the lead for 'Saints In Love'. She also collaborated with Grohl (who used the 'Late' pseudonym) on the dreamy title track, one of the best songs Grohl had yet written. Of the 13 musical pieces, only the urgent, riff-sodden 'How Do You Do?' would have slotted comfortably onto the first – or any – *Foo Fighters* album. That was exactly Grohl's intention: "[With a soundtrack] you're not restricted to the classic pop song structure," he reasoned. "With a soundtrack, you can do anything, and the most important thing is that parts don't have to be repeated continuously. You don't need a catchy chorus."

In other words, he was keeping his more "traditional" rock songs for the next Foo Fighters album.

Grohl's collaboration with Doe was a particularly simple process, as Doe told me via email. "His contribution to the song was a series of chords that have been used many times over, and some humming of a very vague melody. He then told me over the phone that I should write the words and melody because [in Grohl's words] 'I'm kind of a bone-head at that anyway.' I'm sure he could've done it all by himself but . . . I was glad to collaborate. That's the extent of my experience with Dave Grohl."

Grohl completely immersed himself in the experience, declaring it to be the "most fun I've ever had in the studio". The album, however, just like the film, didn't receive the attention it deserved. Most critics dismissed it as a between-serious-albums indulgence on Grohl's part, which wasn't totally accurate. Only a few writers, such as allmusic.com's Stephen Thomas Erlewine, bothered to closely examine the record. "While the soundtrack is a bit too disjointed to work entirely successfully outside of the film," he wrote, "it is nevertheless indicative of Grohl's considerable musical talents, as well as his potential as a film composer."

By 1996 rock'n'roll had entered another of its cyclical downturns. Pearl Jam entered into a long and eventually unfulfilling battle with US promoter Ticketmaster, which effectively sidelined the band for some time, while Bush, Everclear, Stone Temple Pilots and their corporate ilk cynically extracted every last penny from the grunge corpse, or, in the case of Silverchair, considered moving on to the next stage of their musical lives. Hardy perennials like Metallica and Soundgarden headlined Lollapalooza 1996, over acts such as neo-punks Rancid and the overtly political Rage Against The Machine. Indie faves like Tortoise, Trans Am and Built To Spill maintained loyal, but small followings. It was nothing like the golden years of the early Nineties, when Nirvanamania broke out.

MTV had dropped the "alternative" artifice altogether and embraced such acts as the truly execrable Presidents Of The United States Of America, who turned a dumb ditty about canned peaches into a major hit, and Hootie & The Blowfish, possibly the most soulless band ever to be fronted by an African/American. Meanwhile, the mainstream charts were clogged up by the Spice Girls, Mariah Carey, and the slightly edgier Alanis Morissette, whose confused though palatable soundtrack for the disaffected, 1995's *Jagged Little Pill*, was still selling by the unit. For the remarkable breakthrough that Nirvana made five years earlier, there didn't appear to be any comparable phenomenon waiting in the wings.

At the same time, Grohl was going through some unsettling personal times; a stage in his life he later described as "terrible". He'd split with Jennifer Youngblood and hooked up with his *Touch* vocal partner Louise Post. When their relationship ended due to Grohl's infidelity, Post called Grohl a "shag hound" while on stage at a Veruca Salt gig, amongst other uncomplimentary names.* More than one source has told me that Grohl broke up with Post via text message, which might explain her rancour. Having experienced his parents' divorce, Grohl harboured genuine regrets about the breakdown of his marriage, even going so far as to describe it as the biggest failure in his life.

* Like many of Grohl's former paramours, Post declined to be interviewed for this book.

The split can be put down to long absences on the road and the inevitable temptations on offer. "I don't think it was meant to be," he rationalised. "It was such a shame. I was 25, my wife was even younger. We weren't ready to get married. I miss her a ton, she's the funniest goddamn weirdo you ever met in your life. [But] it would have been better had we not got married." As time passed, Grohl was not so affectionate towards Youngblood, stating, "I should have listened to my friends and dumped the bitch." (Though, he soon retracted this outburst.)

With his divorce, Grohl moved from his home in Seattle to Los Angeles, where he continues to base himself, with the occasional retreat to Virginia and his family. Strangely, for a musician who had accumulated a considerable fortune by this time, Grohl chose to slum it during his first days in the City of Angels. "I was living out of my duffel bag on this cat-piss-stained mattress in my friend's back room with 12 people in the house," he recalled. It was hardly the five-star lifestyle to which the man was now accustomed.

In this emotionally and personally trying climate, Grohl resolved to make an album that was the complete antithesis of *Foo Fighters* – or in Grohl's words, a "big budget rock'n'roll opus", mirroring the anthemic qualities of the records he had loved as a kid, including most of the recorded output of Led Zeppelin and Queen. In order to do this, he needed a producer who was comfortable working on such a scale. Englishman Gil Norton seemed the right man for the job. Grohl opted to work with Norton on the strength of one key album: The Pixies'★ *Trompe Le Monde*. "I love it for the way you can hear the band falling apart," Grohl said, "getting scattered, shooting off in a million directions."

Ironically, Norton told Grohl that making that album was one of the most difficult recording experiences of his life – not helped by guitarist/singer Black Francis sacking bassist and foil, Kim Deal, just prior to the sessions. "It's not that I disliked *Trompe*," Norton told me, "it's just that the band was falling apart."

Norton had started his career in Liverpool, working at Amazon Studios, where bands as diverse as Orchestral Manoeuvres In The Dark and Black Sabbath recorded. By the time he was hired by Grohl, Norton had built an

---

★ The influential Boston group were a key inspiration for the slow–fast, soft–loud dynamics that Nirvana took and ran with.

impressive CV of production work including Echo and the Bunnymen, Del Amitri, James, the Triffids, Throwing Muses and Belly.

The first sessions for what would become *The Colour And The Shape*[*] took place at Bear Creek Studios, in Woodinville, Washington, on November 18, after two weeks of pre-production with Norton. As he had done with Black Francis, Norton spent several days in his hotel room with Grohl, stripping the songs back to their absolute basics. However, in light of the recent marathon touring, some band members felt they were going into the album prematurely. Most of the new songs had been slapped together during soundchecks over the previous 18 months, hardly the ideal environment for creativity. "We didn't want people to feel that it [Foo Fighters] was a side project," Grohl explained, when asked why he'd got the band back into the studio so quickly.

The studio also offered a retreat from his messy personal life. "Me and Grohl got on great," Norton said, "he was going through his divorce, so we'd hang out, have drinks."

With *Foo Fighters*, Grohl had hoped to bury Nirvana's spectre; for *The Colour And The Shape*, he had more personal demons to exorcise. For the first time as a lyricist, words and feelings came pouring out. "I sat down and I felt like I had nothing to hide," Grohl said. "I just let it all come on paper. With the first record, I spent so much time trying to disguise and mask things . . . This time I didn't even have time for that."

Such lugubrious numbers as 'Walking After You', which, unlike much of the album, was recorded very quickly in the studio, and 'New Way Home' were very clearly influenced by his turbulent personal life, with the latter featuring references to the Seattle neighbourhood where Grohl lived, including the King Dome football arena and Highway 99. Grohl described 'New Way Home', the album's closer, as emblematic of much of what had come before. "Winding your way through all of these songs [are] emotions and pitfalls and ups and downs, but at the end of the day, you realise you're not scared any more and you're gonna make it." Grohl would even liken the album to a rollercoaster ride, or "like a setlist when a band plays live. There should be a beginning and an end. It's so important and so few

---

[*] Oddly for an American band the title conformed to the English spelling. It was a phrase often repeated by a former Foos' tour manager who bought things because he simply liked their "colour and shape".

records I hear these days make me think, 'This is the intro and this is the finale.' It just makes a better journey through 13 songs." This was clearly a different proposition to 'Just Another Story About Skeeter Thompson'.

At one stage, Grohl even toyed with the idea of using a shot of a therapist's couch for the album's front cover, although he later insisted this was purely a joke. However, such an idea would not have been wide of the mark. When Grohl heard the playback for the first time, he considered that the track sequencing, with its mix of musical emotions and moods, "runs like a therapy session."

The sessions took an unexpected turn just before Christmas 1996. With 12 tracks recorded, including 'Monkey Wrench', 'Everlong' and 'Hey, Johnny Park!', a shout out to a long-lost high school buddy of Grohl's, the band parted for the holidays, agreeing to reconvene in the New Year at a different studio. During the break, Norton listened to the tracks that had been completed, and decided he wasn't entirely happy with the drum tracks. Norton called Grohl and told him that he thought they could be improved. A short while later, Grohl phoned him back in agreement, offering to try drumming on a track.[*] Initially, he only drummed on 'Monkey Wrench', which Norton felt was the one track that especially needed work. "It was brilliant," Norton said of Grohl's new drum track, "and it spiralled out of that." In the end, only two of Goldsmith's parts – for the tracks 'Doll' and 'Up In Arms' – would remain on the finished album. Obviously, Grohl was still tempted to view the band as *his* project, having been a virtual one-man band for both the *Pocketwatch* album and *Foo Fighters*.[†]

Norton offered to call Goldsmith to advise him of their plans, but Grohl said that he would make the call. Ultimately, Goldsmith remained in the dark. "I still feel bad about that," said Norton, who had struck up a friendship with the drummer during those first sessions. However, Goldsmith didn't make the situation any easier, according to Norton. "William shot himself, really – he lost his head and went AWOL."

While the band completed work on the album in LA at Grand Master Recorders over four weeks starting in February, Goldsmith was at home

---

[*] This order of events is contrary to popular belief – it was Norton, not Grohl, who raised the problem of Goldsmith's drumming. Grohl, according to Norton, had no intention of drumming on the album.

[†] Grohl also added guitar parts to the album, but this didn't seem to affect Pat Smear in the same way that it did Goldsmith.

in Seattle with his family. On March 4, 1997 he officially became an ex-Foo Fighter.

To his credit, Goldsmith has rarely spoken publicly about his falling out with Grohl,* although in 2001 he did tell www.firesideometer.com that the situation in the Foos had become "slightly poisonous". Grohl was of the opinion that Goldsmith was more interested in playing somewhere else and wasn't built for the Foo's hectic touring schedule. "He also had a hard time when we were in the studio," Grohl said. Goldsmith's discomfort working with "click tracks" and his unfamiliarity with Pro Tools, a software program that was revolutionising the recording industry, were other key factors in his downfall. "William was over-hitting the drums," Norton told me, "and he'd get tired after a couple of takes. He was losing his confidence." It should also be noted that the band was at least $200,000 in the red when the sessions were aborted; Goldsmith's uncertainty in the studio was proving costly.

Grohl referred to Goldsmith "bumming out" when he learned that his parts had been redone, which was perfectly justified. "That turned into a breakdown and I realised he wasn't coming back." Significantly, Goldsmith and Mendel's "stay together/play together" pact was broken when Mendel remained with the band.

Goldsmith's confidence must surely have been tested by Norton's relentless perfectionism, with some of the tracks on *The Colour And The Shape* being redone 30 times.† Grohl had total respect for the producer. "That recording session was a lesson in patience," he admitted. "We wanted to make a tight, hard rock record . . . but Gil taught me the meaning of 'spot on'."

"There was a really good vibe during the making of *The Colour And The Shape*," Norton confirmed to me.‡

---

* Goldsmith had agreed to be interviewed for this book but then he suffered a double family tragedy – his brother died and his father became ill. Understandably he was still unavailable as the book's deadline approached.

† An actual track called 'The Colour And The Shape' – a fast, hard rocker in the style of 'Weenie Beanie' – was recorded, but to Grohl "it was a step backwards," so it didn't make the final cut.

‡ Significantly, Grohl and Norton have not recorded together since, although Norton was earmarked to work on *One By One*. In his post-Foos career, Norton has worked with emo-core bands Dashboard Confessional and Jimmy Eat World, plus Counting Crows, Feeder and the Distillers.

Foo Fighters' second album achieved the desired goal of being a totally different beast to their debut. Sonically, it is not unlike *Nevermind* – a slick-sounding, well-crafted album. That's not to say that the record is flawless. 'Monkey Wrench', despite its FM-radio friendly adrenaline rush, is little more than formulaic, although it did help further define what would become the band's signature sound of churning guitars, deeply melodic vocals and pulse-racing rhythms. Grohl would grow to despise the overwrought ballad 'February Stars'; he hated it even more than the Foo Fighters' throwaway, 'Oh, George'. During an early live outing for the song, a person in the audience bellowed "Boring!" during a lull in the song. Enough said. Grohl later offered the song as Foo Fighters' donation to the hypothetical album *Crap Songs Of Our Time*, if someone was brave enough to compile such an LP.

If 'Monkey Wrench' did its best (or worst, depending on your response to the song) to establish the Foos' sonic template, that was even further driven home by such *Colour And Shape* cuts as 'Up In Arms', 'My Poor Brain' and 'Hey, Johnny Park!' The latter, with its half-spoken, gently strummed verses and explosive breakdowns, gave Grohl the chance to flex his muscles on rock's holy trinity: drums, guitar and voice. Like so much of the Foos' output, it was hard to get a real fix on what Grohl was singing about, but like some of rock's best vocals, lyrics didn't really matter: when he roared his lungs dry as the song raced to a close, you felt like the guy had the weight of the world on his shoulders. The song failed, however, to bring Grohl's old schoolmate out of the shadows. "I wanna talk to that guy," Grohl laughed. "I'll find him."

Tracks such as 'Everlong' – a close cousin of Neil Young's 'Winterlong' – and 'My Hero' would become Foo standards. 'Everlong' would be the album's second single, after 'Monkey Wrench', and help the album maintain a Pink Floyd-like life in the *Billboard* album chart. The song was a hit across the numerous rock radio formats, and also did serious business in *Billboard*'s many singles listings, hanging around the Modern Rock Charts for a whopping 28 weeks. While Grohl confessed that the sweetly melodic 'Everlong' was the perfect "make-out" song, 'My Hero', like 'I'll Stick Around' before it, was thought to be another song for Kurt Cobain. As usual, Grohl dismissed the suggestion, explaining that it was a celebration of "ordinary heroes", "people who were like friends of the family, [such as] the guy who would take me out to the country when I

was young, and try to introduce me to wildlife and camping and fishing."
Grohl further claimed that it was a tribute to a neighbour who sat alongside Grohl as a kid and "watched *Sesame Street* with me . . . and helped me
to read." With reluctance, Grohl accepted that there was "an element of
Kurt in that song", but stuck by his "everyday heroes" explanation. The
song also captured one of Grohl's most thunderous drum tracks since he
launched 'Smells Like Teen Spirit' into the stratosphere. The drums on
the album may have been recorded under less-than-ideal circumstances,
but here it sounded as though Grohl was back in his DC bedroom, lost in
a teenage flashback, thumping the hell out of his bedclothes. The song
was a pure adrenaline rush, a natural high, and his drumming was the
key.

Elsewhere, 'See You' was a jazzy strum, with hints of the back-porch
melody of *Touch*'s 'Making Popcorn', proof that Grohl was willing, in his
own way, to mess with the formula. The tearaway 'Enough Space', meanwhile, was a furious rave-up that also echoed another of Grohl's *Touch*
songs (in this case 'Bill Hill Theme'); it was the ideal set-closer. Even
though it wasn't obvious at first – Grohl's larynx-shredding vocal renders
his lyrics almost indecipherable – it turned out that this was Grohl's way of
asking journalists to lighten up on the UFO questions, hence the song's
title. "I'm a sci-fi buff; I'm a UFO buff," Grohl readily admitted. "I love
reading about it, I love science fiction movies, but I don't pray to the
alien god in my fucking pyramid temple. So I just thought, enough of this
space shit."

With *The Colour And The Shape* having been efficiently mixed by Chris
Sheldon in LA, Foo Fighters were ready to go back on the road. The
problem was that they were without a drummer.

Equal parts Californian stoner and blond-haired toothy surfer dude,
Taylor Hawkins would prove to be the perfect professional and personal
foil for Dave Grohl. Easy-going, affable and with that distinct west coast
tendency to begin each utterance with "like" and end with "dude",*
Hawkins was an energetic powerhouse drummer, who also shared a lot of
Grohl's best qualities.

---

* During a 10-minute phone conversation, a colleague counted the number of times
Hawkins used the word "like". It came to a grand total of 44.

Although born in Texas on February 17, 1972, in Fort Worth, Hawkins was raised in Laguna Beach, California, in an extremely musical household. "Some of my earliest memories are of music," he said in 2005. "I remember being three or four years old and we had a record player out on the back patio playing music." Hawkins shared an early musical common denominator with Grohl – "We listened to the Jackson 5 and the hits of the Seventies," Hawkins recalled. "It all hit me emotionally, even soundtrack stuff like *Star Wars*."

As a teenager, Hawkins split his time between drumming, surfing and smoking weed. Although drug addiction would come to play a huge role in Hawkins' future, with his mother being an alcoholic he stayed away from booze. "I saw her beat herself up every day," he said in 2002. Like many American suburban teens including Grohl, Hawkins was a borderline ADD candidate as a kid so the drums were a natural outlet.

Thanks to an older brother and sister, Hawkins was exposed to AOR rock early on, listening to Boston, the Police and, especially, Queen. When absorbed in the band's 1978 album *News Of The World*, Hawkins found a new hero in Queen timekeeper Roger Taylor.*

Hawkins' Laguna Beach neighbour, one Kent Kleater, had a "crappy little drum kit and a couple of acoustic guitars in his house." It was the perfect outlet for Hawkins, who began to spend more time hanging out there than he did checking out the surf. At first he tried to master the acoustic guitar, but failed "for whatever reason," as he tried to recall.

Hawkins hadn't really considered learning to drum; to him, it "was for idiots – you know, no one notices the drummer." Kleater persisted, taking him through the simplest of rock rhythms. To his shock, Hawkins was a natural; within a week he was playing along to *News Of The World*, just like a younger Roger Taylor. "And then my life just became drums, drums, drums."

Hawkins' first paying gig was with some buddies in a band called Sylvia – "sort of like an early Nineties Jane's Addiction thing," he explained. From there he connected with a Canadian singer, Sass Jordan, who had a European tour booked and was in need of a drummer. Hawkins signed up

---

* Years later, they would become friendly when Taylor and Queen guitarist Brian May befriended the Foos. Grohl insisted that Hawkins actually "stalked" May until he agreed to play on their *One By One* album.

straightaway, partly because he knew that another of his classic rock heroes, Aerosmith, were on the bill.

Just when Hawkins started to think that his only move might be selling drum kits from the back of a music store, he got a call from Scott Welch, the same contact who had got him the Sass Jordan job. Another Canadian singer/songwriter, Alanis Morissette, needed a drummer. Although Hawkins thought her soon-to-be-huge *Jagged Little Pill* proved she was "a really clever songwriter," to him it was simply another gig.

It was while Morissette was playing at a European festival in 1996 that Hawkins first met Dave Grohl. The pair met up again at the KROQ Christmas party and this time had a real chance to bond. Soon after, at the Whiskey in LA, they got loaded, played "slap in the face" while watching Jason (the son of "Bonzo") Bonham's band. Their connection was immediate; as soon as Grohl started speaking, Hawkins had a sudden realisation: "This guy's exactly like me." Soon after, when Hawkins learned that the Foos were without a drummer, he got in touch with Grohl via Franz Stahl, and offered his services. Grohl was enthusiastic but, at the same time, confused. Hawkins was drumming for a female artist with platinum sales; why would he want to "be in our little band"?

Grohl asked him, point blank: "Why play with us?" Hawkins replied that he loved Foo Fighters and was hoping to play in a "real" rock band. "I wanted to be part of something like that," Hawkins said, "not just part of this machine supporting someone else." His enlistment was sealed when Grohl drove by Hawkins' house and dropped off an advance copy of *The Colour And The Shape*.

However, soon after joining, Hawkins found that there were further upheavals in the band. With Goldsmith gone, Pat Smear also wanted out. "That was a splintered fucking band at that point," Hawkins later observed. "The band was just holding on by our fingertips this whole time." Nonetheless, although sitting at the back, Hawkins had enough onstage charisma to make up for Smear's departure. Hawkins was also fast becoming Grohl's biggest ally in the band, intensified when they moved into a bachelor pad in Laurel Canyon.

Grohl and Hawkins – a man sometimes referred to as "Grohl's evil twin" – rapidly became Hollywood party animals. "We would just go drag the Sunset Strip and bring it back to the house," he said. Grohl was more succinct. "It was a fucking shag cabin," he described, adding that the two spent the next year "fucking everybody and partying".

Hawkins made his Foos' debut a week before the release of *The Colour And The Shape*, with a secret show at Santa Monica's Alligator Lounge on April 19, followed by another unannounced set, two days later, at LA's Opium Den. This was followed by a run of promo dates, including another of their many *Letterman* appearances on May 15, a private party in Paris for the release of the movie *Blackout*, a Tower Records in-store event and a recording at MTV's London studios; they even Foo-ed Cannes, the site of the film world's most upscale festival. Their tour "proper" began with a date at Cambridge's Corn Exchange on May 19; by the end of the year, the band had played more than 80 shows across several continents with another 50 dates in support of the album following in 1998. It didn't take long for both the media and punters to recognise Hawkins' inner-Grohl; although slighter than his Foo leader, Hawkins hit the kit hard and often. "The Foos' new drummer, Taylor Hawkins," noted one writer, "is a shirtless blur of heavy pounding arms. Not bad for a man who used to play for Alanis Morissette." The tour finally wound down at the Reading Festival, playing the main stage to avoid another riot.

As monumental as that was for the band, however, their chance appearance on Ozzfest 98 fulfilled another of Dave Grohl's teenage dreams. This was the first time that the metal franchise had set up camp on UK soil, and a gaping hole opened up in the bill when nu-metallers Korn had to head back to LA for "personal reasons" days before the show at the Milton Keynes Bowl on June 20. Sharon Osbourne called Grohl, and offered him and the band the 55-minute slot. Then she casually mentioned that their spot on the bill was immediately before the Prince of Darkness himself and the re-formed Black Sabbath. Grohl's reponse was brief and to the point: "What? Are you on drugs? Are you insane?" As uncertain as Grohl was, he was relieved, not just by the response of the black T-shirt clad masses, but by the sight of Pantera's Phil Anselmo and Scott Ian of Anthrax, sidestage during the Foos' set, screaming along to 'My Hero' and 'I'll Stick Around'. It wasn't quite 'Iron Man', but the Foos were all right.

The lead-off single from *The Colour And The Shape*, 'Monkey Wrench', may have been mediocre, but it was an immediate radio hit, reaching the Top 10 of *Billboard*'s Mainstream Rock and Modern Rock Tracks charts, as well as charting highly in both England and Australia. Subsequent singles – 'Everlong', 'My Hero' and 'Walking After You' – all scored just as successfully. 'Everlong', in particular, reached a new Foos' high when it peaked at number three in the Modern Rock Tracks chart and four in the Mainstream Rock Tracks list.

Although *The Colour And The Shape* would eventually become the band's biggest album in the USA, shifting nearly two million copies and staying in the *Billboard* album chart for the best part of a year, the immediate critical response to the album was indifferent. At a time when such acts as the Chemical Brothers and the Prodigy were considered cutting edge, Foo Fighters seemed worryingly passé.

Rolling Stone, who'd championed the raw and ragged debut, awarded the album only three stars, astutely noting that Grohl was "working out some romantic issues". The review also found, a touch condescendingly, that "*Colour* has a big, radio-ready, modern-rock sound", exactly what Grohl was hoping to achieve.

Spin gave the album a six-out-of-10 rating, ambivalently observing that Grohl was "a simple rock guy in a simple rock band who occasionally manages to write some really good songs."

While the US press was undecided, over the water there was no such uncertainty. *The Independent* went as far as to cite the album as a symbol of the creative downturn of US rock bands in Nirvana's wake.

The *Daily Mail* couldn't find anything original amid the 13 tracks. "The resulting racket lacks nothing in terms of spirit, but has simply been played too many times before."

"At its worst," *Select* wrote, "[the album] puts remarkably little distance between Foo Fighters and any run-of-the-mill band with tattoos, big shorts, bleached hair and a bug up their ass."

In spite of these disparaging words *The Colour And The Shape* eventually reached *Q* magazine's "100 Greatest Albums Ever" list, while it became number 10 Reader's Choice in the *Kerrang!* list of "100 Albums You Must Hear Before You Die".

Grohl had no regrets about the spit and polish applied, insisting that the songs "deserved some serious production" in order to achieve his goal of making the album "sound as pristine, precise and powerful as possible". The popular consensus is that *The Colour . . .* was Grohl's "divorce album".

Internet whispers had been circulating in early 1997 about Pat Smear's departure from Foo Fighters. It was suggested that he had ideological conflicts towards their upcoming dates supporting the Rolling Stones, which conflicted with what Nate Mendel wryly termed "his Patness". There were also rumours of a power struggle between Smear and Grohl that Gold Mountain were keen to stamp on.

Smear wasn't the type to toe the line and, early in 1997, he let his bandmates know that he'd had enough of touring. He was starting to hate flying almost as much as he hated interviews (which he rarely granted in the first place). On the upside, he had bonded with new kid Hawkins over a shared love of Queen, Pink Floyd and the Police. Hawkins said that life with Smear was "like having a big sister in the band". Smear took the time to teach Grohl the guitar chords to the Beatles' 'Blackbird' and Grohl would talk up Smear at every opportunity, crowning him "a great guitar player", "the punkest of punk" and "the coolest guy in the world". Foo Fighters was the longest tour of duty that Smear had served with a band since the Germs, but he was ready to move on.

On September 4, the band arrived at the MTV Awards in New York with some trepidation. Smear had told them that he'd be announcing his departure on stage, during the band's three-song set. After performing 'My Hero', Smear threw his guitar on the ground and stalked off stage. As the crowd attempted to make sense of what was going on, Smear reappeared with Franz Stahl.

"I'd like to introduce Franz Stahl, who will be taking over," Smear told the confused audience. "Rock on guys. Foo Fighters!" With that he was gone, and the band broke into 'Everlong' as though nothing untoward had occurred. When Stahl disbanded Wool, Grohl inquired about him replacing Smear. Stahl was an easy fit: he'd known Grohl for years and his warp-speed style of playing was tailor-made for Foo Fighters' propulsive live sound. Grohl first approached him in 1995 about joining the original Foo Fighters, so in some ways it was a wish fulfilled. With Pete Stahl currently part of the Foos' road crew, his transition was made that much easier.

As for Smear, he found a new gig hosting MTV's House Of Style. "I just love to dress up," he prophetically said, just prior to leaving Foo Fighters. "It could be designer clothes or a clown suit, it doesn't matter."*

---

* Smear is currently involved with a Germs re-formation as well as the production of the Germs' biopic, *What We Do Is Secret*; Rick Gonzalez, most recently seen in *War Of The Worlds*, is portraying him in the film.

When approached by Grohl, Franz Stahl had been in Japan, helping a singer named Jay, who'd led a popular local act called Luncay, tour his solo record. Although he'd known about Smear's departure, Stahl hadn't been given a definite time and place for his Foos' debut, so he went ahead with the Japanese dates. He then got the call from Grohl, which resulted in him flying from Japan to LA, then changing planes for New York, in order to practise briefly before being led on stage in front of an MTV audience of millions. "It was only one song," Stahl said later, "but it was still the longest moment of my life."

Pat Smear may have considered opening for the Rolling Stones an act of heresy, but Grohl – who had tried to play Stones covers in his first neighbourhood band – had no such qualms. Prior to the two dates, on October 16 and 17, 1997, at Giant's Stadium in New Jersey, Grohl could barely control his enthusiasm. "Opening for the Rolling Stones will be such a profound moment in my life," he stated. "It's an honour. They're one of the last great rock bands." Stahl was more phlegmatic: "I'm just looking forward to hanging out with Keith Richards."

The reality of the gigs was slightly less appealing. The Stones may have been raking in millions of dollars, but their organisation operated with a notoriously tight fist. As support act the Foo's weren't granted the luxury of a guest list and were told that although they had 100 tickets reserved for them, they had to cough up $64 apiece to buy them. The Foos didn't even rate a dressing room; the band got ready for one of their biggest ever shows in a trailer in the car park. "That was fucked up," Grohl surmised. "That was bullshit." The Stones' frugality became even harder to swallow when reviewing the gross ticket sales over the two nights: the pensionable rockers raked in a useful US $6,823,242.

A more rewarding gig was the Bumbershoot Festival in Seattle, held a few weeks prior to the Stones debacle. For the first time since their impromptu free-for-all with the Stinky Puffs, Grohl was joined onstage by his erstwhile bandmate, Chris Novoselic. Hawkins was especially thrilled. "I was like, 'Wow, I'm in Nirvana right now.'"

Their stage jam was a happy accident. Mendel was fed up getting hit in the face with "shit from the audience". The band only had themselves to blame for this. Like the Beatles being showered with jelly babies during the height of Beatlemania, it literally rained sweets during some Foos' gigs after their piss-take of a Mentos ad in the 1996 video for 'Big Me'. When

Mendel stormed off stage, Novoselic casually picked up the bass and launched into Led Zeppelin's 'Communication Breakdown'. "It was awesome," Grohl summed up afterwards.

In spite of all the setbacks – the departure of Goldsmith and Smear, the need to break in two new members, the uneasy critical response to their second album – Grohl insisted Foo Fighters was at "a great level" in 1997.

Dave Grohl had had his fill of the Hollywood lifestyle. "I fucking despise this city," he said, just before relocating. "I think everything about it is just vile . . . what I call the 'Hollywood element' has started to dominate a lot of popular music and that greatly upsets me. Nothing seems sacred here. The whole thing here in Hollywood about fame and beauty and the glorification of the celebrity just made me want to go crazy and kill everyone."

As much as Grohl and Hawkins immersed themselves in the hedonistic lifestyle of the city, the cons eventually outweighed the pros, as Grohl described, "Every evening that you went out, you would be surrounded by people trying to be something they weren't."

Grohl had also had his fill of mouthy rockers who "think that they're omni-important or something more than human. It broke my heart to see people whose one desire was to be larger than life." Hawkins was prepared to name names. "Marilyn Manson had nothing to say on his last album, so . . . he goes to Hollywood and does a bunch of cocaine with a bunch of assholes and got an album [*Mechanical Animals*] out of it. Courtney fucking Love had nothing to say . . . they end up saying fuck all." This hatred of Tinsel Town would permeate the third Foo Fighters' album.

Grohl had the foresight to apply the brake on his debauchery before it got out of hand. After toying with the idea of buying a farm, he opted instead for a spread in Virginia located roughly a mile from his former high school. Hawkins shifted base to the more tranquil Topanga Canyon.

Grohl had contemplated going back to his roots for more than a year. The notion first came about when he was asked to produce an album by an Alabama band called Verbena.* Grohl admitted that he "really didn't know how to produce anything", but agreed to produce the record if

---

* *Into The Pink*, released in 1999.

Adam Kasper, who'd engineered the final Nirvana demos, was also hired. Verbena had enough of a budget to build their own studio. Grohl was impressed enough to inform Kasper, "I'm going to build my own studio, too."

What Grohl had in mind was a totally self-contained recording and rehearsal complex, where the Foos could operate with an absolute minimum of industry interference. "I want to be the David Koresh* of rock'n'roll," he chuckled. Like Barrett Jones before him, Kasper was an ideal studio collaborator with whom Grohl had immediately connected when working on Nirvana's 'You Know You're Right' back in 1994. "He's just a super mellow guy," was Grohl's character assessment.

Kasper had a good set of ears and was a first-rate engineer, everything Grohl required in a studio sidekick. The Seattle-based Kasper engineered Pearl Jam's *Vs* and *Vitalogy* albums, and would also produce their *Riot Act* LP. He had also worked with the Posies on their excellent *Frosting On The Beater* set, Sunny Day Real Estate's 1998 comeback, *How It Feels To Be Something On*, and produced records for Cat Power and Soundgarden (engineering and producing their 1996 swansong, *Down On The Upside*). The latter association came in handy when borrowing equipment to help Grohl set up his studio in time for the Foos' forthcoming recording sessions.

Grohl and Kasper visited Ocean Way Studio in Nashville, where they found the right mixing desk, formerly used by Allen Sides, a respected engineer/producer and the owner of Ocean Way's parent studio in LA. The sale was clinched when Grohl heard that his teenage heroes Lynyrd Skynyrd may have used the board. He and Kasper then flew to New York to pick up an analogue tape machine. These acquisitions were brought back to the basement of Grohl's Virginia home – the site of the new studio he christened Studio 606.

Grohl's intentions for the Foos' third album were made clear: he wanted to make a record that was "real and natural", to avoid "any fucking computers, anything digital or any of that auto-tuning shit". If each successive record Grohl made was a reaction to the one that came

---

* The infamous head of a religious cult based near Waco, Texas, who became embroiled in a gunfight with a rival leader in 1987. Koresh was later tried for and acquitted on an attempted murder charge.

before, this was never more evident than with *There Is Nothing Left To Lose*.

He also rejected the idea of any kind of imposed recording schedule and took the ultimate step in making this a reality by severing the band's contract with Capitol. With Gary Gersh gone from the label, Grohl invoked the "key man" clause leaving the Foos looking for a new home.

Initially, Franz Stahl had spoken excitedly about his new role in Foo Fighters, saying that his "brightest moments" playing music had been with Grohl in Scream. Some months before recording began on the third Foos' album, Stahl said, "I can't wait to start recording and writing songs, leaving my mark on tape and playing my own parts."

However when the band got together in a small practice space to work through the new songs earmarked for *There Is Nothing Left To Lose*, the room began to feel uncomfortably small. Put simply, Stahl was left unmoved by the songs* and was not the type to conceal his feelings – hardly surprising for somebody who had controlled the destinies of virtually all the bands he'd been involved with.

"It just seemed like the three of us were moving in one direction and Franz wasn't," a disappointed Grohl later reflected. "With Franz it was a musical decision. I was in tears. He was one of my oldest friends and we wanted it to work out so badly, but it didn't." Mendel was equally upset by Stahl's departure, revealing it was a "traumatic experience for me". Stahl had been a Foo Fighter for less than a year but he clearly left his mark.

With the band only days from commencing work at Studio 606, Grohl boldly decided to record as a trio – more out of necessity than choice, he had no time to teach a new guitarist the parts for the songs despite the relaxed schedule he'd imposed.†

Grohl's approach to finding a new record label was to pitch the Foo's "as if we were a new band". There was a slight risk in Grohl's cavalier plan, because the music industry was going through another of its cyclical slumps. However, Grohl was in the enviable position of being a desirable

---

* Allegedly, Stahl felt the songs lacked "muscle".

† During this time, Tracii Guns, a member of Eighties glam-metallers LA Guns, slipped Grohl his phone number after hearing of the guitarist vacancy. "Fuck him," was Grohl's prompt response.

commodity after two successful albums, not to mention his impressive track record with Nirvana. The first direct question he asked of each prospective candidate was: "OK, how fucked up is your label now?" According to Grohl, "Everyone seemed a little shaky. There were many labels that had been solid and doing the same thing for years and years, and there were a lot of new labels that were trying to make their way up." A logical move would have been for Grohl to sign with a healthy corporate major but he chose RCA, a label that he admitted "didn't have much of a rock roster".

Grohl was seduced by RCA's enthusiasm.* At their first meeting, he was told: "We really want to work with you guys. We really want you here." The deal was clinched, all on the strength of two new Foo Fighters tracks. It also helped that RCA's offer was, in the words of their new signing, "fucking crazy-ass".†

With the deal done, Grohl, Hawkins and Mendel retreated to Grohl's basement, recording for four months. "There was no clock ticking, no phone ringing off the hook, nothing," Grohl recalled. "It was just us living in the same house in Virginia for four months. It was great." (Two tracks – 'Live-In Skin' and 'Learn To Fly' – were later taped at Conway Studios in LA.) The band's approach to each song was just as straightforward: Grohl would sketch something out on acoustic guitar, then Hawkins and Mendel would flesh it out. As Grohl described, "The three of us would sit down with the basic structure of the song and say, 'OK, which way are we going to fuck this song up?'"

Their first instinct was to "grunge" up the sound, but they decided not to go the obvious route. Taking a cue from Tom Petty (which Grohl readily admitted), the trio moved in another direction altogether. "We thought, 'What happens if we have a song where the dynamics don't go from quiet to loud? What happens if the riff in the verse is the same as the chorus, but we just turn it into something else when it hits the chorus?'"

When not laying down guitar tracks, Grohl was also moving forward

---

* RCA's A&R man, Bruce Flohr, could sometimes be spotted in the thick of Foo Fighters' moshpits.
† So "crazy-ass", in fact, that Grohl's lawyer denied my request to determine the deal's exact amount. Suffice it to say that several more zeroes made their way onto Grohl's next bank statement.

with his vocals; attempting to sing more and scream less. He and Kasper
dubbed all the vocals in the control room, rather than in some isolated
booth – a move Kasper considered a "very bold jump" on Grohl's part.
Grohl also drummed on a large part of the album, because Hawkins was in
what he later described as a "fucked-up state of mind". While Grohl had
made the smart choice of removing himself from LA's myriad temptations,
Hawkins was still indulging in the kind of rock star stupidity which would
almost bring about his undoing. Despite this, Grohl described the sessions
as "laid-back"; there was no repeat of the perfectionism of *The Colour And
The Shape* or the rough-hewn method recording of *Foo Fighters*. Grohl,
Mendel and Hawkins (when he showed up) made the album they wanted
at their own leisurely pace.

They may have been searching for new directions in the studio, but
there was a certain unmistakable "Foo-ness" to *There Is Nothing Left To
Lose*, which roared into life with 'Stacked Actors', Grohl's anti-Hollywood
diatribe, sporting the dirtiest fuzz riff heard on a Grohl recording since
Chris Novoselic's bass strangling on Nirvana's 'Territorial Pissings'. Grohl
had actually come up with the riff when approached to write a song for
one of his heroes, Ozzy Osbourne. Grohl had been trying to imitate the
type of lick that powered such Ozzy tracks as 'Crazy Train', but when
stumbling upon the 'Stacked Actors' riff he knew it was a keeper.

Lyrically, Grohl took no prisoners. "I wrote 'Stacked Actors' about
everything that is fake and everything that is plastic and glamorous and
unreal [in Hollywood] . . . truth be told, I fucking hated Hollywood,
hated the whole life, hated most of the people we met. That's what I'm
saying in 'Stacked Actors'." Of course, many conjectured that one of
Grohl's likely targets was Courtney Love, but once again Grohl sidestepped a public sparring match with the woman Steve Albini once
dubbed a "psycho hosebeast". "I dropped out of high school to get away
from that kind of shit, y'know?" he pleaded.

The fury of 'Stacked Actors' wasn't the sonic template for the whole
album, although there was an unmistakable anger powering such tracks as
'Gimme Stitches', 'Breakout' and 'Live-In Skin', which all gave Grohl the
chance to spill his guts and scream until his face turned blue, while
Hawkins and Mendel did their best to keep up with Grohl's warp-speed
riffing. (Hawkins proved that he was up to the challenge; his drumming
throughout the album strikes the same mix of precision and urgency that

Grohl delivered, on Gil Norton's suggestion, for *The Colour And The Shape*.) But there was more to *There Is Nothing Left To Lose* than punk rock and venting. Grohl's melodic strengths shone through on the nostalgic strum of 'Next Year', which would make for another odd video, with the band cast as astronauts, and 'Learn To Fly', a song which, when released as a single, became the album's biggest hit,* despite Grohl feeling it wasn't truly representative. "[It's] one of the more middle-of-the-road songs from the record," he insisted. He also disliked the harmless, gentle strum of 'Next Year', which became the theme song for the TV sitcom *Ed*, bluntly dismissing it as "a piece of shit".

The success of 'Learn To Fly' – the song spent six months on *Billboard*'s Modern Rock Tracks chart, almost eclipsing 'Everlong's 28 week stay – was considerably helped by the Jesse Peretz-directed promo, which eventually won a Grammy for Best Short Form Video. Inspired by the Zucker Brothers' 1980 comedy classic *Airplane!*† it cast the Foos as both saviours of a seemingly doomed aircraft and as goofy, grinning members of the flight crew. Grohl also starred as a camp flight attendant and Tenacious D, comprising actor Jack Black and his sideman Kyle Gass, made a cameo. Grohl grew to dislike the clip intensely, once attributing the Foo's entire success to "that fucking airplane video".

Just like such previous Foo tracks as 'February Stars' and 'Oh, George', Grohl wasn't mad about 'Learn To Fly', admitting that it was one of his least favourite songs on the record. He also had some trouble trying to explain the song's lyric, which was his attempt to give due credit to his friends and family, who'd stuck with him after his messy divorce and rough patch in Hollywood. "It's kind of [about] looking for inspiration, just trying to find life," was the best Grohl could manage. Grohl wasn't even sure that the song was the ideal single, which showed how little he understood about the machinations of US rock radio, or the tastes of the great unwashed. "On the last record it was simple," he admitted, "the first one ['Monkey Wrench'] was rocking, the second one ['Everlong'] melodic, the third one ['My Hero'] a ballad. This is a more diverse album; every song has its own direction."

* It reached the top of *Billboard*'s Modern Rock Tracks chart, two on *Billboard*'s Mainstream Rock Tracks chart and peaked at 13 on the Hot 100.
† Re-titled *Flying High* in some territories.

No less than five charting singles were lifted from *There Is Nothing Left To Lose*, which, like both its predecessors, sold more than a million copies in the US alone within six weeks of its early November 1999 release, going on to score a Grammy for Best Rock Album.* The mundane 'Generator', featuring the dodgiest voice-box solo this side of Peter Frampton's 'Do You Feel Like I Do', became another radio hit and live staple, as did four-on-the-floor rocker 'Breakout', which made serious inroads in various *Billboard* charts (ditto 'Stacked Actors', scaling the Mainstream Rock Tracks Top 10). The latter was one track that Grohl was happy to talk up; it would also become a live staple for the band. "It just fucking kills, man," Grohl insisted. "I'm so glad that it's the first song on the album. It opens the record with a sledgehammer. It's us saying, 'Fuck it,' again." Mendel and Hawkins would also publicly pledge their allegiance to 'Stacked Actors'.

Grohl, however, was also in favour of the album's less-obvious tunes, especially the slowburning 'Aurora', a track he described as "a nostalgic look back at Seattle and the life I once had. It's probably the heaviest thing I've ever written." In an interview with *Kerrang!*, Grohl went further by declaring that 'Aurora' was "probably the greatest song we've ever written – because it makes everything else just look like shit. In a good way, of course." There was a second key influence on 'Aurora'. Grohl's grandmother had recently died and the song's introspective, meditative lyric reflected his thoughts on her passing. "Whenever you go through something as deep and profound as the death of a family member or friend, you really get knocked back by how huge and at the same time insignificant life can seem," Grohl profoundly stated. And he was right; the song had all the anthemic qualities of a failed track like 'February Stars' – the military drumming, the repetitive riff, a slow-burning melody – but didn't lose itself in schmaltz or production overkill. Like the best Foo Fighters tracks (think 'I'll Stick Around', 'My Hero') 'Aurora' succeeded because Grohl sang his heartfelt lyric with conviction and the band played with absolute intent.

For an album that set out its stall with the noisy 'Stacked Actors', *There Is Nothing Left To Lose* wasn't quite the dirty, scruffy animal that Grohl and

---

* *There Is Nothing Left To Lose* climbed to the tenth spot in the *Billboard* 200 album list and also reached the same position in the UK.

co. had planned. The radio-friendly mix of white-knuckled rockers and heartfelt tunes was in many ways a consolidation of the Foos' formula. Grohl, however, was insistent that the album – or at least its title – was a righteous statement on his part – down to the Danny Clinch cover shot of the Foo Fighters' logo tattooed on his neck.

"I was talking with a friend," Grohl said, "about when you experience these emotions after you've been through a long, difficult period and you finally give into this feeling that, quite simply, there is nothing left to lose. It can seem . . . positive, desperate and reckless." Grohl joked that he considered titling the album *Fuck It*, but it's unlikely that Wal-Mart let alone his new label, RCA, would have gone for the idea. After the one-man-band effort of *Foo Fighters* and the troubled sessions of *The Colour And The Shape*, Grohl felt that *There Is Nothing Left To Lose* was the closest Foo Fighters had yet come to making a genuine "band" album. Of course, that was a little easier to achieve, given that there were only three of them making the record. "The . . . album was the closest we got to that approach," Grohl said. "Taylor, Nate and myself, just the three of us."

What Grohl wasn't giving away, however, was that he and Hawkins were sharing drumming duties, as "Grohl's evil twin" started to disappear into a drug-induced funk, which added a little mystery to the meaning behind the track 'MIA'. Grohl would never reveal who played drums on each track, or who did the share of songwriting. The album credit simply read: "Written by Foo Fighters". (Elsewhere on the liner notes, Grohl stated, for some mysterious reason: "Jimmy Swanson is God.") Grohl would play down Hawkins' slide, simply stating that their playing methods were now almost identical. "Even my best friends, who I've known for 15 years and recorded with, can't tell the difference between us, because Taylor and I have adopted each other's styles." Grohl let his guard down slightly just once, when he admitted to drumming on "about four or five songs". Eventually, Hawkins would come clean and confess that he only played on roughly half the LP, due to his "fucked up state of mind" at the time.

One thing that the album did achieve was to distance the band from the precision and studiocraft of *The Colour And The Shape*. It wasn't their best set of songs, but it did have more energy to it than their second LP, as most obviously shown by 'Stacked Actors'. In a comment that could easily be read as a dig at Gil Norton, even though the producer maintains that there was, and still is, absolutely no grief between him and the Foo leader, Grohl said of the album, "You don't need an über-producer twiddling things into fiddliness, you don't need ten grand's worth of NASA's computers, you don't need to be near the industry to create something worthwhile. In fact, it's absolutely the reverse."

Once again, the press response to the album was mixed. *Rolling Stone* increased their rating to three-and-a-half stars, writer Greg Kot noting that Grohl "attempts to sneak up" on writing an out-and-out power ballad in the vein of the Goo Goo Dolls' 'Iris' (a hit at the time). "There are few quicker tickets to platinum for a former alt-rocker than a power ballad," Kot opined. The review acknowledged that Grohl had expanded on his once-limited vocal range, adopting "a jazzy cadence on 'Stacked Actors' and a hint of twang on 'Ain't It The Life'."

NME were less complimentary. "Nothing left to lose? Oh, I wouldn't say that," the review snapped, contrasting the "promising opening gambit" of 'Stacked Actors' with lesser tracks "[that] can . . . bore the pants off you". The reviewer accepted that 'Learn To Fly' and 'MIA' were "still as good tunes [sic] as this band has ever produced".

The responses from fans on the internet forum "Rate It All" summed up the wildly differing opinions as to the album's merits. "The worst Foo Fighters' album, but it's still good," declared one confused fan. "This one was way too mellow for me," wrote another, who admitted to "enjoy[ing] their harder rock songs more". "You suck," wrote another, a comment one could only assume was directed at Grohl.

For the first time, Grohl was in the unfamiliar role of auditioning guitarists in the search for Franz Stahl's replacement (neither Stahl nor Smear had formally auditioned when joining). He had committed Foo Fighters to almost 18 globe-trotting months on the road to promote *There Is Nothing Left To Lose* – featuring over 100 gigs, interspersed with TV appearances and radio spots.

Of the 35 hopefuls who auditioned, Chris Shiflett seemed to be the least likely candidate. Lacking Smear's charisma or Stahl's punk roots, his playing style was very much like Mendel's – he remained stationary, peeling off riffs and power chords while maintaining an impassive mask, like some kind of punk Buddha.

Christopher Aubrey Shiflett was born in LA on May 6, 1971, and grew up in the comfortable surroundings of Santa Barbara, a predominantly white, relatively well-heeled city of 90,000 – sometimes referred to as the "American Riviera" – situated an hour north of the city. The Shifletts lived next door to a Mexican family, who played Mariachi music day and night. "I still hate Mariachi music," Shiflett declared in 2003.

Just like Grohl and Hawkins, Shiflett grew up listening to FM radio, and his first rock gig was seeing pint-sized belter Ronnie James Dio, on his 'Holy Diver' tour, followed by Night Ranger and Alcatraz. Shiflett then hooked up with a couple of guys old enough to drive, travelling to LA where he caught early versions of Poison, Guns N' Roses, Faster Pussycat and Jet Boy, "all . . . before they got record deals". As much as Shiflett enjoyed LA's sleaziest rock acts, his true hero was Ace Frehley, from grease-painted, cartoon rockers Kiss, whose music his older brothers introduced him to. While in Santa Barbara, Shiflett played guitar in a non-descript outfit that opened for Scream, although he and Grohl did not meet that night. Along with music, Shiflett was a dedicated boxing fan and later, in his early thirties, he took up the sport.

A high-school dropout, Shiflett shared an apartment in LA with his brother for a time, but he repeatedly clashed with the neighbours and moved out. "The people downstairs thought we were playing sports in the apartment," he recalled. Along with friend Joey Cape (vocalist of the punk band Lag Wagon), Shiflett's next stop was San Francisco, working in the office of Fat Wreck Chords, a well-regarded punk-pop outlet, and the label of choice for NoFX, Sick Of It All and many others. After playing in punk acts 22 Jacks and Me First & the Gimme Gimmes,* Shiflett landed his first paying gig in No Use For A Name, who also recorded for Fat Wreck.

The band had lost their guitarist, and Fat Mike, No Use's vocalist, walked into the Fat Wreck offices, asking, "Does anybody know anyone who plays guitar who wants to try out?" Seeing his chance, Shiflett volunteered his services. He auditioned for the band on a Thursday and by the following Monday he was on tour, the start of a four-and-a-half year tenure with No Use For A Name.

Shiflett only applied for the Foos' job at the eleventh hour, when he learned about the auditions via a friend, who was a colleague of Grohl's

---

* The words "gimme gimme" are tattooed inside Shiflett's lower lip.

lawyer, Jill Berliner. Shiflett was sent a tape containing four songs: a pair of straight-ahead rockers ('Everlong' and 'Off The Ground') and two slightly more complex tracks ('A320', from the *Godzilla* soundtrack, and 'Aurora'). By the time an extremely nervous Shiflett arrived in LA for his audition, Grohl's patience was rapidly running out. "After a while," he said of the audition process, "you felt like you were a hooker in a red light area, just one after another." Despite his lack of stagecraft, Shiflett seemed to fit in with the band on a personal level, having spent most of his initial try-out talking rather than playing. "There was no real interrogation process," Shiflett later said. "We just shot the shit and talked about tour stuff, band stuff and silly stories."

Shiflett left the audition feeling upbeat. Even if he didn't pass the audition, he'd lived out his dream, because for the past few years, No Use For A Name had tried everything to land a Foo Fighters support slot. A week later, Grohl called and invited Shiflett to LA for a second jam, following which they continued bonding by getting cheerfully smashed back at the band's hotel. Late the following afternoon, Grohl called to tell a hungover Shiflett that he'd scored the gig. Shiflett went out and tasted the hair of the dog with some LA buddies.

Shiflett had very little time to savour his good fortune as Foo Fighters hit the road, spending a lengthy stretch playing arenas in support of Red Hot Chili Peppers. In much the same way he'd talked up Smear and Stahl, Grohl praised the new recruit. "He is the best guitarist and the best vocalist we've had in the band yet," Grohl gushed. "He's enthusiastic, excited and genuinely stoked to be in the band. It makes us all excited; it makes us feel like we're starting over again."

CHAPTER ELEVEN

The Million Dollar Demos

"When I was young, my favourite bands were fucking Bad Brains, Void, Minor Threat . . . and here I am playing music that sounds like the fucking Eagles."
— Dave Grohl

THROUGHOUT 2000 into 2001, Foo Fighters spent the best part of 18 months touring North America, Europe, New Zealand and Australia. They may have been the support act on the Red Hot Chili Peppers bill, but the full houses didn't hold back. Twelve thousand Baltimore fans treated them like homecoming heroes, as *Kerrang!* reported — after all, Grohl did own a house in nearby Virginia, which almost made it a home game for the head Foo. "The Foos are received like headliners by the capacity crowd," they noted. The Peppers themselves were part of the FF fan club; their drummer Chad Smith was spotted feeding grapes to an indulged Hawkins while he played. Life on the bus was a vast improvement for Shiflett, who'd been "jamming econo" for years as part of No Use For A Name. Their tour bus was the size of a house, equipped with the obligatory Playstation, stereo and video; it was one smooth ride. Shiflett was also quickly establishing himself as a ladies' man. When Grohl was asked how the band managed to avoid the usual "if-it-moves-shag-it" lifestyle, Grohl simply replied: "You've obviously not been out on the road with Chris. You should follow him around for a week. Go on, ask him about the Swedish au pairs." Shiflett smirked and went back to enjoying his post-show beer.

The band spent five months on the Chili Peppers roadshow. Looking back, Grohl preferred the first half of the tour, where they played indoor venues. "There were a lot of nights when it really felt like our show, not like we were opening for somebody," Grohl said. "And that was the best feeling." The second half of the tour wasn't so fulfilling. The band were now playing cavernous arenas, concrete bunkers better suited for basketball games. "You're playing . . . at 7.30 pm, it's all seated, and you feel like Steely Dan or something," Grohl grumbled. "It's just not conducive to our frenetic, energetic live shows." The trade-off, of course, were the handsome fees deposited into various Foos accounts at the end of the tour.

Grohl, who'd first toured Australia with Nirvana almost a decade earlier as part of the inaugural Big Day Out, once declared it the "coolest country on the planet. All they want to do is drink and fuck on the beach. And there's nothing wrong with that." His impression of Oz soured slightly in January 2000.

The key event in the southern rock'n'roll summer, the Big Day Out was known to insiders as the "Big Day Off", and with good reason. The festival offered big money, great weather, excellent conditions and an easy schedule, with half a dozen dates spread over a fortnight in January. There was an anything-goes attitude among the 50,000-plus crowd at each show, who were usually well and truly loaded by the time the headlining act hit the stage. Indulgence was also tolerated backstage, where dope and booze were consumed, along with the first class on-site catering for the artistes.

Foo Fighters rented mopeds for the tour and Grohl had become so enamoured of his new bike that he even used it to arrive onstage. (The look complemented his trucker's sideburns, which he felt created "that whole Lynyrd Skynyrd redneck vibe".) After a few post-gig beers on the Gold Coast checking out Primal Scream and the Hellacopters, Grohl headed back to his nearby hotel, not taking into consideration Australia's tough drink-driving laws which were tightened even further during the Christmas/New Year period.

When Grohl saw a police roadblock ahead, where drivers were being breath-tested, he assumed he would be waved through. Grohl was very wrong. A burly cop pulled him over and asked him to blow into the bag that measured blood alcohol levels. Anyone registering 0.05 and over was considered DUI (Driving Under Influence) and Grohl scored somewhere near 0.15.

Initially, Grohl thought the situation funny, especially when concert-goers drove past, recognised the Foo Fighter and beeped their horns, yelling: "All right Dave! Great show!" When told he was over the limit,

Grohl offered to leave his moped behind and walk back to the hotel. Grohl didn't quite realise what a jam he was in.

"Sorry, mate," the burly cop replied. "Gonna have to put you in the watch house tonight." What made an embarrassing situation even more humbling for Grohl was the company he kept in the lock-up: he was squeezed into a cell with Big Day Out punters who'd overindulged. At three in the morning, Grohl used his obligatory one phone call to Mendel to organise his bail.

A few months later, Grohl copped an $800 fine and, somewhat point-lessly, was suspended from driving in Australia for three months. Although no conviction was recorded the incident remained problematic. "Now, every time I go to Australia, I get stopped at immigration and have to tell my ridiculous story," he groaned.

Back from touring, a restless Grohl placed a call to Adam Kasper. Grohl had a vague idea for a side project, a sort of hardcore "all-stars" album, where he would write and record backing tracks and invite his favourite metal vocalists to scream over the top. Grohl "borrowed" the idea from Black Sabbath guitarist, Tony Iommi, who had recently recorded 12 tracks, each with a different vocalist (including Grohl). Thus, Probot was born, although in this case, Grohl decided only to use singers from under-ground metal bands who'd peaked in the mid to late Eighties. He'd also repay numerous favours from his days in Scream; more than one Probot guest had offered Grohl and the band their floors for the night in the late Eighties.

One of the other inspirations for Probot was the Foos' use of Sepultura as warm-up music for their most recent tour dates, as Grohl recalled: "I would find myself listening to Sepultura's *Chaos AD* before going on stage, and then singing a song like 'Learn To Fly', which I thought was funny, 'Like, what am I doing with my life, man?' When I was young, my favourite bands were fucking Bad Brains, Void, Minor Threat . . . and here I am playing music that sounds like the fucking Eagles."

The basic tracks for the Probot album came quickly. Grohl would sit on his couch, in front of a big-screen TV, a guitar slung over his shoulder, a beer handy, and a Peavey practice amp plugged in. A set of sludgy, indus-trial riffs came to him as naturally as his first cigarette and coffee of the morning. He'd then yell out to Kasper, "Come on, let's go downstairs," where a rough arrangement was worked out on drums, which Kasper caught on tape. "[They] were basically just riff instrumentals, with no suggestion of melody or vocals or anything."

Grohl didn't approach the project seriously – for him it was just a way of blowing off steam after touring an album of Foos' songs that he felt weren't the easiest or most satisfying to play on stage. Over the course of a few days, several beers and numerous trips from the couch to the downstairs studio, Grohl and Kasper had enough material. A few copies were made of the master tape and, on a whim, the name Probot was written on the reel and placed on the shelf in Grohl's studio. With yet another series of Foo Fighters UK dates imminent in August 2001, Grohl didn't have any further time to dedicate to the project.

The Foos had last convened on March 19, at the annual Rock and Roll Hall of Fame dinner, when Grohl and Hawkins inducted Queen and jammed with their heroes Brian May and Roger Taylor. If Grohl had stated that 2000 was "the best year we've ever had", 2001 was to prove the Foos' *annus horribilis*.

After playing a few dates at the Bizarre Festival in Germany on August 17, followed by two V2001 shows – the first at Staffordshire on August 18, the second at Hylands Park at Chelmsford the following day – the band were set to travel to Portugal for another festival when Grohl was informed that Hawkins had OD'd at the band's Kensington Hotel and was on his way to the Accident and Emergency ward. The remaining tour dates were cancelled and the Foos' press people immediately went into spin mode, releasing a statement that Hawkins was suffering from "exhaustion".

Ever since he and Grohl had shared a Hollywood "shag pad", Hawkins was known as a party animal. Grohl was fully aware of his drummer's off-stage recreational activities – they shared the occasional joint, a rare concession by the resolutely drug-free Grohl – and made a point of letting him know he "wasn't stoked about it". According to Hawkins, Grohl told him, "Hey, it's your life. I care about you, but if you're going to fuck up, I don't want to talk to you about it."

The first rumour to emerge was that Hawkins had hoovered up three grams of coke and suffered serious heart trouble. The truth was that he'd been taking painkillers for some time and, in Hawkins' own words, "I took too many of them and went into a coma for two days. It was very serious." Although reluctant to discuss the source of his problem, Hawkins admitted that "relationship stuff outside the band" contributed to his near-downfall, which compounded his "insecurities". "In a lot of ways, I felt very intimidated drumming in a band with the best drummer in the world," he said, uncannily echoing William Goldsmith's sentiments. "I think that contributed to my insecurities."

As Hawkins lay near death in a coma, Grohl wandered long into the night around London's streets, talking out loud like a madman. He felt exactly the same way when Kurt Cobain had flown too close to the sun. Grohl hadn't prayed since Catholic school, but as he later revealed, "I was asking myself, 'How could this happen to me twice in my life?' It felt like a member of my family had fallen ill."

Having witnessed Cobain's disintegration at close hand, Grohl even seriously considered ending the band right there. "I just remember saying that day, 'For right now, our band doesn't exist and I don't want to talk about any band things at all.'"

Thankfully, Hawkins gradually emerged from his coma. As he regained strength, his immediate reaction to his near-death experience was one of embarrassment. "Believe me," Hawkins later said, "I'm not proud of what happened. [A] member of a rock band – the drummer of a rock band, no less – takes too many drugs, becomes ill, has to go into rehab [as Hawkins did upon returning to the USA]. If you spell it out like that," Hawkins admitted, "it's just so embarrassing."

While Hawkins convalesced and prepared himself, both mentally and physically, for the Foos' fourth album sessions, in yet another burst of energy, Grohl laid down roughly 20 drum tracks for an upcoming album by Tenacious D. It was the perfect release for Grohl the drummer, who wailed on the drums like some kind of pagan rock god. As *Hot Press* magazine noted, drumming behind Tenacious D gave Grohl "the opportunity to air the kind of Spinal Tap chops that would've got him laughed out of rehearsals with any of his other bands. [He's] playing like he's been let out of a cage." Grohl was one of the most vocal fans of the LA-based duo who guest-starred in the Foos' 'Learn To Fly' video.* Grohl spotted in

---

* Grohl eventually appeared in the video for Tenacious D's hit single 'Tribute', unrecognisable in his role as a shiny demon. Black and Grohl also jammed 'My Hero' together on *Letterman*.

Tenacious D's wild, sometimes out-of-control sense of humour something that was missing in modern rock. Modern rock was leaving Grohl cold. "I roll on the ground laughing with tears rolling down my cheeks when I see some new rock band with a sexy lead singer with his shirt off, all oiled down, singing about Jesus." When Grohl admitted that "everyone else is becoming a little too earnest," he may have been thinking about life within his own band, something Hawkins' ordeal had made all too clear.

In December 2001, Foos began recording at Grohl's Virginia studio, with the intention of recapturing the stripped-back sound they'd found for *There Is Nothing Left To Lose*. Grohl had about 20 ideas for songs, which he brought into the studio. The band would bang out a rudimentary backing track, and then Grohl would take his first run at a vocal. But things weren't coming together. "I'd get halfway through . . . and scrap the whole fucking song," said Grohl, "something we'd [just] spent a week on." Grohl wasn't alone in feeling that something wasn't right with these early tracks. Was it because the band was rusty, or Hawkins needed further recuperation, or Grohl still hadn't got his side interests out of his system?

Nobody was willing, or able, to specify quite what the problem was, until Grohl realised that the band were simply trying too hard. They were unconsciously making another "big rock record that everyone could latch onto and sing along with" like *The Colour And The Shape*, that drained any spontaneity from the recordings, as Grohl later recalled. "We wound up in the studio acting as surgeons; we were too fucking clinical."

"No one was happy with it," Shiflett confirmed.

Grohl's next move was to call the band's manager, John Silva, for some much-needed perspective. After listening to the work to date, Silva offered Grohl some useful advice: "Stop trying to write hit singles, and go back to being weird."

The band was faced with a dilemma. They were 10 songs, several months and at least US $500,000 into a project which, to date, had produced unsatisfactory results. Grohl decided to shelve the album. "We just fucking scrapped the whole thing," he said. "It was not good enough." Grohl later confirmed to me exactly what the original recordings lacked. "By focusing on production," he said, "we lost focus on the best part of the band – raw energy. It didn't have that spark, man." As word of the aborted sessions leaked out, the original recordings became known as "The Million Dollar Demos". When the *NME* asked, "Is it over for the Foos?" it was a pertinent question, especially as no official rebuttal followed.

During the 2002 northern winter, Foo Fighters agreed to play two shows at the Winter Olympics at Mormon HQ, Salt Lake City; a "secret show" on February 9 and an official show two nights later. It was an offer hard to resist. Despite the freezing cold, the money was considerable, while the potential television audience totalled somewhere in the billions. Just before showtime, Grohl was told that he had an urgent phone call. To his utter amazement, his hero Jim Craig* was on the line.

"He gave me this pep talk," Grohl recalled, "that, I swear to God, changed my life. I can't remember exactly what he said, but it was something along the lines of, 'Well, tonight you'll do what the US hockey team did in 1980.'"

Following these hyper gigs, the Foos' began an enforced period of hibernation, where each member went "side project crazy", in the words of Chris Shiflett, who formed a band, Jackson United. Mendel played a one-off gig with No Use For A Name at a club in San Jose, and also jammed with Fire Theft, a group which included former Foos drummer William Goldsmith. Hawkins, meanwhile, led Taylor Hawkins and the Coattail Riders,† drummed in a covers outfit called Chevy Metal and wrote songs with former Jane's Addiction bassist, Eric Avery. Although reluctant to say so, each of them feared for the future of Foo Fighters. "It felt like we were in limbo," said Mendel, while Shiflett admitted, "I was pretty scared." These fears turned out to be very real when Grohl called a meeting to announce he was joining Queens Of The Stone Age.

By 2001 Queens Of The Stone Age had quite a CV – being proudly independent, hugely credible, proficient on their instruments and above playing the corporate game in order to sell records and fill concerts.

The band's mainstays – singer/guitarist Josh Homme and bassist Nick Oliveri – were outcasts from the Californian desert and had first played

---

* Craig was a member of the 1980 US hockey team that beat the Russians in what was seen by many as the Cold War on ice. "I thought he was the coolest guy," said Grohl, who played both lacrosse and ice hockey at school. "He was just, like, ugly, short, fat, straight out of nowhere."

† The band released their debut album in March 2006.

together in a psychedelic hardcore outfit called Kyuss that split in 1995. Homme then moved to Seattle to tour with Screaming Trees. Not unlike Buzz Osbourne, Homme was the kind of guy to whom like-minded rockers gravitated, and while in Seattle he started recording with a loose-knit crew that included members of Soundgarden (Matt Cameron) and Dinosaur Jr (Mike Johnson), as well as Van Conner from Screaming Trees. They released a series of seven-inch singles under the name Gamma Ray, before morphing into Queens Of The Stone Age. The band's self-titled long-playing debut – "a vital place between art-metal serious-ness and pop pleasure," in the words of *Rolling Stone* – appeared in 1998.

Biker look-alike Oliveri rejoined Homme in 1999 and by mid 2000, the QOTSA album *Rated R* appeared, which, like its forerunner, copped praiseworthy notices. "Queens Of The Stone Age," noted *Rolling Stone*'s Ben Ratliff, "are settling in as kings of the rock riff at the beginning of the new century." Clearly, their time had come.

It may have been the kudos, or such an unorthodox lyric as "nicotine, Valium, Vicodin, marijuana, ecstasy and alcohol", which Homme recited like a toxic shopping list during 'Feel Good Hit Of The Summer' off the album,* that appealed to Grohl who offered the band several support slots during the Foos' 2000 tour. It was a sizeable step-up for the Queens, as the pair filled such venues as the 6,000-seat Universal Amphitheatre in Universal City in California, the slightly smaller State Theatre in Detroit and the Electric Factory in Philadelphia.

Grohl had actually been a Kyuss fan; when their *Blues For The Red Sun* album was released in 1992, he played it upwards of three times daily. Kyuss cut a Nirvana tribute, the "secret track" 'Day One', which closed their final album, *And The Circus Leaves Town* (1995). There was clearly a lot of mutual respect, made even stronger through their shared love of Black Flag. Grohl crowned the Queens "the great white hope for American rock". He'd first witnessed the band's sonic assault at legendary New York venue CBGBs in 1999. Grohl stood alone, right at the front of the stage, rapidly emptying a bottle of his much-loved Crown Royal whisky as the band kicked into overdrive. By the end of the show, Grohl was both legless and a serious Queens convert.

---

* When the *NME* asked Grohl about the lyric from 'Feel Good Hit Of The Summer', he replied with tongue-in-cheek, "That's how you *should* prepare for a festival."

While being interviewed for *Kerrang!*'s year-end round-up (2000), when asked about his biggest disappointment that year, Grohl replied that he didn't get to play on *Rated R*. Upon reading this, Homme asked Grohl if he could somehow make it up to him by having him drum on the next Queens record. It was a no-brainer, especially considering the unfortunate state of Foo Fighters at the time.

The natural flow of the sessions was nothing like the disjointed, stop-start nature of the recently abandoned Foos' recordings and Grohl eventually drummed on the entire *Songs For The Deaf* album, bar one track. He was so turned on by the Queens' album that he insisted it would "change the face of music". Hawkins, Mendel and Shiflett looked on with understandable concern.

"Playing with the Queens Of The Stone Age [is] for one reason and one reason only," Grohl said, "and that's the feeling that every musician waits for and dreams of: playing with people and having it just fit. In eight years, I haven't found anyone that made sense, [but] they definitely did. We didn't have to talk about anything it was just so fucking easy." At such a delicate period in the Foos' career, his words couldn't have been more poorly chosen.

Grohl hadn't forgotten about the Foos' aborted album but obviously felt that a change was as good as a rest. When Homme asked if was free to tour the album in 2002, Grohl accepted the offer. "I just said, 'Fuck it, I'm going to go off and play with the Queens . . . for a while and see how I feel when I get back.'" Just as Grohl was fast becoming a cheerleader for the Queens, Homme was a serious fan of Grohl's playing. He was convinced that drumming for the Queens brought out the animal in Grohl. "Behind a kit is where he fucking should be," Homme said. "Dave's an amazing player; he plays his fuckin' ass off."

Despite having played on some of the world's biggest stages, Grohl found his public QOTSA debut in March 2002, at West Hollywood's Troubadour – billed as "An Evening of Communion and Fellowship" – to be one of the more harrowing gigs of his career. It was the first time since Nirvana that Grohl had been part of a band, rather than a band leader, and he was feeling the pressure of performing.

"Let me tell you," Grohl admitted, "I am not a great drummer, not by a long way. And so the gig with the Queens was the most pressure I've felt in a long time." Grohl later described the show as "liberating", a night when he rediscovered his "fearless side". It was enough to convince him that the best thing he could do was get on the road with the Queens, thereby avoiding, at least for the time being, the mess that was the Foos' fourth album. For the first time in almost a decade, he rehearsed and worked out for days on end in preparation for the upcoming tour, "getting fitter than I've ever been". While on the road, he avoided the kind of intoxicants incanted in 'Feel Good Hit . . .' sticking with his beloved cigarettes, coffee, smelly cheese and Crown Royal whisky. Within a few days of the tour, having fielded one too many questions about the future of the Foos, Grohl refused to do any press, insisting that he was just the hired help.

During the Queens' tour, Grohl put in a call to Mendel who, after some small talk, cautiously asked if the Foos time was up. Grohl firmly and clearly informed his bassist, "Man, the Foo Fighters are like my family. I can play drums with another band, and that's fun. But at the end of the day, you come back to the thing that's yours. I mean, fuck," he added, "I've got [our logo] tattooed on the back of my neck. I never want it to end."

When we spoke about his band in Sydney in late 2002, Grohl put it another way. "It's like having a child and watching it mature and then baby's all grown up. You can't abandon that, no way."

The Foos' reunion was hardly the smooth process that Grohl inferred it was going to be. Instead of returning to the studio in Virginia, which was starting to feel more claustrophobic by the minute, Grohl opted to spend some time with his "evil twin", Taylor Hawkins, in Topanga Canyon.

An exclusive community tucked away in a rocky hillside about a half-hour's drive from Hollywood, Topanga Canyon had become the tranquil location of choice for a fair number of singer/songwriters over the past 30 odd years. Neil Young wrote *After The Gold Rush* there; Young later told *Rolling Stone* writer Cameron Crowe that the album captured "the spirit of Topanga Canyon". Young's former band Buffalo Springfield had based themselves there in the late Sixties, as did former Byrd David Crosby (who once chased serial killer Charles Manson off his Topanga property). Joni Mitchell dedicated her 1970 album, *Ladies Of The Canyon*, to the women of Topanga.

The beaches of Malibu were only a short drive away, which suited

Hawkins perfectly. Geography not being his strong point, when asked to describe the community spirit of the Canyon, Hawkins likened it to "maybe the hills of Surrey. Are there hills in Surrey?" Hawkins lived in a home which one visitor described as "modern-ish". Dogs ran around the backyard, using the swimming pool and trampoline as their own play things. Downstairs, next to the garage, was Hawkins' own play thing: a custom-built 24-track studio.

While recording at Grohl's home studio in Virginia, Hawkins decided to build his own after Grohl explained the advantages: "There's no clock on the wall, it's your fucking house, which also means that you decide who's allowed to come by the studio and who's not." During the early stages of what would become *One By One*, a typical day's recording for Grohl and Hawkins would begin with a swim at 10 am, followed by two hours of recording, a barbeque, another swim, ad infinitum.

The songs laboured under such working titles as 'Tom Petty', 'Knucklehead', 'Spooky Tune', 'Full Mount' and 'Tears For Beers', none of which made it to the final album but Grohl and Hawkins did sketch out instrumental versions of 'Low' and 'Times Like These' during the Topanga sessions. The experience was enough to encourage the pair to return to Virginia for another stab at the album.

In what must have felt reminiscent of the first Foo Fighters album for Grohl, he and Hawkins recorded the basic tracks for the entire album in just under a fortnight. Part of Grohl's haste was out of necessity: he still had some Queens Of The Stone Age dates to complete. After reviewing the previous two weeks' work, Grohl called Mendel and Shiflett. "Hey," he informed them, "I think we just re-recorded the whole record here."

While the Foos' bassist and guitarist were relieved to be informed that the band had been reactivated, they were stunned when Grohl told them, "Guys, you're going to have to finish your parts by yourselves." With the band already several hundred thousand dollars in debt to RCA, Grohl was desperate to get the album completed, his philosophy being: "Whatever it takes to make it work, shit, that's what it takes."

Prior to heading back out on the road with the Queens, Grohl spent a day listening to the demos with Shiflett, Mendel and producer Nick Raskulinecz, to work out exactly where the bass and guitar parts belonged. Shiflett, in particular, was bewildered by this working process. "[Grohl] just left me and Nick to record my guitars and that was that; I didn't even know what was going to make it on the disc or not. It was a weird, broken-up way of making a record." Even Hawkins felt that *One By One*'s creation was "a little bit shoddy". "But it is a picture of the time," he added. "We nearly broke up."

For an album recorded in piecemeal fashion, *One By One* has its moments. Like previous Foo Fighters' records, it led out with a typically turbocharged few minutes of Foos' riffage and rhythm called 'All My Life', a song that, among other things, revealed Grohl's attitude to oral sex. "Don't let it go to waste," he roared, "I love it but I hate the taste." In the tradition of 'Stacked Actors' and 'This Is A Call', the Foos were once again leading with their ace: 'All My Life' was a barely restrained outpouring, Grohl roaring the lyrics breathlessly, while Hawkins pounded a hole in his kit. It was the perfect reminder to Foos fans of what the band did best.

Sex played a key role throughout the album – Grohl euphemistically described 'All My Life' as "a little dirty", while 'Low' concerned itself with "two people getting together because they realise they have more fun fucking each other than anyone else – it's kinda deep." To emphasise this angle, Grohl and his Tenacious D pal Jack Black romped together in a seedy hotel room for the accompanying video, which was promptly banned by MTV. The song itself was surprisingly subdued and under-stated, even though it felt as though the band was busting to explode into widescreen sound at any second. For one of the few times in the Foos' recorded career, Grohl resisted the temptation to scream his vocal; instead he whispered the song's suggestive lyric like some kind of heavy-breather.

As the band completed recording the album at Conway Studios, teen sexpot and RCA labelmate Christina Aguilera was working in the studio next door. When the band found out, they dropped by and invited the 'Dirrty' girl into sharing their "beer bong". "She finished every last drop," Grohl reported with pride. A few days later, his home phone rang and girlfriend Jordyn Blum took the call. When Grohl noticed the bemused look on her face, he asked what was up. "The local radio station's saying you're dating Christina Aguilera," she replied. Grohl quickly called the station to inform them, "It's not true. Let's face it, I'm, like, 33 – she's a kid." Grohl found it hard to shake the Lothario tag.

Elsewhere on *One By One*, 'Times Like These' was a Grohl personal favourite, with echoes of Television and post-punk act Mission Of Burma. It was also a sure-fire radio hit, with an obvious connection to such past

Foos' favourites as 'Learn To Fly' and 'I'll Stick Around'. The song was built around another of Grohl's deeply melodic vocals and a nagging, insistent riff from new guy Shiflett that stuck in your head and refused to budge. And, as it transpired, it was also a key song for the recently reborn Foos. Although the lyric wasn't transparently clear on first listen, Grohl had documented his mixed feelings about the band's uncertain future. It was one of the songs that Grohl had played for Hawkins during the album's Topanga Canyon sessions. According to Hawkins, the song "was kind of about the band breaking up and remembering why we're doing it and all that stuff." After one run-through, Hawkins knew that it would be a key song for the album. US rock radio agreed, because, just like 'Learn To Fly' back in 2000, 'Times Like These' was an across-the-boards hit, spending more than six months in *Billboard*'s Modern Rock Tracks chart. It was one of the biggest hits of a career that wasn't short in high chart placings and hefty sales.

'Halo' owed a debt to Tom Petty, although Grohl added that it was also influenced by Cheap Trick and Guided by Voices. Grohl may have only been a Heartbreaker for a few minutes on *Saturday Night Live*, but he'd clearly studied the man's work. When asked about Petty's influence, Grohl replied that he'd completely reviewed his approach to songwriting. "What happens if we have a song where the dynamics don't go from quiet to loud? What happens if the riff in the verse is the same as the chorus, but we just turn it into something else when it hits the chorus? Tom Petty does it all the time, and it seems to work for him." 'Have It All' was another of the several slow burners on the album, a chance for Grohl and co. to experiment with mood, rather than menace. ('Tired Of You' was another example of this.) And yet again, Grohl proved how effortlessly he could pull off an addictive vocal melody when he felt in the mood. Curiously, despite the album's collection of mid-tempo strums, none of the songs had been written on acoustic guitar, which was Grohl's pre-ferred method for *There Is Nothing Left To Lose*. (Grohl had actually written the bulk of that album while lying in bed, in front of his television, with his acoustic guitar for company.)

'Burn Away' typified the more romantic tunes on the album. Developments in Grohl's personal life were reflected in his lyrics, being some of the most revealing songs he'd attempted to write since "the divorce album", *The Colour And The Shape*. As Grohl explained to me, his new love, Jordyn Blum, was very much on his mind when penning much of the album.

"When you fall in love and you're in a romantic headspace," he said, "you open yourself up to a person and you realise so much because you're exposed: your good side, your bad side, your insecurities, vulnerabilities, blah, blah, blah. It's a creepy process. On other albums, I'd always held back lyrically because you don't want to tell everyone your secrets. But this time, there was an emotional level we were hitting with the music that I wanted the lyrics to match. And," he added, "with a song like 'Tired', you can't rightly sing about chicks and weed." Queen's Brian May was invited to overdub four guitar parts on 'Tired Of You', which Grohl, the ultimate Queen fan, was obviously thrilled by. This was one of the few moments saved from the album's original sessions. The Grohl/May relationship was strong; the Foos had covered Pink Floyd's 'Have A Cigar' for the *M:I2* soundtrack, with May guest-starring on guitar. Grohl was thrilled by the experience; to him it was like "living in a comic book, because you always think of these people as super-heroes when you're a little kid." May would often turn up at the band's many UK shows, even inviting Grohl back to his country manor, where the awestruck drummer took the time to drink a whisky while seated at Freddie Mercury's piano. So the chance of a guest spot on *One By One* seemed only natural. "He's gentle and cordial and sweet and a fuckin' genius," Grohl said. "He's really the nicest person I've ever met."

At almost eight minutes, the album's closer, 'Come Back', was by far the lengthiest Foo Fighters' track ever recorded, but it was actually two songs spliced together. "It's our epic opus," Grohl laughed. Lyrically, it was the most honest he'd been since 'Friend Of A Friend'. According to Grohl, "I'm revealing all these dark, shitty sides of myself . . . like, this is how I can be an asshole."

The record buying public didn't seem to mind if Grohl was an asshole, or how fragmented the creative process had been. When finally released on October 22, 2002, *One By One* – with a striking piece of Raymond Pettibon art adorning the cover, another nod to Grohl's punk past – generated a further enviable sequence of hit radio and chart singles. 'All My Life' reached number five in the UK singles chart, topped *Billboard*'s Modern Rock Tracks chart and reached the number three spot on the

Mainstream Rock Tracks listing.* The follow-up, 'Times Like These', achieved similar business worldwide, as did subsequent singles 'Low' and 'Have It All'. Foo Fighters were now competing with such revered acts as R.E.M. and Pearl Jam for sheer chart consistency. Their singer even acquired a new tag: "Golden Grohl".

The critical response to the album was, for once, almost universally positive. It was summed up by the well-chosen words of the *Austin Chronicle*, who noted: "Let's just hope it doesn't take another near-death experience for their next album to be this good."

Uncut magazine agreed. "The joyous hooks and choruses remain," they wrote, "but they're tempered by a welcome moodiness."

Rolling Stone, who'd failed to fully embrace the Foos' last two albums, also noted this new sense of resolve. "It's rock that draws power from its determination to struggle onward," Jon Pareles observed, also shrewdly noting how Grohl had name-checked a Hüsker Du album (*New Day Rising*) during 'Times Like These'. Pareles also spotted the influence that such perennials as The Beatles and Neil Young had had on Grohl's songwriting. "[They] mean as much to the Foos as grunge progenitors such as the Melvins."

Trade bible *Billboard* saw the album as a flashback to Grohl's fearless love of classic rock. "*One By One*, in all its thunderous angst and desperate expressions of hope, represents a full-on exploration of the Foos' Seventies influences."

The UK press was equally generous with its praise; *NME* noted that "everything they had, they still have – but now every note is ten times more focused and urgent."

"They may have just failed to make a Great Rock Album," *Mojo* declared, "but they have unquestionably become a Great Rock Band." (*One By One* was crowned their November 2002 Album of the Month.) Of all the major music press, only *Q* magazine remained unconvinced. They agreed that the album started with a bang that would register on the Richter scale, but felt that the album faded. "It doesn't deliver track-upon-track," was their summation of the Foos' fourth LP.

The album became a massive success to rival the three previous Foo albums, reaching number one in Australia, three in the USA – spending 50

---

* It also charted highly in Australia, Italy, Germany, and throughout much of Scandinavia.

weeks on the *Billboard* Top 200 (shifting platinum, having sold 1.2 million copies by the second week of November), as well as blitzing lists in Canada, New Zealand, Finland, France, Switzerland, Italy, Denmark, Austria and Germany. In the UK, it debuted at number one only to be knocked off the top spot – in a peculiar twist of fate – by a Nirvana greatest hits collection. No matter how successful Foo Fighters had become, Grohl's past continued to haunt him.

Courtney Love became an unwanted distraction during the difficult creation of *One By One*. On September 28, 2001, Love filed a suit in the Los Angeles Superior Court against Grohl, Novoselic and the Universal Music Group for control of Nirvana's master recordings, as well as seeking to dissolve LLC, the company she formed with Grohl and Novoselic in September 1997 to oversee Nirvana's music and control their legacy.

Grohl was required to give testimony in court several days before *One By One*'s release. The night before, documentary maker Nick Broomfield's rumour-mongering film *Kurt & Courtney*, about the doomed relationship of Cobain and Love, was broadcast. Grohl reached for the off switch on his remote 10 minutes in. "Is this what it's really become?" he asked himself. "Documentaries and murder-conspiracy theories?"

Grohl felt the same disdain towards the protracted court case. "I don't consider the lawsuit reality a lot of the time," he admitted, "because it's so far beyond anything the band ever stood for. It has nothing to do with what Nirvana was." Grohl considered wearing a T-shirt reading "Count-down To The Foo Fighters Album Release" in court in order to alleviate his discomfort.

I asked Grohl whether Love had influenced any of the more bitter lyrics on *One By One*, having clearly been the subliminal target on 'I'll Stick Around' and 'Stacked Actors'. "No, no Courtney snuck in [to the lyrics]," he insisted. "I'm surprised, too, usually it does. [But] I'm a lover, not a hater. And I'm an optimist; I always see the good in everything. When it comes to exterior bullshit, you can block it out by considering it a waste of your time. My head was totally in the album and I was totally in love. Still am."

At the heart of Love's court action was the unreleased track, 'You Know You're Right', recorded in January 1994 shortly before Cobain's death, which Grohl and Novoselic had hoped to include in a boxed set of Nirvana demos, rarities and alternate mixes that was planned for release towards the end of 2001. Love was especially incensed about the use of the "missing" Nirvana track – she considered it more than a "rarity" and wanted it used on a single-disc Nirvana best-of.

The facts of the case were clearly laid out in a memorandum filed in the State of Washington, in the case of *Courtney Love Cobain, et al, versus David Grohl, et al*, dated June 11, 2001. It read, in part: "Defendants Grohl and Novoselic would like to go forward with Geffen/Universal in the preparation and ultimate release of a Boxed Set coordinated with the tenth anniversary of the release of Nirvana's first hit album *Nevermind*. Plaintiff Courtney Love, who has succeeded to her husband's interest in the matter, has expressed concerns about the contents of the Boxed Set, particularly the possible inclusion of the Kurt Cobain recording 'You Know You're Right'. All parties believe that that recording, which has never before been released, has the potential to be a significant hit."

The mood in court turned ugly when Grohl and Novoselic requested that Love undergo a psychiatric evaluation, because they considered her too "incapacitated" to deal with the case. "In her professional dealings, Love is irrational, mercurial, self-centred, unmanageable, inconsistent and unpredictable," the court filing read. A judge eventually rejected the proposal, stating that Grohl and Novoselic "provided no professional support for the proposition", although his decision came before Love's very public meltdown in 2004/05.*

After more than a year of unsettling and occasionally bizarre courtroom manoeuvring, the parties reached an agreement. 'You Know You're Right' was included on the best-of package, simply entitled *Nirvana*, the album that knocked Grohl's *One By One* off the top of the UK album chart (ironically producing a handy windfall for Love, as a result).

With their renewed popularity over the water, in July 2002 Foo Fighters undertook their biggest UK tour yet, becoming the second-hottest ticket that summer just behind Oasis. Included among the dates was a Manchester headliner in front of 15,000, who helped to deposit a handy £250,000 into the Foo Fighters coffers. Although at the time of their Chili Peppers support, the band swore off stadium-sized shows, it appeared as though

---

* The full court documents of Love vs. Grohl, and the soap opera that is Courtney Love's life, can be viewed at www.thesmokinggun.com.

they'd surrendered to their success. As one writer noted before their mammoth show at the Cardiff International Arena, the band were now "four small components in the industrial rock entertainment delivery system."

Grohl and Shiflett shared one double-decker tour bus, Mendell and Hawkins another, which contained a queen sized bed that Hawkins quickly laid claim to. (For their next tour, in 2003, Grohl graduated to his own private bus that contained, amongst the usual indulgences, a complimentary fruit bowl.) Grohl, however, insisted that this wasn't how the band toured around the rest of the world. "It's only in the UK it's gone crazy," he said. When his tour manager wrapped a towel around his neck after one UK gig, Grohl did a double take. "I just thought that was so weird," he commented afterwards. "I mean, that's what they did for Elvis." The Foos' backstage area was designed for maximum band comfort: a massage table, staffed by a woman wearing a badge that read, "Serious Sports Injuries", took pride of place, amidst the silver candle settings and an abundant collection of CDs. Many of the band's partners, including Jordyn Blum, were along for the fabulously well-paid ride.

Over the course of their numerous trans-Atlantic trips, Grohl had gradually warmed to the UK. So much so, in fact, that by this time he was telling anyone who bothered to ask that London was "our second home". This was certainly backed up by the numbers that Foo Fighters pulled in during this tour; the money they'd pocket from this one UK visit would be enough to help some bands retire for life. "I used to hate London," Grohl admitted, "but only last year did I start to realise that London is my favourite city outside of the States. It's a whole new scene [now]. The first time I came to London it was all fish-and-chips, but now it's [upscale sushi house] Nobu and the Metropolitan Hotel."

At Scotland's T In The Park, as a misguided show of support after Grohl's "defection" to the Queens Of The Stone Age, Grohl's record label had installed placards around the site reading that "contrary to public opinion", Grohl wasn't leaving the band. Grohl was more than a little bemused. "I didn't know people were that worried," he said, prior to plugging in and bringing the house down.

On August 24, the Foos headlined the second night of the Reading Festival, topping a bill that also featured prog heroes Muse, Ireland's Ash, Swedish rockers The Hives and Foo Fighters wannabes Sum 41. The show was attended by up to 70,000 people, a fittingly explosive finale to a UK summer of festivals. There was a poignancy to the occasion, as it marked 10 years since Nirvana had appeared at the festival – their last-ever UK gig. For Grohl the show represented both a celebration of Nirvana's legacy and a clear indication of how successful Foo Fighters had become. "The place has so much history in general – and so many memories for me in particular," he said, "that it is a really special place to play." With Virginia Grohl and Jordyn Blum sidestage, he was unequivocal in considering it "the single greatest day of my life".

"I [was] looking out over all the people, and wondering, 'My God, are they all here to see us?' I just could not believe it, that all those thousands of people were watching us. It felt great. It felt like, you know, we'd arrived."

CHAPTER TWELVE

Honour Roll

"I looked at a lot of warehouses around here, and thought, 'Do I want to record my album right where people have been taking it in the ass?'"

– Dave Grohl

EVER since his Hollywood high times with Taylor Hawkins, Grohl had become a homebody when not on the road. After moving back to Los Angeles, he bought a house for his mother and sister within walking distance of his own home. If anybody could keep him in line, it was his family. Having been romantically linked (accurately or otherwise) with Hole and Smashing Pumpkin bassist Melissa Auf der Maur and such starlets as Winona Ryder, Katie Holmes and Christina Aguilera, Grohl insisted that his relationship with MTV producer Jordyn Blum was built to last. "I've settled down a bit, that's for sure," Grohl said in 2003. "And I would love to have a family. That's the one thing I don't have."

Grohl set a wedding date for August 2, that year. His stag party occurred after the final date on the Foos' latest US tour when Grohl and a posse of 60 hit Las Vegas for a long night's journey into day. Wary of any press, Grohl had his crew sworn to silence and was typically cagey when later asked for the gory details. "Use your imagination and then multiply it by 10," he said. "It was a bachelor party, you know?"

Grohl had the perfect plan for the evening and morning leading up to the wedding. Having already had his buck's night, he slept over at Hawkins' house, where they woke early, cooked breakfast and sat by the pool, before disappearing into Hawkins' studio for a couple of hours. ("We came up with a bunch of new riffs," workaholic Grohl revealed.) Then, after a swim and a barbeque lunch, they got ready for the big event held in the backyard of Grohl's new home. Grohl invited plenty of his old school buddies from Virginia, including Jimmy "God" Swanson, who was an usher, as was Hawkins. Kris Novoselic was Grohl's best man. Family relatives flew in from Ohio and Louisiana, while Blum's family travelled from Baltimore and elsewhere in California. Among the 250 or so guests was Tenacious D along with the ex-members of Led Zeppelin.

Despite his calm morning, Grohl was every bit as nervous at the altar as he was performing in front of thousands of festival goers. Grohl fought back tears when he saw Blum walking down the aisle towards him. "I had to keep the fucking pipes from leaking," he laughingly recalled.

Grohl had toyed with the idea of inviting legendary soulman, the Reverend Al Green, to perform the service and provide the evening's entertainment, but instead he hired The Fab Four, the ultimate Beatles' tribute band. "They start in Hamburg," Grohl said, "wind up in *Sgt Pepper*'s suits and before you know it, they're doing 'Let It Be'." When asked why he didn't just approach Paul McCartney for the gig, Grohl drolly replied: "Because we didn't have a million dollars to donate to his favourite charity."

Typically, only weeks after saying "I do" for the second – and, Grohl insists – last time, he and the Foos were back playing several European festival dates. The year 2003 had started off as busy as any other year for the individual members. Mendel toured with Fire Theft during March, while Shiflett's band Jackson United made their public debut at LA club King King, with Grohl and Mendel urging them on from the moshpit. Shiflett also set up his own label, specifically to cater for the band's debut EP. Foo Fighters scored another "Best Hard Rock Song" Grammy for the track 'All My Life', but missed out on the silverware for "Best Hard Rock Performance". It was the band's second Grammy win, and another big night for Grohl, who, along with Bruce Springsteen, Elvis Costello and No Doubt bassist Tony Kanal, took part in an all-star jam that marked the passing of the Clash's Joe Strummer. Grohl's role was to scream "a nuclear err-or" during their take on 'London Calling', leaving the "phony Beatlemania" line to Springsteen and Costello. "Standing next to Springsteen freaked me out," said Grohl. "It's like meeting Abraham Lincoln without the hat." As proudly punk rock as Grohl claimed to be, he did have a soft spot for music's so-called "night of nights". When the Foos scored in 2001, he stood at the dais, grinned a million-dollar smile, and came clean. "I bet we're the only band that's nominated who made a record in their basement."

The Foos also played a low-key invites-only show on May 1 at Washington, DC's Black Cat club, a venue partly owned by Grohl. By dividing their show into two sets – one electric, one acoustic – they unintentionally foreshadowed the split personality of their next album.

In February, Grohl's "death metal all-stars" project, Probot, was finally released, thanks, in no small part, to sometimes Zwan guitarist Matt Sweeney, who helped connect Grohl with almost all the vocalists who contributed. The line-up for Probot, dubbed a "Satanic *Supernatural*", in a cheeky dig at the recent resurrection of Carlos Santana's career – it was also tagged the "heavy metal Wu-Tang" – was suitably impressive. Max Cavalera, of Soulfly and Sepultura, wailed like a wounded beast on 'Red War', Mike Dean from Corrosion Of Conformity did likewise on 'Access Babylon', while Cronos from Venom, King Diamond of Mercyful Fate and Wino from the Obsessed, along with members of such hardcore superstars as Celtic Frost, Napalm Death and Voivod, provided the album with an appropriate dark and dirty metallic flavour.

The album cost around US $100,000 to make, which, given the line-up and the logistical difficulties of bringing the project together, was "cheap as shit", according to Grohl. A fair chunk of that was actually spent on Fedex charges, as Grohl used the postal system to keep in touch with the galaxy of guest vocalists. At least one major label – most likely Geffen, although RCA were also interested – had offered "crazy money" to release *Probot* but Grohl knew that a major wouldn't "get" the record. If it landed in the wrong hands, it might become "Dave Grohl and Friends", rather than a payback gesture to the people who'd helped him out in the past. Pete Stahl introduced Grohl to Greg Anderson, who ran Southern Lord Records. Having played with Stahl and Mendel in Goatsnake, Anderson became the obvious choice for Grohl because he "knows what the fuck the Probot thing is all about." As Grohl explained, "It got to the point where I was afraid people will expect something of it that it's not. It's not the new Metallica album."

The basic tracks were cut and then posted to potential vocalists, along with a brief note from Grohl inviting their participation. Grohl's enthusiasm for the project increased as the tapes started filtering back to him. The first tape he received was 'Dictatosaurus', as wailed by Snake. Grohl was elated. "When I got that track back, that's when I knew, 'Shit yeah, this idea is going to work.'" Then Grohl received the King Diamond cut, 'Sweet Dreams', and he knew he was onto a winner. Grohl was hoping for one of the King's trademark "wicked little laughs" and he did not let him down. "Everyone involved," Grohl said, "came through with the goods." Some of the contributors improvised – Lee Dorian recorded his part for 'Ice Cold Man' on a DAT tape in a friend's bedroom – while others stuck to their signature, blood-curdling howls. The exception to this "done by Fedex" (Grohl's words) method was 'Shake Your Blood', which was specifically "tailored" for a vocalist – in this case, Lemmy, from Motörhead. Grohl had only met the man once before, and then just long enough to mumble, "Hey, man, I've got a lot of respect for you." This time he had the chance to best appreciate how the hard-living bassist worked a room when Lemmy sauntered into LA's Grandmaster Studio, looking every bit as self-assured and cocky as Grohl had imagined. "The day I met Lemmy," said Grohl, "I realised that of all the rockers I'd met in my life, I'd never met a *real* rocker before. Lemmy is the fucking rocker – he is the one."

After making a fair dent on a bottle of Jack Daniel's in order to lubricate his unmistakable whisky-and-sandpaper growl, Lemmy ripped through the song in two takes, after which he looked up from the vocal booth to ask: "All right! Who wants to go look at some tits?" Mentor and fan spent the rest of the day drinking and ogling dancers in a nearby strip club, with Lemmy maintaining a running commentary that had Grohl doubled-up. "He's like a stand-up comedian," Grohl said. "He could do well up in the Catskills."

Realising that any live Probot show would be a "cunt to organise", Grohl agreed to make a video instead. Once again he leaned on his new best friend, Lemmy, to lip-synch his way through 'Shake Your Blood'. He also recruited Anderson, who played guitar in the clip, and Wino. But the biggest guest spot went to the Suicide Girls, best known from their website (www.suicidegirls.com), a group of LA ladies who specialise in "tattooed, kick-ass burlesque". Someone had slipped Grohl a Suicide Girls sticker, which he happily stuck to his guitar. Grohl admitted to a weakness for femme punk rockers: "I used to go for the tattooed punk chick with a little spike in her tongue," he admitted as the shoot began. The Suicide Girls received a pretty straightforward direction from Grohl: the band would play, "surrounded by 70 Suicide Girls making out with each other, whipping each other. You know, just getting off on each other." To achieve this, the girls were decked out in leathers and fishnets, with their tatts and piercings on full and proud display. One Suicide Girl was strapped to a torture table, another was cuffed to a gallows, while a third hung from a circular cage in the middle of the studio where the clip was shot, during which the band played on, grinning like fools. In between shoots, Grohl smiled. "I feel like I'm running a fucking brothel." It was a long way from the big budget and MTV-ready precision of some of the Foos high-rotation clips.

Although his basement studio in Virginia had been efficient and served as a handy band clubhouse, Grohl had much grander plans to rebuild Studio 606 at his Hollywood home.

Thanks to Foo Fighters' shows now being stadium-sized, with receipts to match, there was sufficient money in the coffers. April 2003 typified a month on the road for the Foos – during a stretch of 13 dates, swinging from Bakersfield, California to Camden, New Jersey, the band generated $1,629,853 in ticket sales, playing to upwards of 65,000 people. A similar run of nine dates three months later, beginning at New York's Hammerstein Ballroom, ending two weeks later in Edmonton, Alberta, also grossed more than $1 million, drawing more than 40,000 punters.

The perfect site for the Foos' new pleasuredome was located in unfashionable Northbridge, a sleepy suburb in the San Fernando Valley, roughly 20 miles northwest of downtown LA. At least it appeared sleepy to outsiders – Northbridge was the porno capital of America.* "I looked at a lot of warehouses around here," Grohl said, "and thought, 'Do I want to record my album right where people have been taking it in the ass?'" The answer was a resounding yes.

The actual site of the new 606 had its own macabre history; it was formerly the home of a woman whose stalker torched the building to the ground. Something about the place and the area's Sodom and Gomorrah qualities appealed to Grohl, who invested $700,000 of band money into the 8,000 square feet site. The next few months were spent converting it into the band's clubhouse, even if the eight feet high iron gate outside made it feel more like a rock'n'roll version of Camp David.

---

* Northbridge was also at the epicentre of the 1994 earthquake that rocked Los Angeles.

Grohl's design was based on Polar Studios, the Abba-owned Stockholm facility where Led Zeppelin cut *In Through The Out Door* during a snow-bound Swedish winter in 1978. The new 606's centrepiece was an enormous live recording room, while the control room was filled with sumptuous leather chairs, a vast mixing desk and speakers that towered over the band and crew like skyscrapers. The year-round temperature inside 606 was kept at a cool 72 degrees. It was a vastly different environment to the previous 606, where nature often played a part. "Back in Virginia," Grohl said, "we'd have to stop doing vocals sometimes because you could hear the crows outside through the microphones."

When it was finished in late 2004, Grohl called it a "giant fucking playground" catering to their every need. The facility housed a rehearsal space, storage room, and a media area. "I honestly think we've managed to make one of the top 10 studios in Los Angeles," Grohl proudly claimed. "I'd rather be here than any other place in the whole fucking world."

The band now finally had a place to hang their many gold and platinum discs from around the world, along with Grohl's personal favourite – Nirvana's first gold disc.* "I've never had a place to put all this stuff," Grohl admitted, "because it always seemed funny to have it in the house." Elsewhere, a toy version of the drum kit pounded by Mötley Crüe's Tommy Lee was on display above the mixing desk, obviously as a motivational tool for the band. Outside, in the chill-out area, DVDs of Manowar, the Scorpions and Van Halen played on a loop. If rock'n'roll, LA-style, had a ground zero, it might be the new Studio 606.

While their "giant fucking playground" was still under construction, Grohl made an important connection that would have a serious influence on the first album that the band recorded there. The 2004 US presidential election was looming, and even though Grohl wasn't a political animal – unlike Chris Novoselic, who had become involved with numerous fund-raisers and organisations since Cobain's death – he wanted to see George W. Bush removed from office. "If Bush gets re-elected, the first thing we'll do is riot, smash shit up and make a big statement," said Grohl, only half facetiously.

---

* Grohl understood the value of his Nirvana gold and platinum discs, all desirable collector's items, which he kept stored at his mother's house.

In early July 2004, Grohl put in an acoustic set, alongside Tenacious D and Liz Phair, at the Henry Ford Theater in LA, as part of a fund-raiser in support of Democrat contender John Kerry. Grohl's involvement in this and subsequent Kerry-related events was a statement of his intent. (Grohl had voted Democrat in the previous presidential election.) "I really believed in getting Bush out of office," he said afterwards.

In the words of one of Grohl's role models, Neil Young, John Kerry was "an innaresting character". Born at an army hospital just outside Denver on December 11, 1943, Kerry was raised in a comfortable, upper-middle-class home in Massachusetts. His maternal grandfather, James Grant Forbes, who was born in Shanghai, had acquired a hefty fortune dealing in opium and china. Through Forbes' marriage to Margaret Tyndal Winthrop, who came from a political family, John Kerry was distantly related to four US presidents and various European royals.

After his stint in the US Army Air Corps as a test pilot, Kerry's father, Richard, worked for the Foreign Service and for the Bureau of United Nations Affairs. With this bloodline, it seemed inevitable that Kerry would become involved in politics. Kerry also had a yen for rock'n'roll – while studying at St Paul's School in New Hampshire, he played bass for the prep school band, the Pandas, who cut an album in 1961.*

While attending Yale, Kerry volunteered for Edward Kennedy's first Senatorial campaign; he also dated Janet Auchincloss, Jacqueline Kennedy's half-sister, who invited him to visit the family estate in Rhode Island, where Kerry met JFK for the first time.† Soon after, Kerry enlisted and became a lieutenant, serving two tours of duty in Vietnam, and spending four months as commanding officer of a Swift boat. He received numerous decorations for his service, including a Silver Star and three Purple Hearts. When returning from Vietnam, Kerry became a vocal anti-war opponent, joining the Vietnam Veterans Against The War, becoming the first Vietnam vet to testify before Congress in 1971. For two hours he railed against the war, alleging that the military had "created a monster" in the form of violent American soldiers, who were running amok, raping and/or murdering Vietnamese citizens. During an anti-war rally in New

---

* A copy fetched US $2,551 on ebay in 2004.
† A photo of Kerry sailing with the Kennedys off Rhode Island in August 1962 received massive circulation during Kerry's tilt at the US presidency in 2004.

York during the summer of 1972, Kerry marched alongside John Lennon and Yoko Ono.

Kerry then gravitated towards politics, becoming Lieutenant Governor of Massachusetts in 1982 and became a US Senator in January 1985. Three years later Kerry had his first Bush encounter when joking that "if [George HW] Bush is shot, the Secret Service had orders to shoot [vice president] Dan Quayle." In 2000, prior to the presidential election where "Dubya" crept into the White House after the infamous "hanging chad" incident in the Florida primary, Kerry was on the short-list as Al Gore's vice-presidential running mate (Connecticut Senator Joe Lieberman was appointed). At the next election, in 2004, Kerry won the Democratic nomination to run for president against Bush.

Less than a month after Grohl's acoustic spot in LA at the Kerry fund-raiser, Foo Fighters agreed to join Kerry on his road campaign, playing brief sets in Milwaukee, Dubuque, and St Louis. Although Grohl didn't realise it, the *In Your Honour* album was being conceived.

After the Milwaukee gig, Grohl posted some comments on Kerry's campaign blog site. "I must say, I've never seen such a massive group of people move with such organisation and ease, and still make it seem like a family trip. Seeing Mr. Kerry and his wife cool down from an inspiring town hall session, while sitting with his son Andre over lunch . . . you realise the bond that keeps them aloft is the love that they share as a family – very cool, very true." Grohl also compared the difference between the Kerry crowd and a typical Foo Fighters audience. "Can't say that we get many WWII vets at Foo Fighters shows," he noted. "The crowd was great, though, and I think they got what I was trying to say with my song 'My Hero'. I've done a few things in my life that I'm very proud of, but this one might take the cake."

While on the road with Kerry, Grohl received an interesting text message. It came from his father, a life-long conservative who, of course, sat very much on the opposite side of the political fence to Kerry. "I thought he'd go nuts," said Grohl, "but he sent me a message saying, 'I don't agree with you but I'm proud you're standing up for something you believe in.'" At another Kerry campaign stop, in Las Vegas on October 19, Grohl once again shared a stage with former bandmate-turned-activist Chris Novoselic. Although they didn't play any music together – Grohl performed a few acoustic songs in a solo set – it showed a welcoming solidarity in their personal beliefs aside from rock'n'roll.

The final vote count was almost as close as the 2000 nail-biter but Kerry conceded on November 3, 2004, winning about 48 per cent of the popular vote, a few million votes short of a winning margin. "We were all pretty upset," Grohl said. "That was a bad day." Not acting on his promise to "smash shit up" if Bush was re-elected, Grohl took a more pragmatic approach to dealing with his anger and disappointment by writing songs inspired by his time on the Kerry road show. "I thought that if there's anything people want to listen to . . . it would be songs with some sort of message of hope or positivity. Pissed off as I am, you have to deal with what you've got."

Not since *The Colour And The Shape* had Grohl unearthed such weighty subject matter for his songs. Kerry's loss and Bush's return to office were issues that resonated with Grohl personally, evidenced by such songs as 'In Your Honour', which slowly came together during several months of album pre-production.

When a band insider heard an early version of the track, they described it to Taylor Hawkins as "the Who meets Fugazi." The swirling maelstrom of firestorm guitars and roared vocals would become the set opener for most of the Foos' 2005 shows. "It's not really a song," Hawkins said, "it's a manifesto. And it's the heaviest thing we've ever done."

Grohl disagreed with Hawkins' "manifesto" assessment, insisting that all the songs cut for *In Your Honour* did not constitute some big political statement. He was no Billy Bragg. Grohl may have been surrounded by the punk politics in DC, but he had always been wary about making overt judgements, so his allegiance to Kerry was even more unexpected. "It's not a political record," Grohl said, as *In Your Honour* began to take shape at 606. "It has more to do with [the] human reaction to what happened before and after the election. It's more personal politics."

When asked specifically about 'In Your Honour', Grohl accepted that recent time spent on Kerry's campaign trail had affected him subliminally. In many ways, it reminded Grohl of the communal feeling which occurred during the best Foos' shows. "It's that overwhelming feeling of connection with something," he described.

Around the same time as the sessions for the album began, Grohl returned to the therapist's couch. "I'm not a fucking mess," he said, but "there have been moments making this album, when I have questioned what I am doing with my life and whether I am a good person or not."*

Though he may have been an advocate of psychoanalysis, Grohl flatly rejected the idea of "doing a Metallica" and getting the other members into group therapy, as documented in their *Some Kind Of Monster* film. "No fucking way," he said, laughing. "Now that's a bad idea."

As well as Grohl's recent marriage, the cleaned-up Hawkins announced his engagement to his partner Mi Mi, while Shiflett had recently become a father. Inevitably the band wasn't the only important concern in their lives.

Another, larger concept for the new album came to Grohl when first hearing *She's The One*, a recent soundtrack album from Tom Petty. Suitably impressed by its balance of electric and acoustic songs, Grohl initially considered pursuing more soundtrack work; he'd enjoyed making *Touch*, but as he started to demo a series of mellow acoustic songs, Grohl had an idea: why not make two separate albums, the first a typically balls-out Foo Fighters effort, the other more reflective? When the idea was run by him, Hawkins was keen but a little concerned. "Dave," he drawled, "[after] two years of acoustic touring . . . we might [get] really fat."

When Grohl "realised trying to fit these two things on the same [single] album is tricky," he came up with the perfect compromise: a double album. "We have songs that are loud and obnoxious, and we have . . . beautiful acoustic ballads." According to Grohl, the rock album would give them the perfect setlist for their next visit to Reading, "and on the acoustic album we're the Eagles." The more they considered it, the more the Foos were up for the challenge. RCA, however, had some concerns, particularly when Grohl insisted that they not overly inflate the price of the double disc. The label agreed to a price hike of a single dollar, even though Grohl had already frustrated them by refusing to green-light a greatest hits album.

By Christmas 2004, the Foos had 19 tracks finished,† all contenders for the heavier side of *In Your Honour*. Creating the acoustic disc, however, presented a completely new challenge for the band. During the two weeks

---

* During the recording of *In Your Honour*, Grohl half-seriously considered naming the album *Foo Are You*.
† Including a rap piss-take, 'That Ass', that wasn't destined to make the final cut.

of acoustic sessions, Grohl prepared a list of names that he hoped would be available for cameos, including Ry Cooder, Jim James of My Morning Jacket, one of Grohl's recent discoveries, and Greg Norton, former bassist with Hüsker Dü.

None were available but Grohl was successful when contacting John Paul Jones. The connection between Grohl and the remaining members of Led Zeppelin had never been tighter; on January 12, 1995, when his icons were inducted into the Rock and Roll Hall of Fame. Grohl, who was squeezed into a table between Jones and his wife, Jimmy Page and John Bonham's kids Jason and Zoe, couldn't remove the shit-eating grin from his face for the entire evening.

When Jones returned Grohl's call and said that he was available (to work on the tracks 'Miracle' and 'Another Round'), Grohl couldn't control his glee. "I ran around the room screaming, 'Guess who I just got a fucking call from?' " A totally understated Jones strolled into 606 a few days later, with a mandolin tucked under one arm, and casually introduced himself to the rest of the band. "I tried to be cool," Grohl gasped, "but I'm sure I looked like a total fucking idiot. I was shitting my pants. Full diaper."

Jones was the first of many guest stars. Petra Haden – the daughter of renowned jazz bassist Charlie Haden, formerly of the band That Dog and more recently the voice behind an amazing a cappella remake of *The Who Sell Out* – played violin on 'Miracle', Josh Homme added a tasty guitar part to 'Razor', while Rami Jaffee, of the band Wallflowers, chimed in with keyboard fills on six of the ten acoustic tracks, including 'Cold Day In The Sun', which was written and crooned by Taylor Hawkins. When it came to choosing a duet partner for 'Virginia Moon', a bossa nova valentine that Grohl had been kicking around since the time of *There Is Nothing Left To Lose*, his choice was a surprise to some.

Grohl was one of the millions converted to Norah Jones' sultry voice and jazz piano noodling since the low-key release in 2002 of her Grammy-winning album, *Come Away With Me*. Grohl was aware of the implications of working with a mainstream artist like Jones, who hardly registered on the radar of a typical Foos fan. Hawkins, Shiflett and Mendel weren't entirely sold on the idea. "I think the only person who whole-heartedly approved was our guitar tech," said Grohl, "who's had a border-line stalking crush on her for years."

In a neat act of synchronicity, Jones was booked to record on

Valentine's Day. According to Grohl, "We cleaned up, stashed the porn, put some flowers in the studio and she wafted in and did the whole thing in two hours. She is extraordinary."*

At the end of a fortnight's work, the rest of the band was won over by Jones and the entire soft/loud, electric/acoustic concept. Hawkins, for one, felt totally liberated. "To free yourself of any . . . prejudice or whatever, it's a good feeling," he admitted. "I mean, I listen to some music that I would get burned at the stake for in a rock club. But to me, that's the point." Hawkins also took the chance to add one of his own songs, 'Cold Day In The Sun', a twangy soft-rock strum, to the "quiet" side of *In Your Honour.*

Shrewdly, the band didn't sacrifice the sense of mood and menace that flavoured their best tracks while working on *In Your Honour*'s acoustic disc. The opening song, 'Still', was built around Grohl's voice, a gentle guitar and wave upon wave of keyboards, but it still packed the same menacing intent as their most red-hot rock tracks. The first song recorded for *In Your Honour*'s pensive side, the lyric was inspired by an incident Grohl remembered from his youth in Virginia, when a local kid committed suicide by simply sitting on the railroad tracks and waiting for the express. "I remember we rode our bikes to the park that morning," Grohl said, "and there were all these ambulances and shit. We saw pieces of his bones." With 'Still' in the bag, Grohl and the band sat around for the playback. "When we listened back to it, I remember saying, 'That's my favourite thing we've ever recorded.' " Any doubts they had about going soft on their audience were gone.

'What If I Do' followed, another song constructed around a simple acoustic guitar pattern and Grohl's voice, with Rami Jaffee adding some keyboard flavour. Above anything else, the song proved that when Grohl took time out from screaming, he had a more than serviceable singing voice. Those doubts he'd aired early on, which sometimes forced producers to double-track his vocals in order to give them the necessary oomph, were forgotten. Like 'Still', the lyric was another chance for Grohl to flashback to his past. In this case he wrote what he described as an "ode to North Carolina". The next track, 'Miracle', was the first of John Paul Jones' guest spots; he tapped away at a piano while Grohl delivered another quality

---

* So extraordinary that 'Virginia Moon' later received a Grammy nomination.

vocal, all the time resisting the obvious temptation to burst into his signature roar. Petra Haden brought the song home with a tasty violin solo, which was another Foos' first. 'Another Round' was Jones' second cameo; this time he scrubbed at a mandolin, as Grohl crooned a mellow backporch lyric and Danny Clinch, better known as an A-list rock'n'roll photographer, chimed in on harmonica. When Grohl and the band adjourned to the control room, he lost himself in a teenage reverie. "Looking at John Paul Jones, remembering the times I dropped acid listening to 'Going To California' was amazing."

An old/new song, 'Friend Of A Friend', Grohl's nod to Cobain, back in the day when they were roomies in Seattle, was next. This was the leanest of all the tunes on the acoustic album, with Grohl in full coffee shop-minstrel mode. Given the song's history, Grohl was understandably hesitant about including it on *In Your Honour*. He wasn't sure if he was ready for another round of questions about his Nirvana bandmate, particularly after having gone 10 rounds in the courts with Courtney Love. But at the same time, Grohl was resisting the temptation to "edit myself. I recorded it, people thought it was a powerful song and so there it is." The track, of course, was a natural fit for a collection of 10 tunes that were more about veracity and texture than volume. 'Over And Out' wasn't a track written specifically for this album; Grohl had been wrestling with it for five years, when he first cut a version in his basement in Virginia as an "experiment in doing something more mellow". Grohl stated that one of the band's goals with this disc was that there would be little in the way of instrumentation or studio trickery between the singer and the tape. 'Over And Out' is ample proof of this. 'On The Mend', yet another understated strum, came out of a Grohl jam in a London hotel room.

If the unplugged side of *In Your Honour* had a centrepiece, it had to be 'Virginia Moon', the slightly woozy bossa nova duet shared by Grohl and Norah Jones. As soon as Grohl wrote the song, he knew that it needed a female vocal; he could hear a woman singing in his head as he pieced the tune together. He'd been listening to her album, *Come Away With Me*, so it was simply a matter of making the connection. "I thought it would be cool to have some piano on there," Grohl figured, "and I heard a Norah Jones record and thought, 'Cool, maybe she's the one I should call.'" Grohl realised that some Foo true believers may have had trouble with him sharing the mic with such a mainstream star, but to Grohl it was no more peculiar than his recent collaboration with industrial rock master Trent Reznor. "The fact that it's Norah Jones kind of freaks people out," he said. "That's dumb."

'Razor', the quietest jam that Grohl had ever had with Josh Homme, who played guitar, rounded out the sombre side of *In Your Honour*. Grohl had premiered the song at a tsunami benefit gig in LA, prior to the recording session. He'd been up most of the previous night trying to get the song on paper; he was still writing lyrics when a car arrived to take him to the gig. By chance, Homme was sharing a dressing room with Grohl, and overheard him quietly strumming the song. It was then that they agreed that Homme should record the song's near-classical second guitar part, which was as radical a departure for the head Queen as it was for Grohl.

Many pundits refer to *In Your Honour* as the Foos' 'White Album'. While Beatles fan Grohl may have considered this a massive compliment, there was a sting in the tail: many of these same pundits believed that the 'White Album' was a great single album bursting to get out of a double. *In Your Honour* had the same problem of excess.

Once again, the band led with their best hand on the album's rock side, in this case the thunderstruck title track. Grohl felt so strongly about the track that he actually agreed to print the song's lyrics in the CD's inner sleeve, which was the first time since *The Colour And The Shape* that Grohl had agreed to do this. But, of course, this wasn't so much a song lyric as a design for life; when Grohl growled "in your honour I would die tonight" he sang with the steely conviction of a man with a mission, not unlike the guy who inspired the song, John Kerry. 'No Way Back' swiftly followed, delivering a hefty one-two punch, the ideal way to begin the band's bravest album yet. All the Foos signatures were there: a larynx-shredder of a vocal from Grohl, white-knuckled riffing from Shiflett and steel-fisted rhythms courtesy of Hawkins and Mendel. The next track, 'Best Of You', was more trademark Foos, with a melody that was impossible to shake after only a cursory listen. It was the logical first single, too, and, predictably, lodged itself in *Billboard*'s various charts, logging a hefty 29 weeks in their Modern Rock Chart.

Despite its fatalistic lyric – "no one's getting out of here alive," Grohl yelled – 'DOA' was another song that was destined to be added to the list of fan favourites. Another cast-iron riff, another howl-at-the-moon Grohl vocal, and more hammer-of-the-gods contributions from the band's engine room ensured that 'DOA', *In Your Honour*'s third single, did the usual brisk business at the cash register. By now, Grohl and band had so successfully forged their modern rock template, that a legion of imitators – including such bands as Cave In, Default, Hotwater Music, Breaking Point, Good Charlotte, Fuel and numerous others – had emerged in their wake. But none of these acts had Grohl's remarkable ability to keep churning out radio-friendly rock'n'roll anthems. Admittedly, the album track 'Hell', where Hawkins took the chance to unleash his inner Keith Moon, was a curious digression, but the first side of *In Your Honour* was really more about defining the Foos' signature sound rather than straying too far from the blueprint. Such cuts as 'Free Me' and 'The Last Song' drove that point home with typical Foos ferocity.

Grohl was coy when asked who he had in mind when he screamed "this is the last song / I will dedicate to you". Could he be thinking, once again, of a certain notorious grunge rock widow? "All I've got to say," he said defensively, "is that there's a whole lot of people that I love and hate far more than any of the people that you know I know." Waters thoroughly muddied, Grohl refused to comment further.

What Grohl would allude to, however vaguely, was the concept that a double album would make the perfect swansong for the band. "I always imagined that a double record like this was a good way to send it off," he said on its release. "[It's] a good way to say goodbye." But Grohl was only sparring with his interviewer; he knew that he and the band had come way too far and endured far too much together to pull the pin when the Foos were at their commercial peak.

Understandably, Grohl refused to accept that the album was flabby, but he also didn't want to alienate the band's traditional following, so the "loud, obnoxious" disc included such tracks (and future hit singles) as 'Resolve', 'Best Of You' and 'DOA', with a set of gently warped videos to accompany them.

When I spoke to director Michael Palmieri in early 2006, he said that he wasn't RCA's first choice for the 'DOA' and 'Resolve' clips; they didn't even want him involved in the writing of the treatments for the videos. According to Palmieri, "They thought that my aesthetic lacked what the Foos might be looking for, but the label had gone to just about every director in town and nothing had clicked yet, so by a process of elimination I was finally allowed to write [the storyboards]."

The idea he had in mind for the quietly creepy 'DOA' clip was taken from "weird European art films from the Seventies". The band was so into the idea that they left the script unaltered when reading it only a few days after Palmieri was hired. Best known for his work with alt-pop icon Beck, Palmieri acknowledges the influence the Foos' previous videos had on his work. "I always liked their videos, particularly [Michael] Gondry's 'Everlong'," Palmieri told me. When he was recruited by Beck, "I went back and watched some videos that I really loved and one of those was 'Everlong'. It made me remember that music videos can be beautiful art and storytelling. I thought it would be great to try and make videos like that."

With twice the budget of 'DOA' – Palmieri refused to divulge the exact figure – 'Resolve' was "a huge video, giant sets and a lot of CG". It was during the shoot of this more typical Foos clip that Grohl encountered his Oriental doppelgänger, in an eatery in Duarte, California, where the sushi bar sequence was shot. During pre-production, Palmieri's designer, Mike Keeling, called the director with some strange news. As Palmieri recalled, "He said, 'Dude, you're not going to believe this, [but] I just ate at a place called Sushi For Less and I was served by a guy who looks like a Japanese Dave Grohl.'"

Keeling was unaware that Palmieri was working on a Foo Fighters clip at the time. Palmieri had already mapped out the idea of Grohl sinking to the bottom of the ocean to meet a mermaid, but he now had a new twist. "I immediately got this image of a much weirder video – one that takes place in Sushi For Less and then ends up at the bottom of the ocean." After a hasty rewrite, he called Grohl. "Dave got it," Palmieri said, "and was like, 'What the fuck?!' He loved it."

Grohl's reaction might have been different if aware that he was required to be bound, flipped upside down and held underwater in a make-believe shark tank (actually an underwater "greenscreen" at Universal Studios). "I seem to capitalise on every phobia Dave has without realising it," said Palmieri. "He is deathly afraid of being strapped into anything or being turned upside down – and he can't go more than three feet underwater without having a panic attack. I had no idea." As Grohl attempted to settle into the shark tank, Palmieri asked him whether he had any other phobias he should be made aware of. "My biggest phobia is making videos with you," was Grohl's reply.

It was Hawkins who copped the bulk of the rough treatment for the hair-raising 'DOA' clip, in which Grohl's dog makes a cameo. During the first day of shooting, the band was spun upside down "about 30 times in a row"; the following day, Hawkins was given another three or four stomach-churning spins solo. One of his [Hawkins] phobias – vertigo – was also explored in 'DOA'. "I was hanging him about 40 feet above a train," Palmieri said. "It was pretty nuts. I was surprised he didn't just clobber me for making him do it."

To Palmieri, the band seemed devoid of any rock star pretensions. "I've heard so many horror stories . . . working with bands that are awful divas and the like. But Dave, Taylor, Nate and Chris pretty much top it off in terms of how cool things can be on a film set. Dave is a keen film-maker in his own right and he's a damn good editor.* He really helped me out on 'Resolve', which was an incredibly difficult edit. I love working with those guys."

Even if there was excess baggage in the double concept – *Rolling Stone* felt that the album "could easily have been pruned down to one disc" – the public seemed unconcerned. Within weeks of its release, *In Your Honour* was certified platinum in the USA, where it took up a seemingly permanent residence in the charts, on the back of hit singles 'Best Of You' and 'DOA', as well as a day-long celebration of the band '24 Hours Of Foo', hosted by MTV2. The album was the biggest global hit of their careers, to date, topping charts in Australia, Finland, New Zealand and Sweden, peaking at number two in the UK, Norway and Ireland, and reaching the top five in Canada, Germany, Austria and Denmark.

This success was replicated when the band hit the road for their first *In Your Honour* date at the Shoreline Amphitheatre in Mountain View, California, in early June 2005. Foo Fighters were now an A-list touring act, with gate receipts – and backstage riders – to match. In fact, the list of the band's pre- and post-show needs made for one of the more amusing documents ever to cross a promoter's desk.

Among the usual food and drink requests – a dozen bottles of Snapple, a case of Coor's Light, 24 bottles of Gatorade, a bottle of Crown Royal Canadian whisky – were more specific needs, such as "one fresh vegetable

---

* Grohl directed the videos for 'Monkey Wrench', 'My Hero' and 'All My Life'.

and cheese tray", followed by this caveat, in blaring upper case letters: "REMEMBER, CAULIFLOWER BLOWS!" As an indication of Grohl's epicurean tastes the words appeared (again in upper case): "DAVE LOVES STINKY CHEESE." The band also offered useful suggestions for their more esoteric requests; following a listing asking for "10 energy bars" was the suggestion "ask a hippy for better suggestions". Also intermingled among their various needs were such oddities as four pairs of white tube socks (US size 10–13) and four pairs of medium boxer shorts, presumably to counteract post-gig perspiration.

Yet that was only the start. The band requested a "clean and well-lit and well-ventilated dressing room which can comfortably accommodate 20 people", asking that it was not to be shared with anyone: "except Supergrass, Oasis or maybe Led Zeppelin". They also asked for heating or air-conditioning "as is customary in modern times", signing off with "Dearest Reader," the band advised, "this rider is comprised of the things that make the band rock you like a proverbial hurricane. The silly items like gum and candy bars make a difference to these boys that are far from their families and friends. The band travels on its stomach, just like Foreigner or Motörhead."

Clearly their required needs paid huge dividends because Foo Fighters became a streamlined money-making machine as *In Your Honour* stuck fast to the upper end of the charts in the second half of 2005. In a remarkable run of full and almost-full houses, starting in California on June 10 and ending with two sold-out shows in Melbourne, Australia, on December 6 and 7, the band grossed a staggering US $14,179,033 from a total of 36 shows.

If there was one memorable gig from the *In Your Honour* run of dates, it was a "secret" show, organised in conjunction with RealNetworks, webcast live from the New Mexico desert on June 18. The site was of Foos' significance, being the former Walker Air Force Base in Roswell, where the US government allegedly stashed the evidence from the crash site of a mysterious UFO in July 1947.

"This is a long overdue and historic moment for the band," Grohl confirmed, prior to the show. "Despite being in a band called Foo Fighters, having a label called Roswell Records, and being a total UFO nut, I have never been to Roswell. I can't think of a better way to celebrate the band's 10th anniversary."

It was an equally momentous experience for 500 competition winners, who had no idea of their destination until the day of the show. All they knew was that they had won access to a private gig and a Foos barbeque. "You probably only get a chance like this once in a lifetime," gushed Danny Marie. Another of the lucky 500, Tiffany Hu, thought the competition was a hoax and was one step short of deleting the email. "I thought I was getting spam mail," she laughed.

Playing such a show was a rarity on the Foos' 2005 calendar; apart from a promo gig earlier in the year at Sydney's 900-capacity Metro Theatre, and a mid-tour Grohl homecoming at DC's 9.30 Club – most Foo gigs were now in arenas, which didn't make for an especially strong connection between band and crowd.

At Roswell, the band blazed for 90 minutes, mixing live standards with a hefty selection of *In Your Honour* tracks. "Grohl, who was noticeably tickled to be performing in Roswell," reported www.livedaily.com "tore into the tunes like a kid opening up presents on Christmas morning."

As Grohl and the band flew back to Seattle, the significance of the day took hold. It had been a long, strange trip to get to Roswell – 10 years, millions of miles, hundreds of shows, five albums, several departures, and a couple of near break-ups – but Foo Fighters had finally come home.

Grohl's only regret was that he wasn't able to examine the mysterious remains that were once allegedly stored in the hangar. Now *that* really would have made the journey complete.

Sydney Superdome,
December 1, 2005

"In my humble opinion, this is the best motherfucking band in the world!"
– Dave Grohl

O NLY 10 miles distance separates the Hordern Pavilion, the site of Nirvana's Big Day Out performance in January 1992, and the cavernous Sydney Superdome, where Foo Fighters' *In Your Honour* tour checked in just a few weeks before Christmas 2005. It's likely that many of the faithful were at both these events, as well as the numerous Foo Fighters shows that the band has played in Australia, their second-biggest market. Plenty had changed for Dave Grohl during those 13 years.

While on a previous Australian tour, Grohl visited a clairvoyant who, having no idea who Grohl was, advised him that he was one of the luckiest people who'd ever offered her their palm. She was not far off the mark.

While with Scream he was an eager pup eking out an existence from the back of a van, in Nirvana he was the human whirlwind, the guy trying to keep it together while Kurt Cobain was doing his best to undermine everything the band had achieved. While there was no doubt that Grohl played a crucial role, he was initially looked upon as a mere recruit; another in a long line of drummers to pass through the ranks. Leading his own band Foo Fighters, Grohl was singer, songwriter and, occasionally, drummer.

Introducing himself with the words, "Hello, I'm Dave and I'll be your compere for tonight," for the next two hours Grohl tore up and down the Superdome stage, throwing out monster riffs and arena rock poses with the ease of a guy who had been playing this game for almost 20 years.

Foo Fighters had built up their own greatest hits set. Gone was the cheesy cover of Gerry Rafferty's 'Baker Street', gonzo takes on Queen's back catalogue, or guest spots from Grohl's muso pals. From the gargantuan riff opening 'In Your Honour', right on through to the final screeching wails of feedback shutting down 'Monkey Wrench', this show was all Foos. Granted, the band has yet to lay claim to an FM Classic Rock staple in the mould of 'Stairway To Heaven', or 'Smoke On The Water', but they now possess a solid back catalogue of instantly recognisable modern rock tunes, ranging from 'Learn To Fly' to 'Generator', 'Big Me' to 'Everlong', 'Stacked Actors' to 'This Is A Call', 'I'll Stick Around' to 'Best Of You'.

The same band whose amiable public image has been forged via a succession of increasingly funny, self-mocking videos, had also constructed an arena friendly stage act featuring a light show to rival Pink Floyd's. At the Superdome, retina-burning lasers and strobes bounced off the roof, spinning in all directions, as if some alien mothership was about to touch down. When combined with Hawkins' flashy drum solos and Grohl's daring march into the crowd during 'Stacked Actors', complete with 100-yard dash high-fiving his way through the faithful, you had a large-scale show that also attempted to reduce the distance between performer and audience.

At one point during the show, the first of two full houses at this 15,000 seat Sydney steel-and-concrete bunker, Grohl stopped, glanced fondly at the others, then announced: "In my humble opinion, this is the best motherfucking band in the world!" The bellowing Foo devotees concurred heartily. Grohl's admiration for his drummer Taylor Hawkins is especially strong.

"You'd have to go a long way to see a better fucking drummer than this man," Grohl declared, as he invited his sidekick down front to warble his passable country-rock tune, 'Cold Day In The Sun'. Coming from one often praised as the ultimate modern rock drummer – as heard with the Queens Of The Stone Age, let alone Nirvana – this was high praise indeed.

It's unlikely that rock stardom was a part of Dave Grohl's master plan, when he was the best air drummer in Virginia or just another face in the moshpit at DC's 9.30 Club. It wasn't on the agenda when he joined Nirvana, spending dull and dreary afternoons with an uncommunicable Kurt Cobain, and being forced to sleep on a couch designed for someone half his size.

Yet here was Grohl at the age of 36, with the words of his songs being screamed back at him by the Foo faithful, many of them barely able to crawl at the time that Nirvana broke in 1991. When Grohl casually stated, "I could do this shit all night," he wasn't just referring to this one wild gig on a warm Sydney night but the life he'd been living for more than a decade, a life that started with a bedroom drum kit and a few lucky moves.

With all these acknowledgements, why would Grohl want to give it up? He's mentioned more than once that parenthood might slow him down, and he seems genuinely thrilled by the prospect of his first child (due in early 2006). Getting off this treadmill isn't easy – especially when the ride is so smooth and satisfying.

An experiment that started with two friends in a tiny studio, testing how many songs they could cut in the shortest amount of time, has bloomed into a multi-platinum, million-dollar-spinning rock band. Grohl has the best of both worlds – being able to put his band on ice if the mood takes him and record soundtracks, tributes or freelance for recognised acts such as Queens Of The Stone Age and Nine Inch Nails. As long as Grohl maintains this switching of roles, there will always be a Foo Fighters.

Each member has a well-defined role in the band. As Grohl's right-hand man, Taylor Hawkins is the scrawny, chain-smoking surfer dude, whose on-stage moves receive their own fair share of audience rapture, perhaps out of a genuine love that he's still there after his close brush with fate. Chris Shiflett and Nate Mendel seem content to be the quiet achievers, the Foos' engine room.

When the house lights went up, and the satiated Sydney punters reluctantly drifted into the night, Grohl flopped, smiling, into a seat backstage, draining the beer that he'd failed to finish in one swill – an onstage bet made with the crowd. There were no rock star indulgences at this after-show gathering, just a smiling, contented musician, still dripping sweat, surrounded by Foo friends and family, looking forward to the next gig, the next crowd, the next ovation.

As Grohl once told me, there is a mysterious bond that keeps Foo Fighters together. "It's like *Apocalypse Now*," he said, laughing. "We're heading up the river and Chef – that's me – jumps off to get some mangoes and gets spooked by that tiger. He gets back on, screaming, 'Never get off the boat, man, never get off the boat!' Well, man," he said with a grin, "the Foo Fighters is the boat."

Discography

(This discography includes releases only; demos, such as the ones Grohl recorded with Freak Baby and Mission Impossible, have not been included.)

Mission Impossible
Split 7″ with Lünchmeat
Sammich Records
1985
Helpless / Into Your Shell / Am I Alone?

Alive And Kicking (compilation)
WGNS/Metrozine
1985
Helpless / I Can Only Try

Dain Bramage
I Scream Not Coming Down
Fartblossom Records
1987
The Log / I Scream Not Coming Down / Eyes Open / Swear / Flannery / Drag Queen / Stubble / Flicker / Give It Up / Home Sweet Nowhere

Scream
No More Censorship
RAS Records
1988
Hit Me / No More Censorship / Fucked Without A Kiss / No Escape / Building Dreams / Take It From The Top / Something In My Head / It's About Time / Binge / Run To The Sun / In The Beginning★
(★written by Grohl)

Live At Van Hall In Amsterdam
Konkurrel Records
1989
Who Knows – Who Cares? / U Suck A / We're Fed Up / Laissez Faire / This
Side Up / Human Behaviour / Iron Curtain / Total Mash / Still Screaming /
Chokeword / Feel Like That / Came Without Warning / Walk By Myself

Your Choice Live Series 010
Your Choice
1990
CWW Pt II / ICYOUD / The Zoo Closes / Hot Smoke And Sassafras /
Fight / American Justice / Show And Tell / Sunmaker / No Escape / Take It
From The Top / Dancing Madly Backwards / Hit Me
(Recorded live at Oberhaus in Germany, May 4, 1990)

Fumble
Dischord
July 1993
Caffeine Dream / Sunmaker / Mardi Gras / Land Torn Down / Gods Look
Down*/ Crackman / Gas / Dying Days / Poppa Says / Rain
(* written by Grohl)

Nirvana
Nevermind
DGC
September 1991
Smells Like Teen Spirit / In Bloom / Come As You Are / Breed / Lithium /
Polly / Territorial Pissings / Drain You / Lounge Act / Stay Away / On A
Plain / Something In The Way

Incesticide
DGC
December 1992
Dive / Sliver / Stain / Been a Son / Turnaround / Molly's Lips / Son Of A
Gun / (New Wave) Polly / Beeswax / Downer / Mexican Seafood /
Hairspray Queen / Aero Zeppelin / Big Long Now / Aneurysm

In Utero
DGC
September 1993
Serve The Servants / Scentless Apprentice / Heart-Shaped Box / Rape Me /
Frances Farmer Will Have Her Revenge On Seattle / Dumb / Very Ape /
Milk It / Pennyroyal Tea / Radio Friendly Unit Shifter / Tourette's /
All Apologies

MTV Unplugged In New York
DGC
November 1994
About A Girl / Come As You Are / Jesus Doesn't Want Me For A Sunbeam /
The Man Who Sold The World / Pennyroyal Tea / Dumb / Polly /
On A Plain / Something In The Way / Plateau / Oh, Me / Lake Of Fire /
All Apologies / Where Did You Sleep Last Night?

From The Muddy Banks Of The Wishkah
DGC
October 1996
Intro / School / Drain You / Aneurysm / Smells Like Teen Spirit / Been A
Son / Lithium / Sliver / Spank Thru / Scentless Apprentice / Heart-Shaped
Box / Milk It / Negative Creep / Polly / Breed / Tourette's / Blew

With The Lights Out
DGC
November 2004
Heartbreaker / Anorexorcist / White Lace And Strange / Help Me I'm Hungry
/ Mrs. Butterworth / If You Must / Pen Cap Chew / Downer / Floyd The
Barber / Raunchola / Moby Dick / Beans / Don't Want It All / Clean Up
Before She Comes / Polly / About A Girl / Blandest / Dive / They Hung Him
On A Cross / Grey Goose / Ain't It A Shame / Token Eastern Song / Even In
His Youth / Polly / Opinion / Lithium / Been A Son / Sliver / Where Did
You Sleep Last Night? / Pay To Play / Here She Comes Now / Drain You /
Aneurysm / Smells Like Teen Spirit / Breed / Verse Chorus Verse / Old Age /
Endless, Nameless / Dumb / D-7 / Oh The Guilt / Curmudgeon / Return Of
The Rat / Smells Like Teen Spirit / Rape Me / Rape Me / Scentless Apprentice /
Heart-Shaped Box / I Hate Myself And I Want To Die / Milk It / M.V. /
Gallons of Rubbing Alcohol Flow Through The Strip / The Other Improv /

Serve The Servants / Very Ape / Pennyroyal Tea / Marigold / Sappy (A.K.A. Verse Chorus Verse) / Jesus Doesn't Want Me For A Sunbeam / Do Re Mi / You Know You're Right / All Apologies / Love Buzz / Scoff / About A Girl / Big Long Now / Immigrant Song / Spank Thru / Hairspray Queen / School / Mr. Moustache / Big Cheese / In Bloom / Sappy / School / Love Buzz / Pennyroyal Tea / Smells Like Teen Spirit / Territorial Pissings / Jesus Doesn't Want Me For A Sunbeam / Talk To Me / Seasons In The Sun

Dave Grohl

Pocketwatch (released under the name **Late**)
Simple Machines
1993
Pokey The Little Puppy / Petrol CB / Friend Of A Friend / Throwing Needles / Just Another Story About Skeeter Thompson / Colour Pictures Of A Marigold Dream / Hell's Garden / Winnebago / Bruce / Milk

Touch: Music From The Motion Picture
Roswell/Capitol
November 1997
Bill Hill Theme / August Murray Theme / How Do You Do? / Richie Baker's Miracle / Making Popcorn / Outrage / Saints In Love / Spinning Newspapers / Remission My Ass / Scene 6 / This Loving Thing (Lynn's Song) / Final Miracle / Touch

Grohl has also contributed to the following EPs and albums:
King Buzzo, Buzz Osborne, 1992; *Backbeat*, Original Soundtrack, 1994; *Ball-Hog or Tugboat?*, Mike Watt, 1995; *Little Tiny Smelly Bit*, The Stinky Puffs, 1995; *Harlingtox Angel Divine*, 1996; *Tibetan Freedom Concert*, Various Artists, 1997; *It's All About The Benjamins*, Puff Daddy, 1997; *For The Rest Of Us*, John Doe, 1998; *Earthlings?*, The Earthlings, 1998; *Moon Pix*, Cat Power, 1998; *Hell City, Hell*, Various Artists, 1998; *Fox Sports Presents: Game Time!*, Various Artists, 1999; *Into The Pink*, Verbena, 1999; *Ulysses (Della Notte)*, Reeves Gabrels, 1999; *Ever Passing Moment*, MxPx, 2000; *Iommi*, Tony Iommi, 2000; *Tenacious D*, 2001; *Heathen*, David Bowie, 2002; *Songs For The Deaf*, Queens Of The Stone Age, 2002; *Doll Revolution*, The Bangles, 2003; *The Death And Resurrection Show*, Killing Joke, 2003; *Honky Mofo*, 2004; *Probot*, 2004; *Bleed Like Me*, Garbage, 2005; *With Teeth*, Nine Inch Nails, 2005. For a detailed list of credits, see www.allmusic.com

Foo Fighters
Foo Fighters
Roswell/Capitol
July 1995
This Is A Call / I'll Stick Around / Big Me / Alone + Easy Target / Good
Grief / Floaty / Weenie Beenie / Oh, George / For All The Cows / X-Static /
Wattershed / Exhausted

The Colour And The Shape
Roswell/Capitol
May 1997
Doll / Monkey Wrench / Hey, Johnny Park! / My Poor Brain / Wind Up /
Up In Arms / My Hero / See You / Enough Space / February Stars /
Everlong / Walking After You / New Way Home

There Is Nothing Left To Lose
Roswell/RCA
November 1999
Stacked Actors / Breakout / Learn To Fly / Gimme Stitches / Generator /
Aurora / Live-In Skin / Next Year / Headwires / Ain't It The Life / MIA

One By One
Roswell/RCA
October 2002
All My Life / Low / Have It All / Times Like These / Disenchanted Lullaby /
Tired Of You / Halo / Lonely As You / Overdrive / Burn Away / Comeback

In Your Honour
Roswell/RCA
June 2005
In Your Honour / No Way Back / Best Of You / DOA / Hell / The Last
Song / Free Me / Resolve / The Deepest Blues Are Black / End Over End /
Still / What If I Do? / Miracle / Another Round / Friend Of A Friend /
Over And Out / On The Mend / Virginia Moon / Cold Day In The Sun /
Razor

Foo Fighters Videography

Anthologies
Guardian Angels
Unauthorised Foo Fighters documentary, best avoided.
Chrome Dreams 2005

Everywhere But Home
Live footage from One By One world tour, 2002/03.
Roswell/RCA 2003

Promotional Videos
'I'll Stick Around'
1996 Director: Gerald Casale
"The concept I submitted was similar to the one we shot," director Casale
told me, "but the 3D animated 'virus' was literally a bloated, charred, inflated
girl representing Courtney [Love]. Dave and band were understandably afraid
of litigation."

'Big Me'
1996 Director: Jesse Peretz
The band lived to regret this spoof – every night they'd be pelted with Mentos
(known as "Footos" in the clip). Eventually they dropped the song from their
setlist, fearing serious injury. "Mentos hurt like shit," according to Grohl.

'Monkey Wrench'
1997 Director: Dave Grohl
In a trend that would continue through many Foos' videos, another of their
songs – in this case, a Muzak version of 'Big Me' – can be heard in the elevator
scene. The video's concept was lifted directly from one of Grohl's dreams.

'Everlong'
1997 Director: Michael Gondry
This was a particular favourite of future Foos video director, Michael Palmieri.
"It struck me so deeply," he told me in 2006. Director Michael Gondry went
on to big screen acclaim with *Eternal Sunshine Of The Spotless Mind*.

'My Hero'
1998 Director: Dave Grohl
Another Grohl-directed clip – and another song not about Kurt Cobain. This is the only Foos video that includes an appearance by guitarist Franz Stahl, who left the band soon after.

'Walking After You'
1998 Director: Matthew Rolston
A hefty budgeted clip – somewhere on the wrong side of $300,000 – featuring only Grohl and Arly Joven, who appeared in the film *Blade*. The song also turned up on *X Files The Movie*; David "Mulder" Duchovny was approached to direct the video, but passed.

'Learn To Fly'
1999 Director: Jesse Peretz
Featuring Tenacious D, this was the Grammy-winning clip that truly established the Foos rep as video piss-takers par excellence. Grohl would later insist that the band's success was due to "that fucking airplane video".

'Breakout'
2000 Director: The Malloy Brothers
The "other" Foos song to be heard in this clip – which stars Traylor Howard, from *Two Guys, A Girl And A Pizza Place* – is 'Generator'. Another not-so-serious clip. "I can't imagine anyone wanting to break off a relationship just because they have acne," said Grohl.

'Next Year'
2000 Director: Phil Harder
Foos in space. Tired of their lives as gay flight attendants and/or flight crew, the band reinvents themselves as Apollo astronauts, headed for the moon. Grohl didn't like the gently twangy song; he called it "shit".

'Generator'
2000 Director: Uncredited
Cut during a live set on the Australian show, *Live At The Chapel*, this is actually nothing of the sort – the album track is deftly matched to the band's live performance, shot inside a restored Melbourne church, of all places.

'The One'
2001 Director: Jesse Peretz
The band's third video with director Peretz, who, according to Gerald Casale, "got the opportunity to do the videos I would like to have done once Dave got the video bug." This was shot in Brooklyn and featured actress Amy Weaver.

'All My Life'
2002 Director: Dave Grohl
The Foos return to a frequent theme, as 'Big Me' plays in the elevator as Grohl steps inside. One of the song's many lyrical themes is Grohl's ambivalent attitude to cunnilingus, although he later insisted, "I'm very fond of giving oral sex to women."

'Times Like These'
2002 Directors: Liam Lynch / Marc Klasfeld / Bill Yukich
This clip came in three different varieties, including a version directed by one-hit-wonder Liam Lynch, who croaked the 'United States Of Whatever' all the way to the top of the charts.

'Low'
2003 Directors: Jesse Peretz and Les Dudis
A pair of rednecks – Grohl and Tenacious D's Jack Black – meet in a seedy motel and commit a number of perverse acts. Acts of drug and dildo abuse were edited from the final cut; MTV banned it regardless. "I've never had a gay experience," Grohl explained afterwards.

'Have It All'
2003 Director: Uncredited
Just like 'Generator', this was a reminder that the Foos were essentially a live band that sometimes made achingly funny videos. This was shot on stage in Toronto, Canada.

'Best Of You'
2005 Director: Mark Pellington
This was the first single lifted from *In Your Honour*; the clip was shot in an abandoned hospital somewhere in Los Angeles.

'DOA'
2005 Director: Michael Palmieri
"In general," explained director Palmieri, " 'DOA' is all practical rigging tricks, cameras spinning with rigs or counter-rotating with them, and then painting out [the] small wires later. That, and a little bit of magic!" Grohl's dog cameos.

'Resolve'
2005 Director: Michael Palmieri
Featuring the Japanese Dave Grohl – accidentally discovered by production designer Mike Keeling – some scenes were actually shot in the real Sushi For Less restaurant, located in Duarte, California.

Probot
'Shake Your Blood'
2003 Director: Bill Yukich
Grohl was a big fan of the Suicide Girls, who star in this Probot video alongside Grohl, Lemmy from Motörhead and others. "My favourite of them all is Katie," Grohl said. "She's hot as fuck."

Websites
Mission Impossible / Dain Bramage: www.pooldrop.com/dainbramage/
Scream: www.dischord.com/bands/scream.shtml
Nirvana: www.nirvanaclub.com; www.livenirvana.com/digitalnirvana/;
    www.rollingstone.com/artists/nirvana
Foo Fighters: www.foofighters.com; www.fooarchive.com

Bibliography

CHAPTER ONE

Anon: Senate OKs $6billion For Poor, *Chicago Tribune*, September 10, 1971
Anon: Senate Unit OKs Wage Hike, *Chicago Tribune*, May 25, 1972
Anon: Rebellious Jukebox, *Melody Maker*, 1997
Anon: Songs In The Key Of Life, *NME*, 1999
Anon: We Love Festivals, *Q*, 2000
Anon: The Coolest People In Rock, *Melody Maker*, September 2000
Anon: Dear Superstar, *Blender*, May 2003
Anon: Dave Grohl's Christmas Plans, *Melody Maker*, December 2000
Anon: Cash For Questions, *Q*, 2003
Azerrad, Michael: *Come As You Are, The Story Of Nirvana*, Main Street Books, 1993
Ballard, Michael & Newsome, Ted: Dave Grohl's Quest For Heavy Metal And The Birth Of Probot, *Stance*, December 2001
Brannigan, Paul: Big Mouth Strikes Again, *Kerrang!*, September 2002
Connolly, Paul: Rock Warriors, *The Times*, November 2002
Grohl, David: A Led Zeppelin Fan Writes, *Q*, April 2003
Grohl, David: Led Zeppelin: The Immortals, *Rolling Stone*, April 15, 2004
Hundley, Jessica: *Dazed And Confused*, May 2005
Kilian, Michael: Ohio Senate Race Has Many Facets, *Chicago Tribune*, October 29, 1970
Lynskey, Dorian: The Man Who Fell To Earth, *Arena*, November 2002
Micallef, Ken: Returning To His Roots With Probot, *Modern Drummer*, June 2004
Mitchell, Ben: A Life Less Ordinary, *Q*, November 2005
Odell, Michael: Keep It Down In There, *Q*, January 2003
Peake, Mike: The Former Nirvana Drummer – Now Foo Fighters Frontman – On Weapons, Hygiene And His Bedroom Stamina, *FHM*, February 2000
Petkovic, John: Dave Grohl's Music Hasn't Been Much Of A Fight At All, *Cleveland Plain Dealer*, May 2003
Rogers, Ray: A Few Good Foos From A Foo Fighter, *Interview*, May 1997

Rubin, Trudy: The Amnesty Issue, *Chicago Tribune*, January 24, 1972

Saah, Jim: Dave Grohl, *Uno Mas*, undated

Siepe, Dirk: Grohl Speaks, *Visions*, September 2000

Swenson, Kyle: Dave Grohl's No Fuzz Zone, *Guitar Player*, November 1999

True, Everett: Hallo Spaceboys, *Melody Maker*, February 1997

Wall, Mick: No Way Out!, *Mojo*, October 2005

Wiederhorn, Jon: I, Probot, *Revolver*, February 2004

Wolliscroft, Tony: The Man Who Fell To Earth, *Rhythm*, August 2001 (including unedited transcript)

Yates, Ronald: Sen Taft Urges Aid To N. Vietnam, *Chicago Tribune*, February 4, 1973

CHAPTER TWO

Azerrad, Michael: *Our Band Could Be Your Life; Scenes From The American Indie Underground, 1981–1991*, Back Bay Books, 2001

Brannigan, Paul: Big Mouth Strikes Again, *Kerrang!*, September 2002

Everley, Dave: I Was A Teenage Punk Rocker, *Kerrang!*, August 2, 1997

MacKaye, Ian: Brief History of Dischord Records, www.dischord.com

Sherry, James: The Secret Life of Dave Grohl, *Metal Hammer*, June 1997

Various: Young, Loud & Snotty: 50 Greatest US Punk Tracks, *Mojo*, November 2005

CHAPTER THREE

Andersen, Mark; Jenkins, Mark: *Dance Of Days: Two Decades Of Punk In The Nation's Capital*, Akashic Books, 2001

Anon: Dave Grohl is the Evil Head, *NME*, November 2003

Anon: Heavy Mettle, *Time Out*, April 2004

Anon: Untitled story from *Touch And Go* fanzine, no date

Anon: Untitled story from *Flipside*, December 1982

Anon: Untitled story from *Thrillseeker 2* fanzine, no date

Brace, Eric: Dave Grohl (untitled, not dated)

Connolly, Paul: Rock Warriors, *The Times*, November 2002

Doyle, Tom: Weeeeeeeee!, *Q*, June 1996

Everley, David: I Was A Teenage Punk Rocker, *Kerrang!* August 2, 1997

Peake, Mike: The Former Nirvana Drummer – Now Foo Fighters Frontman

– On Weapons, Hygiene And His Bedroom Stamina, *FHM*, February 2000

Saah, Jim: Dave Grohl, *Uno Mas*, undated

Siepe, Dirk: Grohl Speaks, *Visions*, September 2000

Wolliscroft, Tony: The Man Who Fell to Earth, *Rhythm*, August 2001 (including unedited transcript)

CHAPTER FOUR

Andersen, Mark; Jenkins, Mark: *Dance Of Days: Two Decades Of Punk In The Nation's Capital*, Akashic Books, 2001

Anon: Foo Fighters Q&A, InYourEye.com, 1996

Anon: SAM questionnaire, 2000

Anon: Burn It: Dave Grohl, *NME*, 2002

Anon: A Week In The Life – Dave Grohl, *Classic Rock*, 2004

Azerrad, Michael: *Our Band Could Be Your Life; Scenes From The American Indie Underground, 1981–1991*, Back Bay Books, 2001

Brace, Eric: Dave Grohl (untitled, not dated)

Brannigan, Paul: Big Mouth Strikes Again, *Kerrang!*, September 2002

Garden, Marion: Dave Grohl's League Of Extraordinary Gentlemen, *Terrorizer*, January 2004

Grohl, David: Led Zeppelin: The Immortals, *Rolling Stone*, April 15, 2004

Grohl, David: 'Just Another Story About Skeeter Thompson', *Pocketwatch* CD (lyrics)

Segal, Victoria: The Prize Fighter, *X-Ray*, June 2003

Silver, Dan: Get In The Van, *Metal Hammer*, 1998

Udo, Tommy: Mr Incredible, *Metal Hammer*, 2003

Wolliscroft, Tony: Men Behaving Badly, *Kerrang!*, May 2000

www.pooldrop.com/dainbramage/history: Dain Bramage history

CHAPTER FIVE

Brace, Eric: Dave Grohl (untitled, not dated)

Leroy, JT: JT Leroy Meets Dave Grohl, *Flaunt*, 2002

Saah, Jim: Dave Grohl, *Uno Mas*, undated

Silver, Dan: Get In The Van, *Metal Hammer*, 1998

CHAPTER SIX

Anderson, Dawn: It May Be The Devil And It May Be The Lord . . . But It Sure As Hell Ain't Human, *Backlash*, August 1988

Azerrad, Michael: *Come As You Are, The Story Of Nirvana*, Main Street Books, 1993

Borzillo, Carrie: *Nirvana, The Day By Day Eyewitness Chronicle*, Thunder's Mouth Press, 2000

Everley, Dave: I Was A Teenage Punk Rocker, *Kerrang!*, August 2, 1997

Saah, Jim: Dave Grohl, *Uno Mas*, undated

Sub Pop Records: Press release for Nirvana's album *Bleach*, 1989

Thompson, Dave: *Never Fade Away: The Kurt Cobain Story*, St Martin's Paperbacks, 1994

Wolliscroft, Tony: The Man Who Fell To Earth, *Rhythm*, August 2001

CHAPTER SEVEN

Anon: Rebellious Jukebox, *Melody Maker*, 1997

Anon: SAM questionnaire, 2000

Anon: Dear Superstar, *Blender*, May 2003

Anon: *Nirvana, Nevermind, Classic Albums* DVD, Eagle Eye Media / Isis Productions, 2004

Anon: Everyone Has Their Dark Side, *Q*, June 2005

Azerrad, Michael: *Come As You Are, The Story Of Nirvana*, Main Street Books, 1993

Bennett, J: Twice As Nice, *Rock Sound*, June 2005

Borzillo, Carrie: *Nirvana, The Day By Day Eyewitness Chronicle*, Thunder's Mouth Press, 2000

Cameron, Keith: The Foo Epidemic, *NME*, December 1995

Cross, Charles R.: *Heavier Than Heaven, A Biography Of Kurt Cobain*, Hyperion, 2001

Daley, David: Feels Like The First Time, *Alternative Press*, January 1996

Davies, Dan: Foo's Gold, *Big Issue*, October 1999

DiPerna, Alan: Absolutely Foobulous, *Guitar World*, August 1997

Fricke, David: Nevermind 10 Years On, *Rolling Stone*, September 2001

Gaar, Gillian: The Recording History of Nirvana, *Goldmine*, 1997

Lawson, Dom: Into The Void, *Kerrang!*, May 2005

CHAPTER EIGHT

Anon: Icons, Dave Grohl, *Sky*, 1997

Anon: Songs In The Key Of Life, *NME*, 1999

Anon: I Saw The Light, *NME*, 1999

Anon: The 100 Coolest People In Rock, *Melody Maker*, 2000

Anon: Nirvana: Dave Grohl Talks About Their Origins, The Music And The Myth, *NME*, 2002

Anon: Summer Of Rock, *Rolling Stone*, 2003

Anon: Cash For Questions, *Q*, 2003

Azerrad, Michael: *Come As You Are, The Story Of Nirvana*, Main Street Books, 1993

Bailie, Stuart: Happy Dave Is Here Again, *Vox*, June 1997

Borzillo, Carrie: *Nirvana, The Day By Day Eyewitness Chronicle*, Thunder's Mouth Press, 2000

Chirazi, Steffan: What You See Is What You Get, *RIP*, November 1995

DiPerna, Alan: Absolutely Foobulous, *Guitar World*, August 1997

Fricke, David: Nevermind 10 Years On, *Rolling Stone*, September 2001

Mundy, Chris: It's A Band, Damn It (And Don't Mention The 'N' Word), *Rolling Stone*, October 1995

Rigby, Paul: The Pocketwatch Demos, Foo Fighters Collectors' Edition, *Metal Hammer*, 2005

Rogers, Ray: A Few Good Foos From A Foo Fighter, *Interview*, May 1997

Saah, Jim: Dave Grohl, *Uno Mas*, undated

Segal, Victoria: The Prize Fighter, *X-Ray*, June 2003

True, Everett: The Chosen Foo, *Melody Maker*, November 1995

CHAPTER NINE

Anon: Nirvana Was Hilarious, *Raw*, December 1995

Anon: Foo Fighters Q&A, InYourEye.com, 1996

Brace, Eric: Dave Grohl (untitled, not dated)

Brannigan, Paul: Big Mouth Strikes Again, *Kerrang!*, September 2002

Cameron, Keith: The Foo Epidemic, *NME*, December 1995

Daley, David: Feels Like The First Time, *Alternative Press*, January 1996

Gell, Aaron: They Came From Outer Space, *Blender*, Summer 1995

Grohl, David: Led Zeppelin: The Immortals, *Rolling Stone*, April 15, 2004

Higginbotham, Adam: The Tao of Foo, *Time Out*, December 1995

Lynskey, Dorian: The Man Who Fell to Earth, *Arena*, November 2002

Mundy, Chris: It's A Band, Damn It (And Don't Mention The 'N' Word), *Rolling Stone*, October 1995

Murphy, Kevin: Honor Roll, *Classic Rock*, June 2005

Orshoski, Wes: Dave Grohl: Honor Roll, *Harp*, Sept/Oct 2005

Sindell, Joshua: We Have Lift-Off!, *Kerrang!*, May 2001

True, Everett: The Chosen Foo, *Melody Maker*, November 1995

Yates, Henry: Bass Camp, Foo Fighters Collectors' Edition, *Metal Hammer*, 2005

CHAPTER TEN

Anon: The Maverick, *Metal Hammer* Presents Foo Fighters, July 2005

Anon: Lucky Man, *Metal Hammer* Presents Foo Fighters, July 2005

Anon: Rebellious Jukebox, *Melody Maker*, 1997

Anon: I Saw The Light, *NME*, 1999

Anon: Up Close And Personal With The Foo Fighters Frontman, *Kerrang!*, August 2000

Anon: Dave Grohl On Metal, Q, 2004

Anon: Pub Talk, *Kerrang!*, October 2003

Anon: Swaymag.com, September 1999

Anon: For A Loser Redneck From Virginia, I'm Stinking Rich!, *Melody Maker*, September 2000

Bailie, Stuart: Happy Dave Is Here Again, *Vox*, April 1997

Blake, Mark: My! They've Scrubbed Up Well!, Q, November 2002

Brace, Eric: Dave Grohl (untitled, not dated)

Clark, Rachel: Split Personality, *Revolver*, October 2005

DiPerna, Alan: Absolutely Foobulous, *Guitar World*, August 1997

Doyle, Tom: Weeeeeeeeee!, Q, June 1996

Everley, Dave: I Was A Teenage Punk Rocker, *Kerrang!*, August 1997

Flans, Robyn: The Foo Fighters Rock In Ol' Virginny, *Mix*, January 2000

Grohl, David: Led Zeppelin: The Immortals, *Rolling Stone*, April 15, 2004

Hundley, Jessica: Street Fighting Man, *Dazed & Confused*, May 2005

Johnson, Lisa: The New Model Army, *Kerrang!*, October 18, 1997

Kulkarnie, Neil: I Fucking Hated Hollywood, *Metal Hammer*, December 1999

Lancelot 2020: The Metamor-Foo-Sis, *Revolver*, September 1999

Lynskey, Dorian: The Man Who Fell To Earth, *Arena*, November 2002

Murphy, Kevin: Honor Roll, *Classic Rock*, June 2005

Murphy, Peter: What It Feels Like For A Grohl, *Hot Press*, October 2002

Myers, Ben: I'm Still Standing, *Kerrang!*, September 1999

Perrone, Pierre: Overtime Gentlemen Please, *Rock Sound*, January 2001

Plunkett, Danny: Foo, What A Scorcher!, *Loaded*, September 1997

Sherry, James: "I Haven't Vomited Since I Was Fourteen Years Old", *Metal Hammer*, June 1997

Sherry, James: The Secret Life Of Dave Grohl, *Metal Hammer*, June 1997

Siepe, Dirk: Foo For A Day – King For A Lifetime, *Visions*, July 1997

Silver, Dan: Get In The Van, *Metal Hammer*, 1998

Swenson, Kyle: Dave Grohl's No Fuzz Zone, *Guitar Player*, November 1999

True, Everett: The Chosen Foo, *Melody Maker*, November 1995

Turner, Dale: Rockin' Grohl Hoochie Foo, *Guitar One*, December 1999

Wolk, Douglas: Big Us: On The Road With The Foo Fighters, *CMJ*, December 1997

Wood, Mikael: All His Life, *Dallas Observer*, April 2003

www.fooarchive.com: Dave's song guides

Yates, Henry: The Ones That Got Away, *Metal Hammer* Presents The Foo Fighters, 2005

CHAPTER ELEVEN

Anon: Songs In The Key Of Life, *NME*, 1999

Anon: The Coolest People In Rock, *Melody Maker*, September 2000

Anon: The Strange Journey From Kurt To Killing Joke, *Metal Hammer*, July 2003

Anon: We Want Answers!, *Maxim*, 2000

Anon: Essential Reading Material, *NME*, 2000

Anon: Up Close And Personal With The Foo Fighters Frontman, *Kerrang!*, 2000

Anon: Dear Superstar, *Blender*, May 2003

Anon: The Maverick, *Metal Hammer* Presents Foo Fighters, July 2005

Anon: Lucky Man, *Metal Hammer* Presents Foo Fighters, July 2005

Anon: The Strange Journey From Kurt To Killing Joke, *Metal Hammer*, July 2003

Apter, Jeff: Foo Fighters, Australian *Rolling Stone*, January 2003

Blake, Mark: My! They've Scrubbed Up Well!, *Q*, November 2002

Brannigan, Paul: Big Mouth Strikes Again, *Kerrang!*, September 2002

Cameron, Keith: *Mojo*'s Album Of The Month, *Mojo*, 2002

Epstein, Dan: Man Of Steel, *Guitar World*, January 2004

Lynskey, Dorian: The Man Who Fell To Earth, *Arena*, November 2002

Mayhew, Malcolm: Stronger Than Before, *Dallas Observer*, April 2003

Murphy, Kevin: Honor Roll, *Classic Rock*, June 2005

Murphy, Peter: What It Feels Like For A Grohl, *Hot Press*, October 2002

Odell, Michael: Keep It Down In There, Q, January 2003

Pappademas, Alex: The Good Fight, *Spin*, November 2002

Pappademas, Alex: Everything You Ever Wanted To Know About The Foos But Were Afraid To Ask, *Spin*, January 2003

Ratliff, Ben: *Rated R* Review, *Rolling Stone*, June 2000

Silver, Dan: Exhaustion. Insanity. Jail. Dave Grohl's Year in Hell, *Kerrang!*, December 2000

Sindell, Joshua: We Have Lift-Off!, *Kerrang!*, May 2001

Spearwood, Morgan: Retaining Nirvana, *Living Abroad*, December 2002

Turner, Dale: Rockin' Grohl Hoochie Foo, *Guitar One*, December 1999

Winwood, Ian: Courtney. Kurt. Drugs. Rehab., *Kerrang!*, March 2002

Winwood, Ian: *NME* Festival Guide, 2005

Winwood, Ian: Reinventing the Steel, *Kerrang!* 2003

www.thesmokinggun.com: Courtney Love vs Dave Grohl, etc, transcript

CHAPTER TWELVE

Anon: Q: Are We Not Metal? A: We Are Probot, *Spin*, March 2004

Anon: Everyone Has Their Dark Side, Q, 2005

Anon: Something Old, Something New, Something Borrowed, Something Foo, *NME*, 2003

Anon: Cash For Questions, Q, 2003

Anon: Pub Talk, *Kerrang!*, October 2003

Anon: Everyone Has Their Dark Side, Q, June 2005

Anon: In Your Honor, Track By Track, *NME*, May 2005

Anon: Close Encounters Of The Foo Fighters Kind: Foo Fighters And Rhapsody To Hold Exclusive, Free Concert In Roswell, New Mexico, RealNetWorks Press Release, June 1, 2005

Anon: The Strange Journey From Kurt To Killing Joke, *Metal Hammer*, July 2003

Bennett, J: Twice As Nice, *Rock Sound*, June 2005

Doorne, James: The New Metallers In Town, *Bizarre*, January 2004

Epstein, Dan: Man Of Steel, *Guitar World*, September 2005

Garden, Marion: Dave Grohl's League of Extraordinary Gentlemen, *Terrorizer*, January 2004

Grohl, David: *Kerrang!* 2003 Yearbook

Harrington, Jim: Live Review: Foo Fighters In Roswell, NM, www.livedaily.com, June 20, 2005

http://blog.johnkerry.com: Dave Drops In On John Kerry's Blog, 2004

Hundley, Jessica: Street Fighting Man, *Dazed & Confused*, May 2005

Kulkarni, Neil: Have We Got Foos For You!, *Melody Maker*, April 1996

Lawson, Dom: Into The Void, *Kerrang!*, June 2005

Morat: Riders On The Storm, *Kerrang!*, January 2005

Murphy, Kevin: Honor Roll, *Classic Rock*, June 2005

Nailen, Dan: The Foo Fighters Now Play Three Weeks On The Road, Then Spend Two Weeks Home, *Salt Lake Tribune*, May 2003

Wiederhorn, Jon: I, Probot, *Revolver*, February 2004

www.thesmokinggun.com: Details of the Foo Fighters' tour rider

POSTSCRIPT

Apter, Jeff: Foo Fighters, Australian *Rolling Stone*, January 2003

VIDEOGRAPHY

Anon: Cash For Questions, *Q*, 2003

Anon: For A Loser Redneck From Virginia, I'm Stinking Rich!, *Melody Maker*, September 2000

Garden, Marion: Dave Grohl's League Of Extraordinary Gentlemen, *Terrorizer*, January 2004

Heatley, Michael: Living On Video, *Metal Hammer* Presents Foo Fighters Collectors' Edition, 2005

Perrone, Pierre: Overtime Gentlemen Please, *Rock Sound*, January 2001

True, Everett: Hallo Spaceboys, *Melody Maker*, February 1997

1 2 3 4 5 6 7 8 9